Indiana History

PEARSON

Credits appear on R24–R25, which constitute an extension of this copyright page.

Pearson North America, 501 Boylston Street, Suite 900, Boston, MA 02116
A Pearson Education Company
www.pearsoned.com

Printed in the United States of America
7 18

000200010271939631

RR

ISBN 10: 1-323-03204-5
ISBN 13: 978-1-323-03204-6

Program Consulting Authors

The Colonial Williamsburg Foundation
Williamsburg, VA

Dr. Linda Bennett
Associate Dean, Department of Learning, Teaching, & Curriculum
College of Education
University of Missouri
Columbia, MO

Dr. Jim Cummins
Professor of Curriculum, Teaching, and Learning
Ontario Institute for Studies in Education
University of Toronto
Toronto, Ontario

Dr. James B. Kracht
Byrne Chair for Student Success
Executive Associate Dean
College of Education and Human Development
Texas A&M University
College Station, TX

Dr. Alfred Tatum
Associate Professor, Director of the UIC Literacy, Language, and Culture Program
University of Illinois at Chicago
Chicago, IL

Dr. William E. White
Vice President for Productions, Publications and Learning Ventures
The Colonial Williamsburg Foundation
Williamsburg, VA

Dr. A. James Fuller
Professor of History
University of Indianapolis
Chair of Indiana Council for History Education
Indianapolis, IN

Consultants and Reviewers

PROGRAM CONSULTANT

Dr. Grant Wiggins
Coauthor, *Understanding by Design*

ACADEMIC REVIEWERS

Bob Sandman
Adjunct Assistant Professor of Business and Economics,
Wilmington College–Cincinnati Branches
Blue Ash, OH

Jeanette Menendez
Reading Coach,
Doral Academy Elementary
Miami, FL

Kathy T. Glass
Differentiated Instruction
Glass Educational Consulting
Woodside, CA

Roberta Logan
African Studies Specialist Retired,
Boston Public Schools/Mission Hill School
Boston, MA

PROGRAM TEACHER REVIEWERS

Andrea Baerwald
Boise, ID

Ernest Andrew Brewer
Assistant Professor,
Florida Atlantic University
Jupiter, FL

Charity L. Carr
Stroudsburg Area School District
Stroudsburg, PA

Laura Pahr
Holmes Elementary
Chicago, IL

Eretta Rose
MacMillan Elementary School
Montgomery, AL

Nancy Thornblad
Millard Public Schools
Omaha, NE

Megan Zavernik
Howard-Suamico School District
Green Bay, WI

INDIANA PROGRAM TEACHER REVIEWERS

Michelle Aschleman
Perry Hill Elementary
Fort Wayne, IN

Erin Blumenthal
Flint Lake Elementary
Valparaiso, IN

Gretchen Davenport
Perry Hill Elementary
Fort Wayne, IN

Natasha Dommer
New Haven Intermediate
New Haven, IN

Carolyn Harden
Brummitt Elementary
Chesterton, IN

Amy Harrington
Liberty Elementary School
Hobart, IN

Theresa Holmes
Hailmann School
La Porte, IN

Luann Luck
Pleasant Grove Elementary
Greenwood, IN

Wendy McCarthy
Eads Elementary
Munster, IN

Evangeline Palmer
Woodlan Elementary
Woodburn, IN

Becky Pennington
Center Grove Elementary
Greenwood, IN

Melissa Ross
Northwest Elementary
Huntington, IN

Social Studies Handbook

Indiana Academic Standards .... IN 11

Reading and Writing

Main Idea and Details ... IN 18

Summarize .... IN 19

Sequence .... IN 20

Compare and Contrast ... IN 21

Cause and Effect .... IN 22

Draw Conclusions ...... IN 23

21st Century Learning Online Checklist .... IN 24

Keys to Good Writing ... IN 25

Map and Globe Handbook

Five Themes of Geography .... IN 26

Reading Globes .... IN 28

Earth's Hemispheres ..... IN 29

Maps Show Direction .... IN 30

Maps Show Distance .... IN 31

Political Maps .... IN 32

Physical Maps .... IN 33

Elevation Maps .... IN 34

Use a Grid .... IN 35

Use Latitude and Longitude for Exact Location ..... IN 36

Maps Show Events ...... IN 37

Chapter 1

Indiana's Geography

my Story Spark .... IN 38

my Story T.C. Steele 1

Lesson 1
Land and Water 2

Lesson 2
Regions and Resources 10

Map Skills
Use Latitude and Longitude 16

Lesson 3
Indiana Connections 18

Study Guide 24

Review and Assessment 25

my Story Book 27

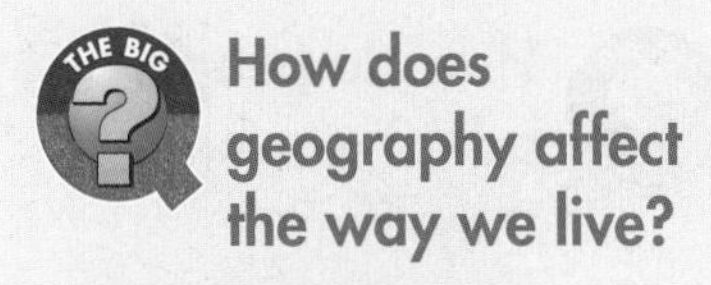

How does geography affect the way we live?

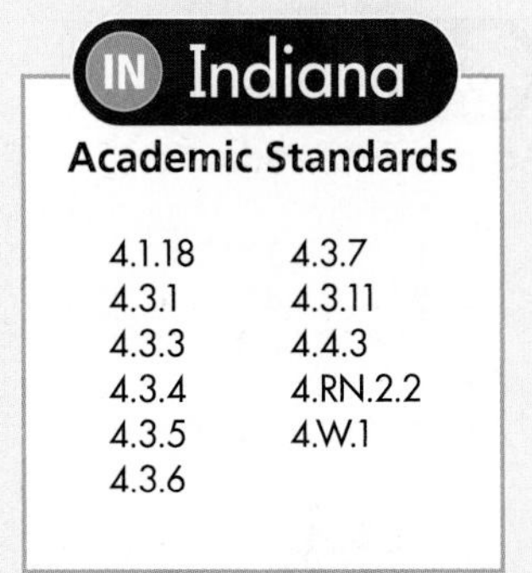

IN Indiana
Academic Standards

4.1.18	4.3.7
4.3.1	4.3.11
4.3.3	4.4.3
4.3.4	4.RN.2.2
4.3.5	4.W.1
4.3.6	

The Central Till Plain

Chapter 2

Indiana's Early History

How do people adapt to where they live?

Indiana
Academic Standards

4.1.1	4.3.13
4.1.2	4.4.1
4.1.3	4.4.3
4.3.8	4.4.6
4.3.9	4.RN.2.2
4.3.12	4.W.1

my Story Spark 28

my Story **Robert de La Salle** 29

Lesson 1
First People 30

Lesson 2
Native Americans of Indiana 36

Lesson 3
Explorers and Settlers 42

21c Map Skills
Interpret Maps 48

Study Guide 50

Review and Assessment 51

my Story Book 53

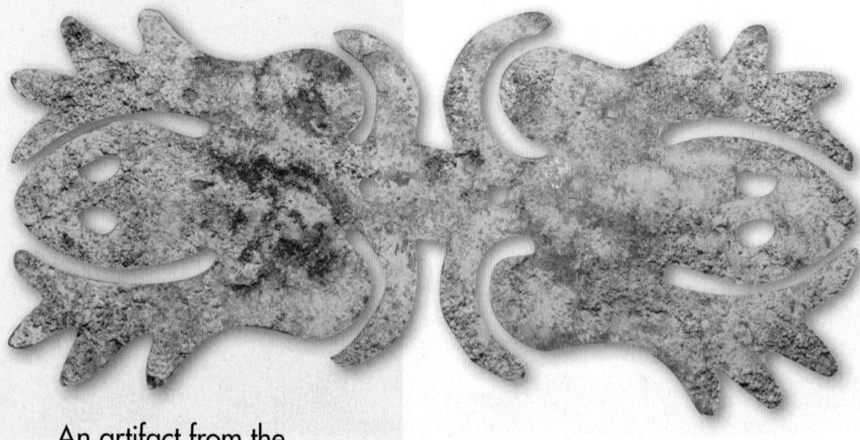

An artifact from the Hopewell people

Chapter 3

American Revolution to Civil War

my Story Spark 54

my Story **Tecumseh** 55

Lesson 1
American Revolution and Indiana 56

Lesson 2
Building and Expanding the Nation 62

Lesson 3
A New State 68

Lesson 4
Civil War and Indiana 74

21C Critical Thinking Skills
Compare Viewpoints 82

Study Guide 84

Review and Assessment 85

my Story Book 87

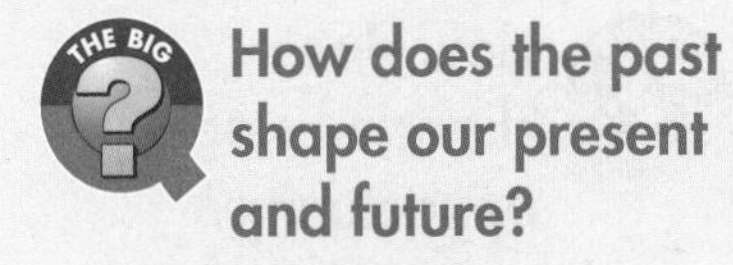

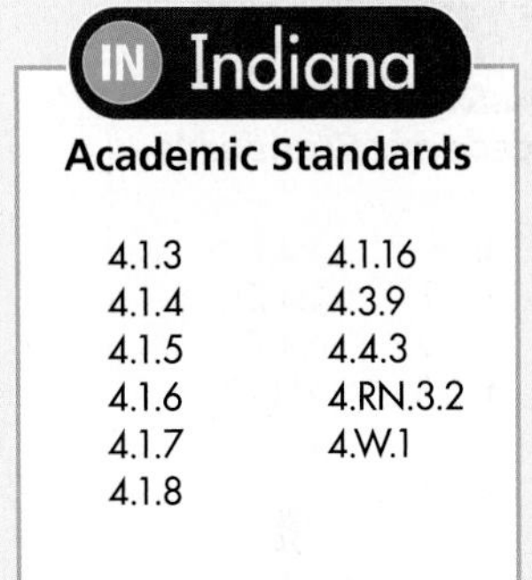

George Washington and American Revolution soldiers

Chapter 4

A Growing State

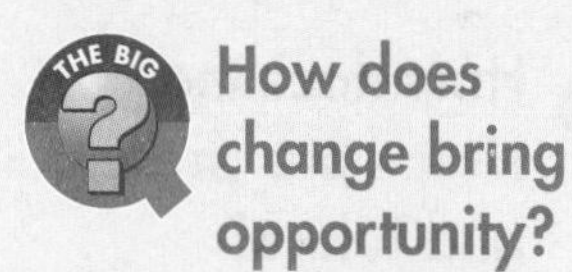

How does change bring opportunity?

Indiana Academic Standards

4.1.9, 4.1.11, 4.1.12, 4.1.15, 4.1.18, 4.3.10, 4.4.1, 4.4.2, 4.4.7, 4.RN.3.3, 4.W.1

my Story Spark 88

my Story **Gene Stratton-Porter** 89

Lesson 1
Economic Changes 90

Lesson 2
New People, New Jobs 96

Lesson 3
Growth and Development 102

21c Graph Skills
Interpret Timelines 110

Study Guide 112

Review and Assessment 113

my Story Book 115

Michigan City train station

Chapter 5

Challenging Times

my Story Spark 116

my Story **Ernie Pyle** 117

Lesson 1
World War I and the 1920s 118

Lesson 2
The Great Depression and World War II 124

Lesson 3
A Changing State 132

Critical Thinking Skills
Primary and Secondary Sources 138

Study Guide 140

Review and Assessment 141

my Story Book 143

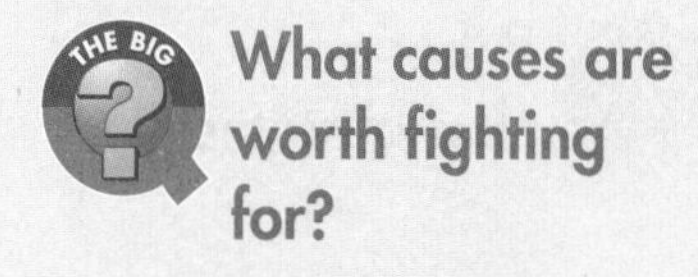

What causes are worth fighting for?

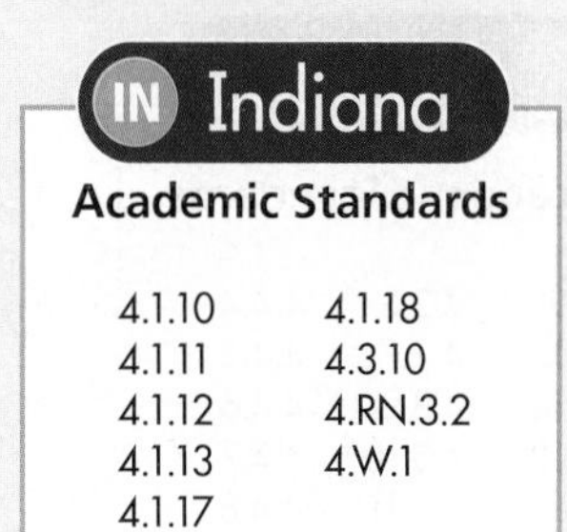

IN Indiana

Academic Standards

4.1.10 4.1.11 4.1.12 4.1.13 4.1.17 4.1.18 4.3.10 4.RN.3.2 4.W.1

World War II Victory Gardens poster

Chapter 6

Indiana Today

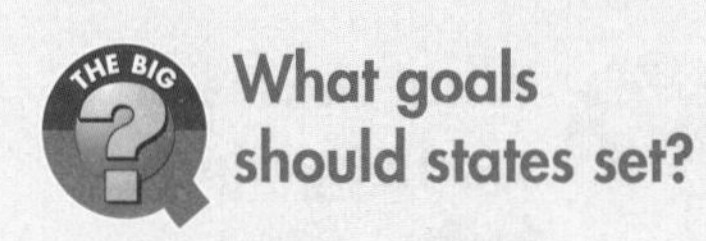

What goals should states set?

IN Indiana

Academic Standards

4.1.9	4.2.6	4.4.4
4.1.13	4.2.7	4.4.5
4.1.14	4.3.8	4.4.6
4.1.18	4.3.10	4.4.7
4.2.1	4.3.11	4.4.8
4.2.2	4.3.12	4.4.9
4.2.3	4.3.13	4.4.10
4.2.4	4.4.1	4.RN.2.1
4.2.5	4.4.2	4.W.1

my Story Spark 144

my Story **Myra Selby** 145

Lesson 1
Indiana's Government 146

Lesson 2
Citizens of Indiana 152

21c Collaboration and Creativity Skills
Solve Problems 158

Lesson 3
Indiana's Economy 160

Lesson 4
Entrepreneurs and Artists 168

Study Guide 176

Review and Assessment 177

my Story Book 179

Atlas 180

Glossary R11

Index R17

Credits R24

Indiana Statehouse rotunda

Indiana Academic Standards

Grade 4: Indiana in the Nation and the World

STANDARD 1: HISTORY	
Students trace the historical periods, places, people, events, and movements that have led to the development of Indiana as a state.	
Historical Knowledge	
American Indians and the Arrival of Europeans to 1770	
4.1.1	Identify and compare the major early cultures that existed in the region that became Indiana prior to contact with Europeans. **Examples:** Paleo-Indians such as the Hopewell, Adena and the Mississippian cultures
4.1.2	Identify and describe historic Native American Indian groups that lived in Indiana at the time of early European exploration, including ways these groups adapted to and interacted with the physical environment. **Examples:** Miami, Shawnee, Potawatomi and Lenape (Delaware)
The American Revolution and the Indiana Territory: 1770s to 1816	
4.1.3	Explain the importance of the Revolutionary War and other key events and people that influenced the development of Indiana as a state. **Examples:** George Rogers Clark and the Fall of Vincennes (1779), development of the Northwest Territory, Indiana becoming a U.S. Territory, Chief Little Turtle, Tecumseh, Tenskwatawa (the Prophet), William Henry Harrison, and the Battle of Tippecanoe (1811)
4.1.4	Summarize and explain the significance of key documents in Indiana's development from a United States territory to statehood. **Examples:** The Land Ordinance of 1784; The Northwest Ordinance (1787), which made Indiana part of the United States territory; and the 1816 Indiana Constitution, which established the first state government
Statehood: 1816 to 1851	
4.1.5	Identify and explain the causes of the removal of Native American Indian groups in the state and their resettlement during the 1830s.
4.1.6	Explain how key individuals and events influenced the early growth and development of Indiana. **Examples:** Indiana's first governor, Jonathan Jennings; Robert Owen and the New Harmony settlement; moving the state capitol from Corydon to Indianapolis; development of roads and canals in Indiana; and the Indiana Constitution of 1851

Grade 4: Indiana in the Nation and the World

The Civil War Era and Later Development: 1850 to 1900	
4.1.7	Explain the roles of various individuals, groups, and movements in the social conflicts leading to the Civil War. **Examples:** Levi and Catherine Coffin, abolition and anti-slavery groups, The Underground Railroad, and the Liberia colonization movement
4.1.8	Summarize the impact of Abraham Lincoln's presidency on Indiana and describe the participation of Indiana citizens in the Civil War. **Examples:** Indiana's volunteer soldiers, the Twenty-eighth Regiment of the United States Colored Troops, Camp Morton, John Hunt Morgan, The Battle of Corydon, Lew Wallace, Benjamin Harrison, and women and children on the home front
4.1.9	Give examples of Indiana's increasing agricultural, industrial, political and business development in the nineteenth century. **Examples:** Growth of railroads and urban centers, such as Indianapolis, South Bend, Evansville, Fort Wayne and Gary; President Benjamin Harrison; expansion of the educational system and universities; the growth of labor unions; and the start of Eli Lilly's pharmaceutical business
Growth and Development: 1900 to 1950	
4.1.10	Describe the participation of Indiana citizens in World War I and World War II. **Examples:** Home front activities such as planting victory gardens, air raid drills and rationing; the use of Indiana steel mills to manufacture weapons; contribution of troops; and the war reports of Ernie Pyle
4.1.11	Identify and describe important events and movements that changed life in Indiana in the early twentieth century. **Examples:** Women's suffrage, the Great Depression, World War I, African-American migration from the South and World War II
4.1.12	Describe the transformation of Indiana through immigration and through developments in agriculture, industry and transportation. **Examples:** The impact of improved farming methods on Indiana agriculture; the development of Indiana's automobile industry such as the Studebaker and the Duesenberg; the glass industry; the Ball Brothers; the growth of the steel industry in northern Indiana; and immigrant influence on cities and coal mining regions of the state
Contemporary Indiana: 1950 – Present	
4.1.13	Identify and describe important events and movements that changed life in Indiana from the mid-twentieth century to the present. **Examples:** The civil rights movement and school integration in Indiana; Indiana's participation in the Korean War; Asian and Hispanic immigration; and growth in advanced manufacturing and the life sciences industry.

Grade 4: Indiana in the Nation and the World

4.1.14	Research Indiana's modern growth emphasizing manufacturing, new technologies, transportation and global connections. **Examples:** Use Indiana government Web sites and other online resources to learn about the development of the interstate highway system, establishment of ports in Indiana, aerospace engineering, and pharmaceutical and high-tech industries.
Chronological Thinking, Historical Comprehension, Analysis and Interpretation, Research	
4.1.15	Create and interpret timelines that show relationships among people, events, and movements in the history of Indiana. **Examples:** Immigration patterns such as the settlement of the French and Germans, and automobile manufacturing
4.1.16	Identify different opinions in historical documents and other information resources and identify the central question each narrative addresses. **Examples:** Identify different opinions regarding Indiana's participation in the Civil War, using political cartoons, newspaper editorials and writings found in digitalized collections of local and state libraries, museums and historic sites.
4.1.17	Construct a brief narrative about an event in Indiana history using primary* and secondary sources*. **Examples:** The first Indianapolis 500 mile race in 1911, The Battle of Tippecanoe 1811, The Ohio River Flood of 1913 and the 1965 Palm Sunday tornadoes ***primary source:** developed by people who experienced the events being studied (i.e., autobiographies, diaries, letters, government documents) ***secondary source:** developed by people who have researched events but did not experience them directly (i.e., articles, biographies, Internet resources, nonfiction books)
4.1.18	Research and describe the contributions of important Indiana artists and writers to the state's cultural landscape. **Examples:** Painters: T.C. Steele, the Hoosier Group and Robert Indiana; Authors: James Whitcomb Riley and Gene Stratton Porter; Musicians: Cole Porter, Hoagy Carmichael, Wes Montgomery, Joshua Bell and John Mellencamp; Other entertainers: Red Skelton and David Letterman

Grade 4: Indiana in the Nation and the World

STANDARD 2: CIVICS AND GOVERNMENT	
Students describe the components and characteristics of Indiana's constitutional form of government; explain the levels and three branches of Indiana's government; understand citizenship rights and responsibilities; investigate civic and political issues and problems; use inquiry and communication skills to report findings in charts, graphs, written and verbal forms; and demonstrate responsible citizenship by exercising civic virtues and participation skills.	
Foundations of Government	
4.2.1	Explain the major purposes of Indiana's Constitution as stated in the Preamble.
4.2.2	Describe individual rights, such as freedom of speech, freedom of religion and the right to public education, which people have under Article I of Indiana's Constitution.
Functions of Government	
4.2.3	Identify and explain the major responsibilities of the legislative (Article 4), executive (Article 5), and judicial branches (Article 7) of state government as written in the Indiana Constitution.
4.2.4	Identify major state offices, the duties and powers associated with them, and how they are chosen, such as by election or appointment. **Examples:** Governor, lieutenant governor, chief justice, state senators and state representatives.
Roles of Citizens	
4.2.5	Give examples of how citizens can participate in their state government and explain the right and responsibility of voting.
4.2.6	Define and provide examples of civic virtues* in a democracy. **Examples:** Individual responsibility, self-discipline/self-governance, civility, respect for the rights and dignity of all individuals, honesty, respect for the law, courage, compassion, patriotism, fairness and commitment to the common good ***civic virtues:** behaviors that contribute to the healthy functioning of a democracy
4.2.7	Use a variety of resources to take a position or recommend a course of action on a public issue relating to Indiana's past or present. Examples: Use local, state and federal Web sites, as well as newspapers, television and video images, to research and write an editorial related to Indiana's environment. **Examples:** Use local, state and federal Web sites, as well as newspapers, television and video images, to research and write an editorial related to Indiana's environment.

Grade 4: Indiana in the Nation and the World

STANDARD 3: GEOGRAPHY	
Students explain how the Earth/sun relationship influences the climate of Indiana; identify the components of Earth's physical systems; describe the major physical and cultural characteristics of Indiana; give examples of how people have adapted to and modified their environment, past and present; identify regions of Indiana, and compare the geographic characteristics of Indiana with states and regions in other parts of the world.	
The World in Spatial Terms	
4.3.1	Use latitude and longitude to identify physical and human features of Indiana. **Examples:** transportation routes and bodies of water (lakes and rivers)
4.3.2	Estimate distances between two places on a map when referring to relative locations.
Places and Regions	
4.3.3	Locate Indiana on a map as one of the 50 United States. Identify and describe the location of the state capital, major cities and rivers in Indiana.
4.3.4	Map and describe the physical regions of Indiana and identify major natural resources and crop regions. **Examples:** Northern Lakes and Moraines, Central Till Plain and Southern Lowlands
Physical Systems	
4.3.5	Explain how glaciers shaped Indiana's landscape and environment.
4.3.6	Describe Indiana's landforms (lithosphere*), water features (hydrosphere*), and plants and animals (biosphere*). ***lithosphere:** the soil and rock that form Earth's surface ***hydrosphere:** all the water on Earth's surface, including the hydrologic cycle (precipitation, evaporation, and condensation) ***biosphere:** all plants and animals
4.3.7	Explain the effect of the Earth/sun relationship on the climate of Indiana. **Examples:** Describe seasonal changes and use USDA hardiness zone maps to select plants and trees for a community park.
4.3.8	Identify the challenges in the physical landscape of Indiana to early settlers and modern day economic development. **Examples:** Forest growth and transportation routes
Human Systems	
4.3.9	Explain the importance of major transportation routes, including rivers, in the exploration, settlement and growth of Indiana and in the state's location as a crossroad of America.

Grade 4: Indiana in the Nation and the World

4.3.10	Identify immigration patterns and describe the impact diverse ethnic and cultural groups has had and has on Indiana. • *E pluribus unum* (out of many, one) • Ellis Island was opened (January 1, 1892) during the administration of President Benjamin Harrison (Indiana's only President)
4.3.11	Examine Indiana's international relationships with states and regions in other parts of the world. **Examples:** Describe cultural exchanges between Indiana and other states and provinces, such as Rio Grande do Sul, Brazil, or Zhejiang Province, China.
Environment and Society	
4.3.12	Create maps of Indiana at different times in history showing regions and major physical and cultural features; give examples of how people in Indiana have modified their environment over time.
4.3.13	Read and interpret texts (written, graphs, maps, timelines, etc.) to answer geographic questions about Indiana in the past and present.
STANDARD 4: ECONOMICS	
Students study and compare the characteristics of Indiana's changing economy in the past and present.	
4.4.1	Give examples of the kinds of goods* and services* produced in Indiana in different historical periods. ***goods:** tangible objects, such as food or toys, that can satisfy people's wants and needs ***services:** actions that someone does for someone else, such as dental care or trash removal
4.4.2	Define productivity* and provide examples of how productivity has changed in Indiana during the past 100 years. **Examples:** Improved farm equipment has helped farms produce more. Technology has helped businesses run more efficiently. Improved education has provided individuals with the knowledge and skills to run businesses and work more productively. ***productivity:** the amount of goods and services produced in a period of time divided by the productive resources used
4.4.3	Explain how both parties can benefit from trade* and give examples of how people in Indiana engaged in trade in different time periods. ***trade:** the voluntary exchange of goods or services

Grade 4: Indiana in the Nation and the World

4.4.4	Explain that prices change as a result of changes in supply* and demand* for specific products. ***supply:** what producers are willing and able to sell at various prices ***demand:** what consumers are willing and able to buy at various prices
4.4.5	Describe Indiana's emerging global connections. **Examples:** Identify international companies in Indiana, such as Toyota, Chrysler (Fiat), Honda, Roche Diagnostics, and Indiana companies that have an international presence such as Biomet, Eli Lilly and Cummins Engine.
4.4.6	List the functions of money* and compare and contrast things that have been used as money in the past in Indiana, the United States and the world. ***functions of money:** helps people trade, measures the value of items, facilitates saving
4.4.7	Identify entrepreneurs* who have influenced Indiana and the local community. **Examples:** The Studebaker brothers, Madam C.J. Walker, Eli Lilly and Marie Webster ***entrepreneur:** a person who takes a risk to start a business
4.4.8	Define profit* and describe how profit is an incentive for entrepreneurs. ***profit:** revenues from selling a good or service minus the costs of producing the good or service
4.4.9	Identify important goods and services provided by state and local governments by giving examples of how state and local tax revenues are used.
4.4.10	Explain how people save, develop a savings plan, and create a budget in order to make a future purchase.

IN **4.RN.2.2** Determine the main idea of a text and explain how it is supported by key details.

Summarize

We summarize, or retell, to check our understanding of what we have read. A summary is usually short. We can sum up what we have read in just a few sentences.

Reading Skills

4.RN.3.2 Describe the organizational structure of events, ideas, concepts, or information in a text.

Sequence

Sequence refers to the order of events in text. We also use sequence when we list the steps in a process.

Compare and Contrast
To compare and contrast is to look for similarities and differences in things.
SPEAKS 5 DIFFERENT LANGUAGES
$23.95
$19.95
ABSOLUTELY NOT PXR201 COMPATIBLE
PXR201 COMPATIBLE
20% OFF!

IN **4.RN.3.2** Describe the organizational structure of events, ideas, concepts, or information in a text.

Draw Conclusions
When we draw conclusions, we think about facts and details and then decide something about them.

21C

21st Century Learning Online Checklist

You can go online to myworldsocialstudies.com to practice the skills listed below. These are skills that will be important to you throughout your life. After you complete each skill tutorial online, check it off here in your book.

Target Reading Skills

- ☐ Main Idea and Details
- ☐ Cause and Effect
- ☐ Categorize
- ☐ Fact and Opinion
- ☐ Draw Conclusions
- ☐ Generalize
- ☐ Compare and Contrast
- ☐ Sequence
- ☐ Summarize

Collaboration and Creativity Skills

- ☐ Solve Problems
- ☐ Work in Cooperative Teams
- ☐ Resolve Conflict
- ☐ Generate New Ideas

Graph Skills

- ☐ Interpret Graphs
- ☐ Create Charts
- ☐ Interpret Timelines

Map Skills

- ☐ Use Longitude and Latitude
- ☐ Interpret Physical Maps
- ☐ Interpret Economic Data on Maps
- ☐ Interpret Cultural Data on Maps

Critical Thinking Skills

- ☐ Compare Viewpoints
- ☐ Use Primary and Secondary Sources
- ☐ Identify Bias
- ☐ Make Decisions
- ☐ Predict Consequences

Media and Technology Skills

- ☐ Conduct Research
- ☐ Use the Internet Safely
- ☐ Analyze Images
- ☐ Evaluate Media Content
- ☐ Deliver an Effective Presentation

Keys to Good Writing

The Writing Process

Good writers follow five steps when they write.

Prewrite	Choose a topic, gather details about it, and plan how to use them.
Draft	Write down all your ideas, and don't worry about making it perfect.
Revise	Review your writing, looking for the traits of good writing. Change parts that are confusing or incomplete.
Edit	Check your spelling, capitalization, punctuation, and grammar. Make a final copy.
Share	Share your writing with others.

The Writing Traits

Good writers look at six qualities of their writing to make it the best writing possible.

Ideas	Share a clear message with specific ideas and details.
Organization	Have a beginning, middle, and end that are easy to follow.
Voice	Use a natural tone in your writing.
Word Choice	Choose strong nouns and verbs and colorful adjectives.
Sentence Flow	Vary your sentence structures and beginnings to create writing that is easy to read.
Conventions	Follow the rules of spelling, capitalization, punctuation, and grammar.

Geography Skills

Five Themes of Geography

Geography is the study of Earth. This study can be divided into five themes: Location, Place, Human/Environmental Interaction, Movement, and Region. You can use the themes to better understand how each place on Earth is different from any other place, as the example of the Great Lakes shows.

Location: Where can the Great Lakes be found?
The Great Lakes are located in the United States and Canada. The five lakes include Lake Erie, Lake Huron, Lake Michigan, Lake Ontario, and Lake Superior.

Location

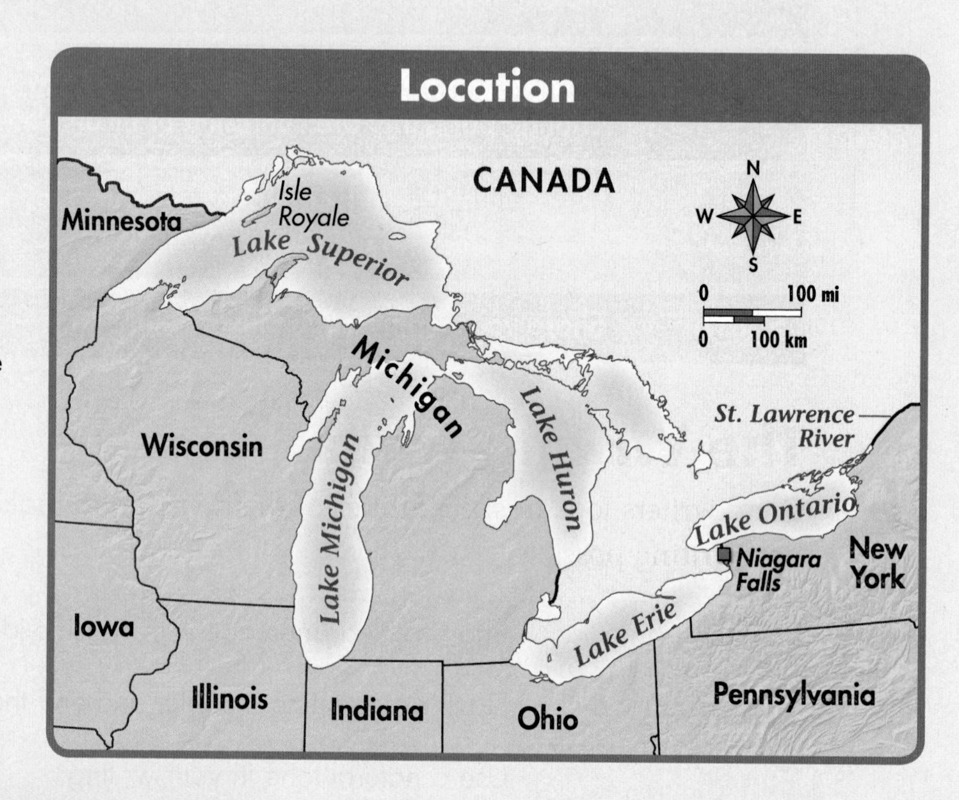

Place

Place: How is this place different from others?
Lake Michigan is the only one of the Great Lakes to sit entirely within the boundaries of the United States. It covers about 22,300 square miles.

Map and Globe Handbook

IN **Indiana Academic Standards**

4.3.1 Use latitude and longitude to identify physical and human features of Indiana.

4.3.2 Estimate distances between two places on a map when referring to relative locations.

4.3.3 Locate Indiana on a map, and identify the location of the state capital, major cities, and rivers.

Human/Environmental Interaction

Human Interaction: How have people changed a place?

Canals are man-made waterways that are dug across land. Canals around the Great Lakes connect these lakes to other lakes and to rivers in the area. In Indiana, for example, a canal connects Lake Michigan to the Grand Calumet River.

Movement

Movement: How has movement changed a place?

Since the Great Lakes connect to the Atlantic Ocean by the St. Lawrence Seaway, shipping is a major industry here.

Region

Region: What is special about the region that includes the Great Lakes?

There are many natural areas where birds can nest or take shelter.

Reading Globes

This is an image of Earth. It shows some of Earth's large landforms, called continents. It also shows Earth's large bodies of water, called oceans.

1. **Name** the two continents shown in this photo of Earth.

....

2. **Name** the two oceans shown.

....

To the right is a **globe**, a round model of Earth. Some globes are small enough to hold in your hands. It shows the true shapes and locations of Earth's continents and oceans.

A globe often shows two lines that divide Earth into halves. These two lines are called the prime meridian and the equator. You can see the equator on this globe.

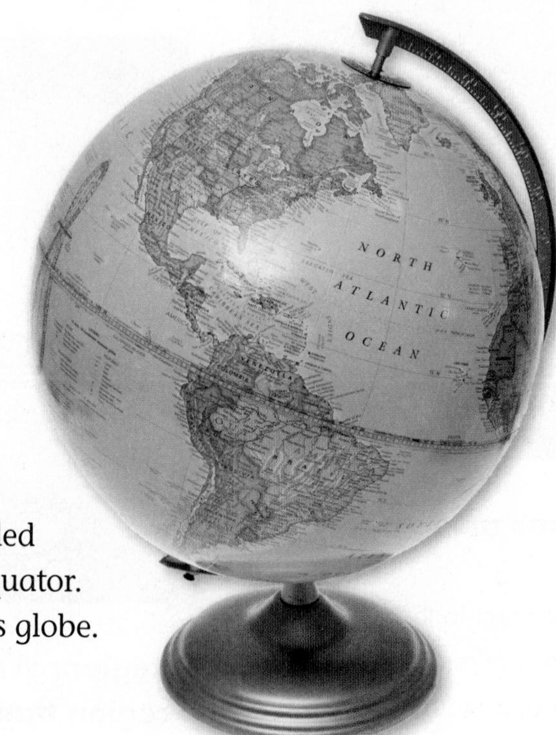

Earth's Hemispheres

The equator and the prime meridian divide Earth into halves called **hemispheres.** The **prime meridian** is a line drawn from the North Pole to the South Pole that passes through Europe and Africa. That line divides Earth into the Western Hemisphere and the Eastern Hemisphere as shown below.

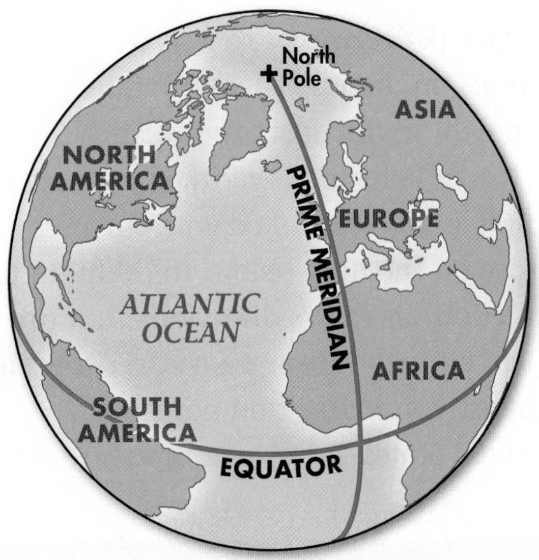

Vocabulary

globe
hemisphere
prime meridian
equator

The **equator** is a line drawn around Earth halfway between the North Pole and the South Pole. It divides Earth into the Northern and Southern Hemispheres.

Because Earth is divided two ways, it has four hemispheres.

Western Hemisphere

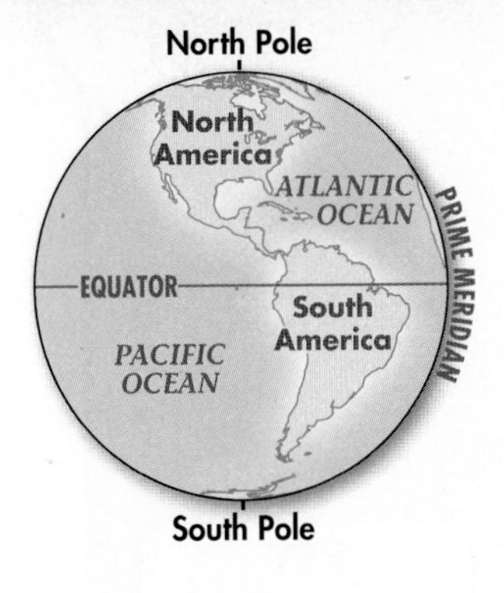

Eastern Hemisphere

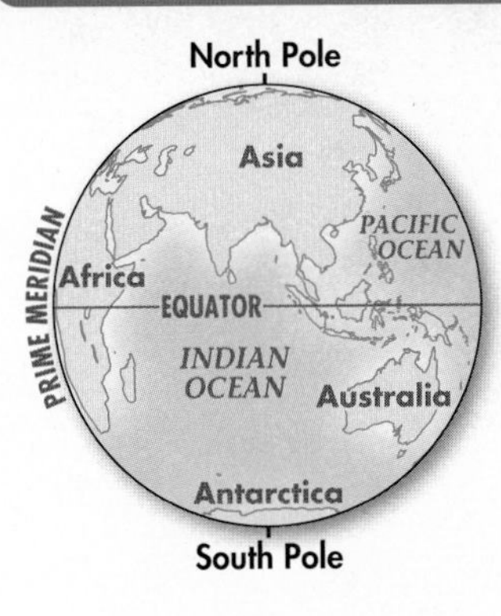

Northern Hemisphere

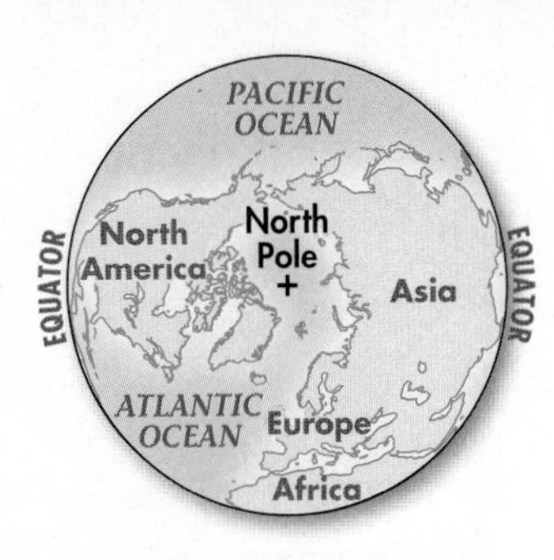

Southern Hemisphere

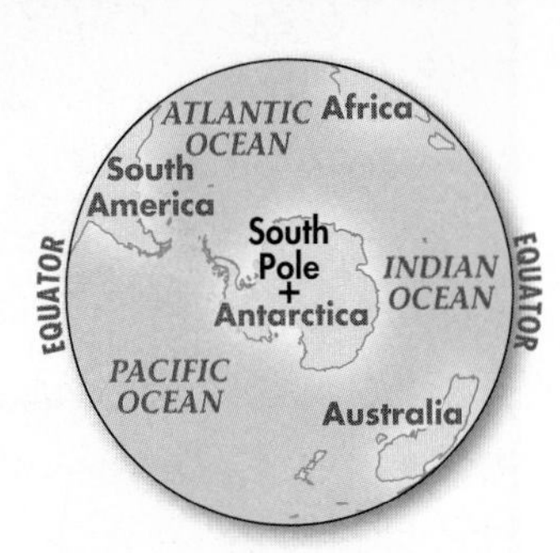

3. Name the two hemispheres that North America is located in.

....

....

4. Identify whether Asia is north or south of the equator.

....

Maps Show Direction

Maps show real directions. A **compass rose** is a symbol that shows directions on a map. There are four **cardinal directions**—north, south, east, and west. North points toward the North Pole and is marked with an *N*. South points to the South Pole and is marked with an *S*.

Look at the compass rose on the map below. In addition to showing the cardinal directions, it shows directions that are midway between them. These are the **intermediate directions.** They are northeast, southeast, southwest, and northwest.

This map shows the United States. It has a compass rose to show direction.

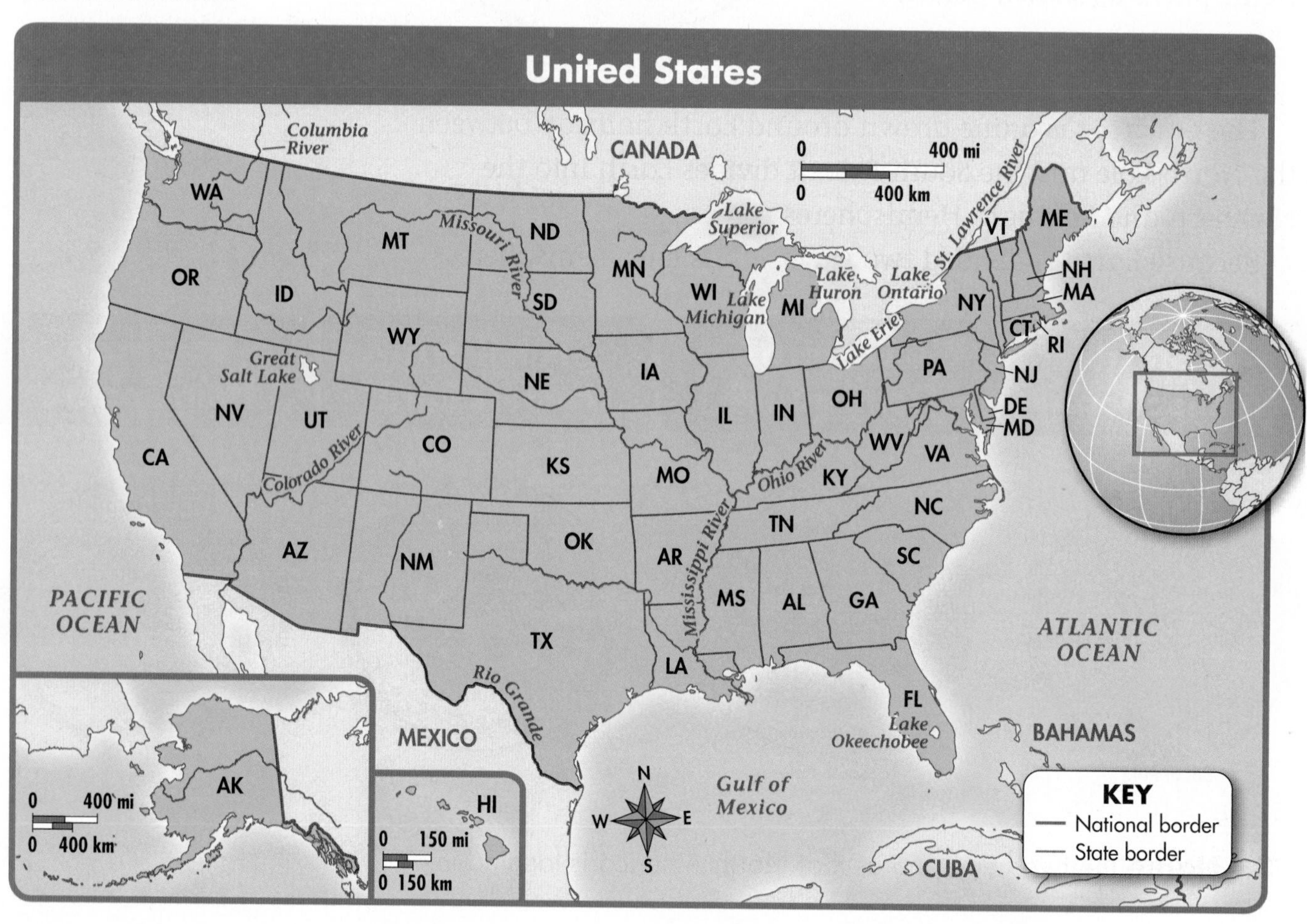

5. **Identify** Indiana. **Circle** it on the map.

6. Using cardinal and intermediate directions, **describe** the location of Indiana in the United States.

....

....

Maps Show Distance

A map is a very small drawing of a large place. However, you can find real distances in miles or kilometers from one point to another on Earth by using a map scale. A **map scale** shows the relationship between distance on the map and distance on Earth. One way to use the scale is to hold the edge of a piece of paper under the scale and copy it. Then place your copy of the scale on the map to measure the distance between two points. Doing this can help you estimate the distance between the two points.

The map below shows the path of Hurricane Katrina. You can use the scale to track the miles the storm traveled.

Vocabulary

compass rose
cardinal direction
intermediate direction
map scale

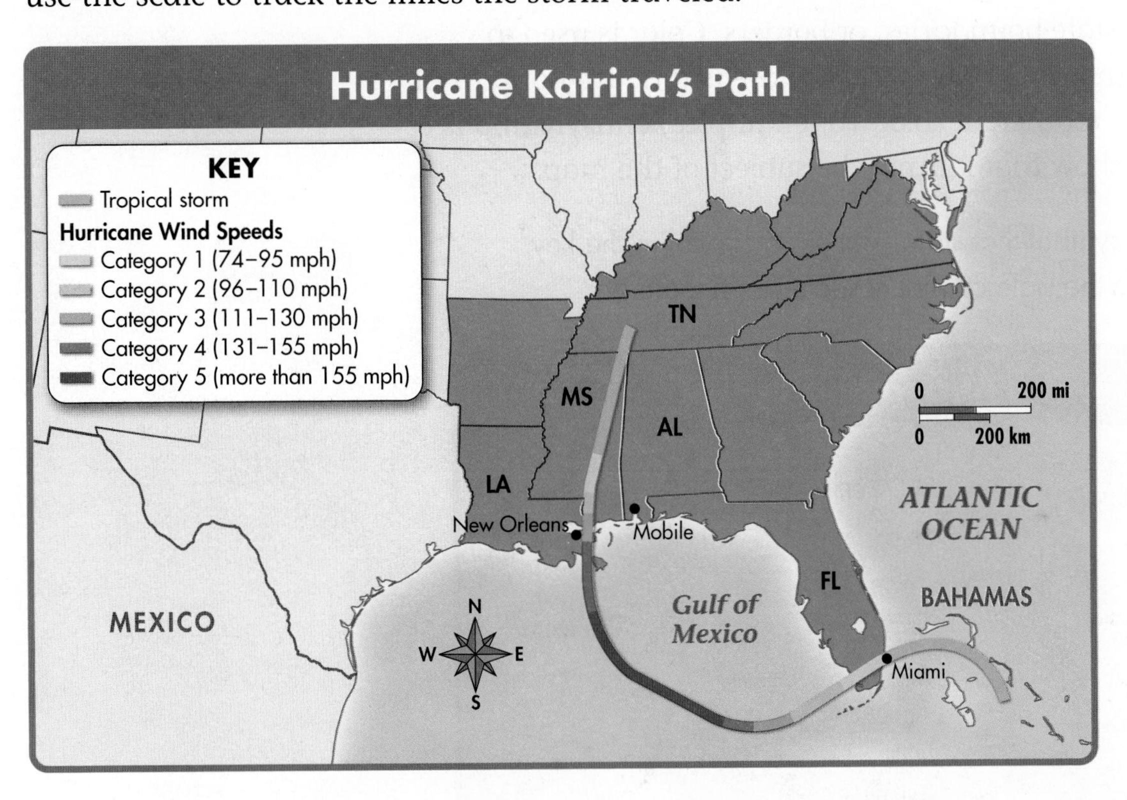

7. Identify the body of water where Hurricane Katrina became a Category 5 hurricane.

....

8. Estimate about how many miles Hurricane Katrina traveled north from New Orleans before it became a tropical storm.

....

....

Political Maps

A map is a flat drawing of all or part of Earth. It shows a place from above.

Different kinds of maps show different information. A map that shows boundaries for counties, states, or nations, as well as capital cities, is called a **political map.** This kind of map often shows major landforms and bodies of water to help locate places.

Each map has a title. The title tells you what the map is about. Maps use symbols to show information. A **symbol** is a small drawing, line, or color that stands for something else. The **map key** or legend tells what each symbol on the map stands for. On this political map, a star stands for the state capital. Lines show the state boundaries, or borders. Color is used to show the area that is the Midwest. The areas that are not part of the Midwest are a different color. For example, Pennsylvania is a lighter color to show that it is not the subject of the map.

9. Circle the symbol that stands for state capital in the key. Then **circle** the state capital of Indiana on the map.

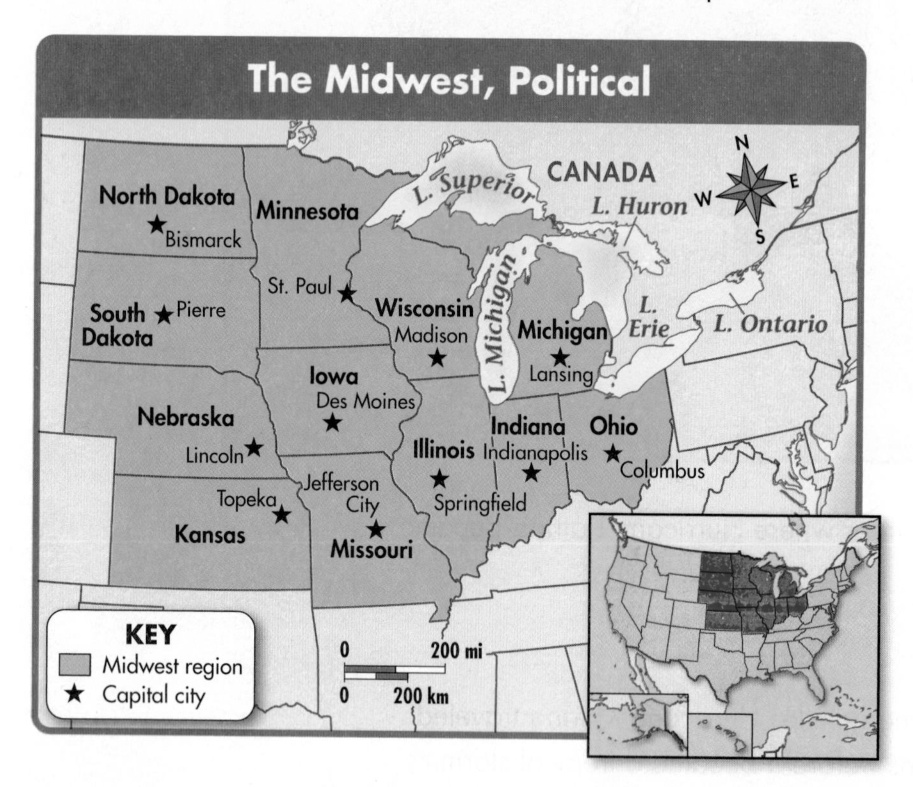

Physical Maps

A **physical map** shows landforms, such as mountains, plains, and deserts. It also shows bodies of water, such as oceans, lakes, and rivers. Physical maps often show borders between states and countries to help locate these landforms. A good place to look for political and physical maps is an atlas. An **atlas** is a collection or book of maps.

The physical map of the Midwest shown below identifies land and water features. It includes labels for peninsulas, or land that sticks out into water and is connected to a larger piece of land. It also has labels for ranges, peaks, plateaus, and plains. A range is a series of mountains. A peak is the top of a mountain. A plateau is an area of flat land that is higher than the land around it. Plains are flat, level land.

Vocabulary

political map
symbol
map key
physical map
atlas

10. Circle the river that makes up Indiana's southern border. **Draw an X** through the lake that touches the northwestern corner of Indiana.

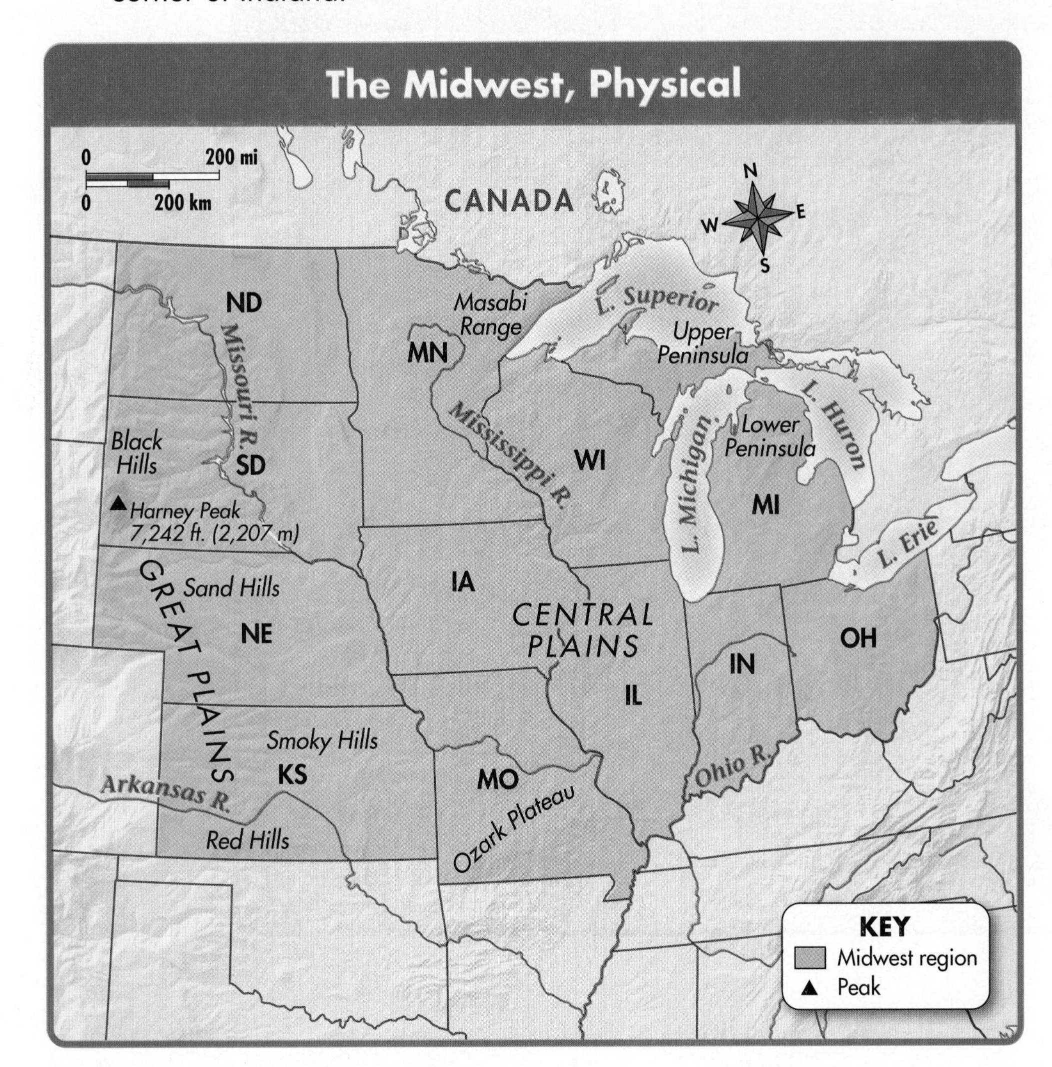

Elevation Maps

An **elevation** map shows you how high the land is. Elevation is height above sea level. A place that is at sea level is at the same height as the surface of ocean's water.

Elevation maps use color to show elevation. To read this kind of map, first look at the map key. Note that there are numbers next to each color on the map key. The numbers show the range of elevation that each color represents. On this Indiana map, dark green represents the lowest elevation. The range for dark green is between 0 and 600 feet above sea level.

11. Identify the elevation range of the Till Plains. How tall is Indiana's highest point?.

....

....

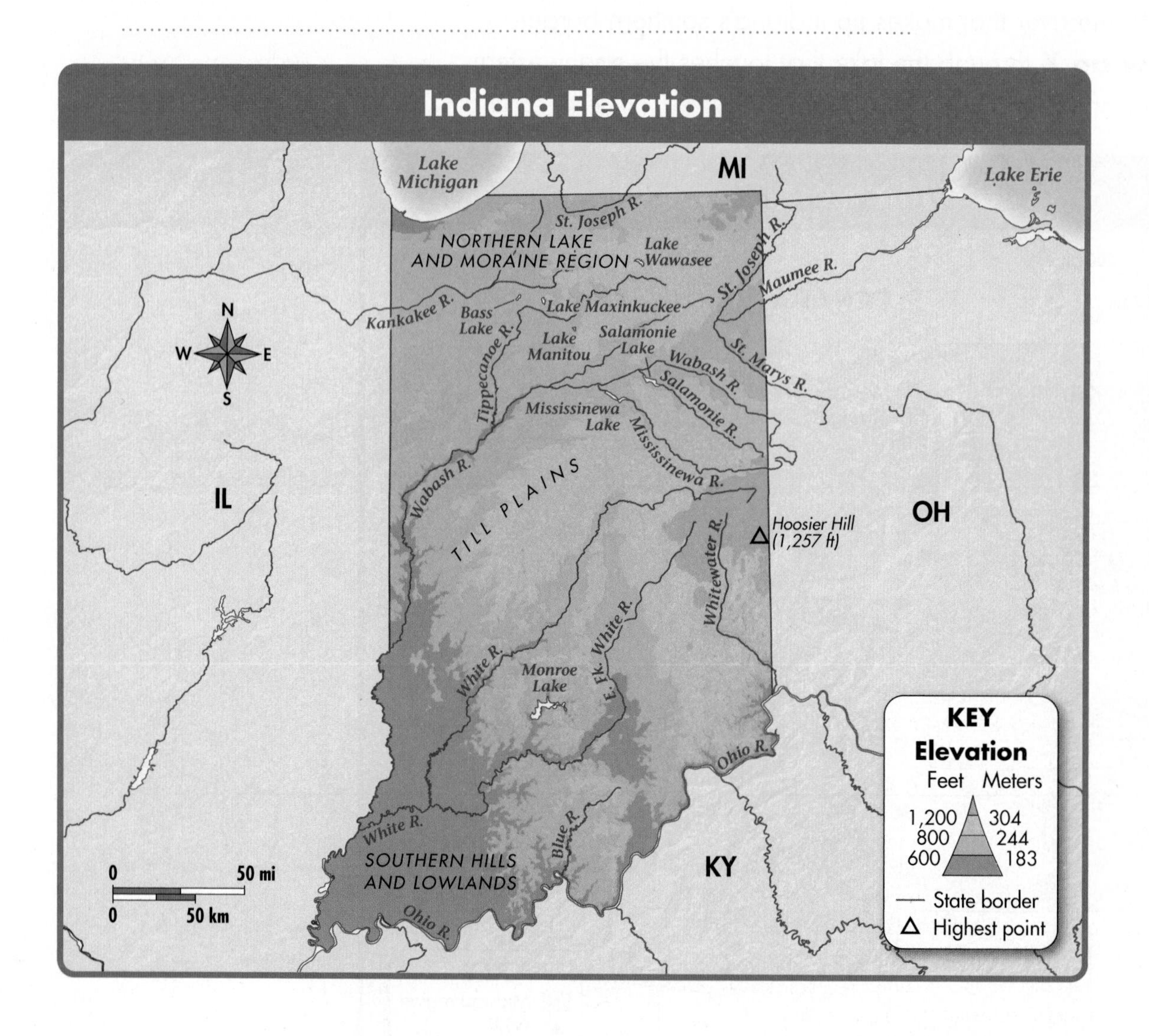

Use a Grid

Vocabulary

elevation
grid

A city map shows the streets of a city. It might also show points of interest and natural features. To help locate places more easily, this city map has a **grid.** A grid is a system of lines that cross each other forming a pattern of squares. The lines are labeled with letters and numbers. These squares give every place on the map a location.

To find a specific location, the map has an index. An index is an alphabetical listing of places. The index gives the letter and number of the square where the place is located.

12. Look at the map. **Add** the number and letter set for the Indianapolis Motor Speedway to the index.

Index	
Indianapolis Motor Speedway	
Fort Harrison State Park	B4
The Children's Museum of Indianapolis	C2

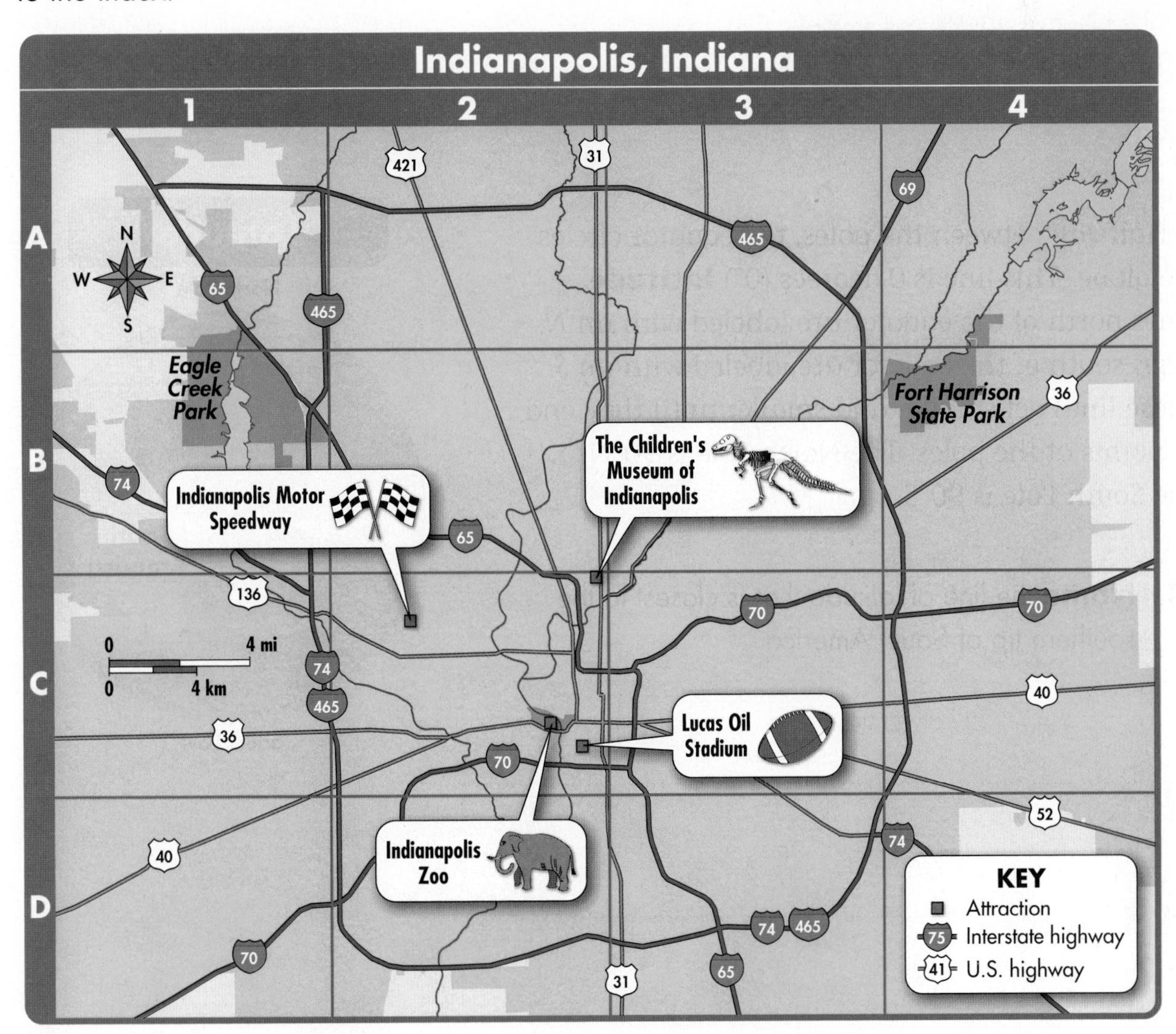

Use Latitude and Longitude for Exact Location

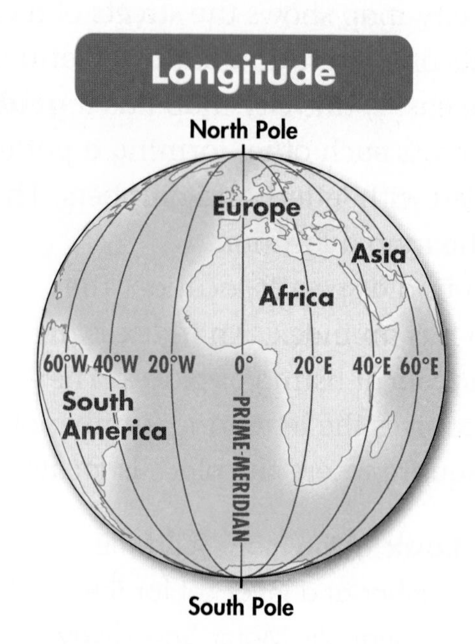

Long ago, mapmakers made a system for locating exact places on Earth. The system uses two sets of lines that form a grid around the globe. These lines are numbered in units called **degrees.**

One set of lines runs from the North Pole to the South Pole. These are lines of **longitude.** The prime meridian is labeled 0 degrees (0°) longitude. Lines of longitude are labeled from 0° to 180°. Lines east of the prime meridian are labeled with an *E*. Lines west of it are labeled with a *W*.

13. Identify about how many degrees east the center of Africa is from the prime meridian.

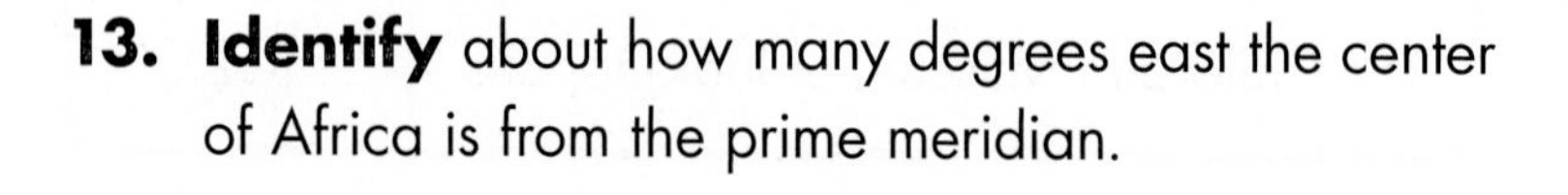

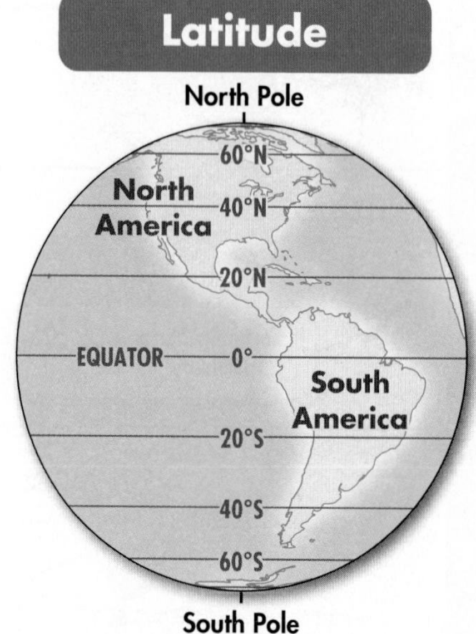

Halfway between the poles, the equator circles the globe. This line is 0 degrees (0°) **latitude.** Lines north of the equator are labeled with an *N*. Lines south of the equator are labeled with an *S*. These lines get smaller and smaller until they end as points at the poles. The North Pole is 90°N. The South Pole is 90°S.

14. Name the line of latitude that is closest to the southern tip of South America.

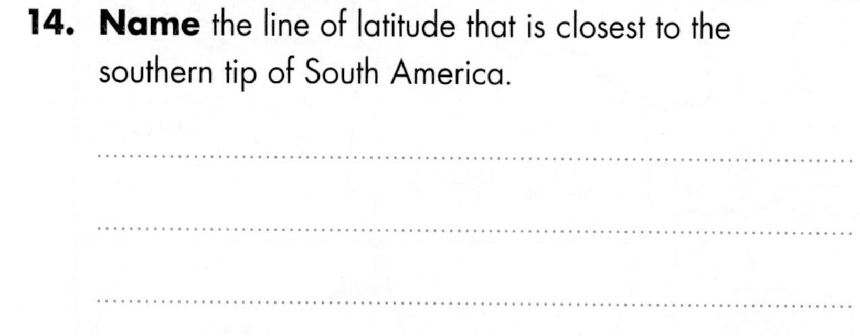

Maps Show Events

Vocabulary

degree
longitude
latitude

Maps can also show events. These might be current events, such as a map of battles that are being fought between different countries, or a weather map that shows the path of a severe storm. Another example of an events map is a map of special activities at a fairground or festival.

Maps can also show events from the past, or historic events. You can use the lines of longitude and latitude on the map of explorers in the Americas shown below to locate and compare events that happened long ago.

15. Circle the island that was explored at 80°W.

16. Identify the explorer who traveled above 50°N.

....

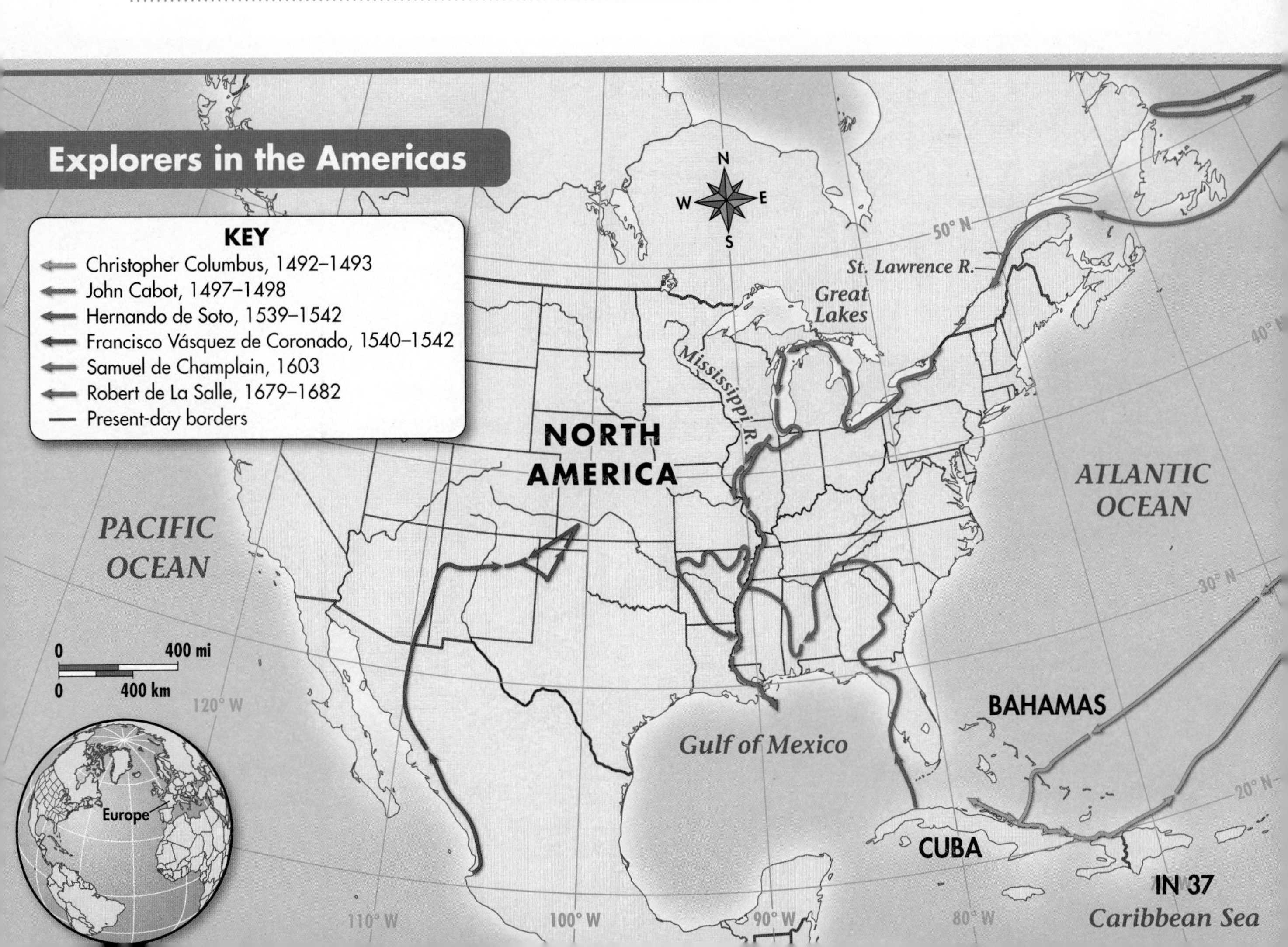

Chapter 1

Indiana's Geography

my Story Spark

How does geography affect the way we live?

Describe how the land or outdoor weather in Indiana affects your daily activities.

Indiana's land has inspired artists such as T.C. Steele, who painted landscapes of the countryside like this one.

Lesson 1 Land and Water
Lesson 2 Regions and Resources
Lesson 3 Indiana Connections

T.C. Steele

Landscape Painter (1847–1926)

Indiana's rolling hills, peaceful forests, and bright autumn colors inspired many, but especially an artist named Theodore Clement (T.C.) Steele. Born in the Indiana countryside in 1847, Steele learned to paint from a young age. By 13, he taught fellow students how to draw at a college prep school.

Steele studied how to make portraits, or pictures of people. He made his living painting portraits. But his true love was painting Indiana's landscapes, or scenes from nature. These paintings made him one of the most famous artists in the state.

In the early 1900s, Steele and his second wife settled in Brown County. This is a beautiful region south of Indianapolis. They built a house on the top of a hill and named it "The House of the Singing Winds." He was the first major artist to settle there. Today, visitors can tour Steele's house and gardens and view the land that inspired him.

The natural beauty of the landscape soon attracted other artists. This group of artists became known as the Hoosier Group of American regional impressionist painters. Their art became one of Indiana's greatest contributions to American art history.

T.C. Steele was one of the most famous artists in the state.

Think About It What does T.C. Steele's story tell you about the landscape of Indiana? As you read this chapter, think about how the geography of a place affects the people who live there.

Lesson 1

Land and Water

Envision It!

Indiana includes many varied landforms, or natural features, and bodies of water.

Indiana is one of the 50 states that make up the United States. The state is known for its beautiful and varied landscapes. These include flat plains, grassy hills, sandy beaches, winding rivers, and large caves.

Indiana's Location

Indiana is located on the continent of North America. It is near the center of the United States and is part of the Midwest region. Several states border Indiana. To the west is Illinois. Kentucky is to the south. Ohio forms the eastern border. To the north is Michigan, as well as part of Lake Michigan. The Ohio River runs along the southern boundary of Indiana. The Wabash River forms part of the state's western border.

Indiana has cities where many people live and work. Indiana's state capital and largest city, Indianapolis, is located in the center of the state. The capital is where the state's goverment is located. Other cities, such as Gary, are located in northern Indiana near Lake Michigan. Evansville and New Albany are located along the Ohio River in the southern part of the state.

Indiana

1. **Label** the capital city, the cities of Gary and Evansville, and the Wabash River on the map. Then **describe** the location of the city closest to where you live.

Label the landform and body of water on the left. In the box above, draw a picture of a landform or body of water where you live, and write its name on the line.

UNLOCK THE BIG ? I will know Indiana's location, that glaciers shaped the land, and the unique landforms and water features in the state.

Vocabulary

glacier	hydrologic cycle
landform	evaporation
lithosphere	precipitation
hydrosphere	biosphere

IN Indiana Academic Standards

4.3.3 Locate Indiana on a map, and identify the location of the state capital, major cities, and rivers.

4.3.4 Map and describe the physical regions of Indiana and identify major natural resources and crop regions.

4.3.5 Explain how glaciers shaped Indiana's landscape and environment.

4.3.6 Describe Indiana's landforms (lithosphere), water features (hydrosphere), and plants and animals (biosphere).

Indiana's Landscape

Long ago, ice and snow covered many parts of North America, including Indiana. This period of time is called the Ice Age. During the Ice Age, glaciers moved from north to south. A **glacier** is a huge mass of ice that moves slowly across the land.

These glaciers helped shape the landscape and environment of Indiana. For nearly 400,000 years, glaciers covered the northern two thirds of Indiana. As the glaciers moved and melted, they changed the natural features of the land. They flattened land, leaving behind rich soil that is good for farming. They dug large holes that became lakes. In northern Indiana, the melting glaciers created swamps and marshes. In the southern part of the state, the icy water helped form caves.

2. Flat land has many uses. It is good for building homes and businesses. It is also good for farms and recreation. This photograph shows different uses of Indiana's flat landscape. **Label** three uses of the land that you see.

Wyandotte Cave is in Crawford County in southern Indiana. This room is called Rothrock Cathedral.

Indiana's Landforms

Indiana has many different landforms. A **landform** is a natural feature of Earth's surface, such as a mountain, hill, valley, or even an island. These features are part of the lithosphere. The **lithosphere** is the soil and rock that form Earth's surface.

Indiana is a varied land. It has flat plains, hills, and valleys. It also has forests and beaches. Most of the land in central and northern Indiana is flat. Many large farms are located there. The highest point in the state is Hoosier Hill near the Ohio border. It has an elevation of 1,257 feet. Elevation is the height of the land above sea level. In the south-central part of the state, the rolling hills of Brown County are a popular tourist attraction. Many large caves are also found in southern Indiana. Wyandotte Cave is about 30 miles west of New Albany. In one of its huge underground rooms, a rock pile called Monument Mountain stands 175 feet tall.

The sand dunes along the shores of Lake Michigan are one of the most unique landforms in Indiana. Winds off Lake Michigan pile the sand on the shore forming tall dunes. Plants and grasses cover some sand dunes. The winds push and change other sand dunes. Plants cannot grow on these dunes because they move too much. For example, Mount Baldy is a tall dune that is more than 120 feet high. It remains mostly bare. Along with hills of sand, the Lake Michigan area also includes sandy beaches, swamps, grassy hills, and forests.

3. Write four landforms that can be found in Indiana.

....

....

Mount Baldy sand dune on Indiana Dunes National Lakeshore

The Wabash River is often muddy and slow-moving.

Water Features and the Hydrologic Cycle

Indiana's water features include lakes and rivers. Glaciers carved hundreds of lakes into the northern region of Indiana. The state's largest natural lake is Lake Wawasee. It has 25 miles of shoreline.

The 43 miles of shoreline on Lake Michigan form part of Indiana's northern border. Lake Michigan links Indiana to Canada and to the Atlantic Ocean.

Indiana also has several reservoirs created by dams. A reservoir is a lake where water is stored. Monroe Lake is the largest human-made lake in the state. It is also the largest body of water in Indiana.

Most of Indiana's rivers flow into the Ohio River, which flows into the Mississippi River. Businesses in the state use rivers to ship products to other places. The Mississippi River flows into the Gulf of Mexico. From there, products can be shipped all over the world. The Wabash River is the longest river in the state. Because it drains Indiana's farmland, it is often muddy and slow-moving. The Ohio River is the state's second longest river. It runs along the state's southern boundary for about 350 miles.

Indiana's water features are part of the hydrosphere. The **hydrosphere** is all the water on Earth's surface. It includes lakes, rivers, and streams.

Indiana's water is also part of the **hydrologic cycle**, or the cycle that describes the movement of water on, in, and above Earth. The water on Earth is always moving and changing forms, from rain to ice to vapor, or gas.

In the hydrologic cycle, the sun heats water in the oceans. Through evaporation, some of the water becomes vapor. **Evaporation** is the change of a liquid to a vapor. The vapor rises into Earth's atmosphere and turns into clouds. This process is called condensation. Then, water drops form in the clouds and fall to Earth as precipitation. **Precipitation** is the amount of moisture that falls as rain or snow. Most precipitation on land flows into streams and rivers and ends up back in the oceans, where the process begins again.

4. Label *Evaporation* and *Precipitation* on the diagram. **Trace** the arrows showing the sequence of the steps.

The Hydrologic Cycle

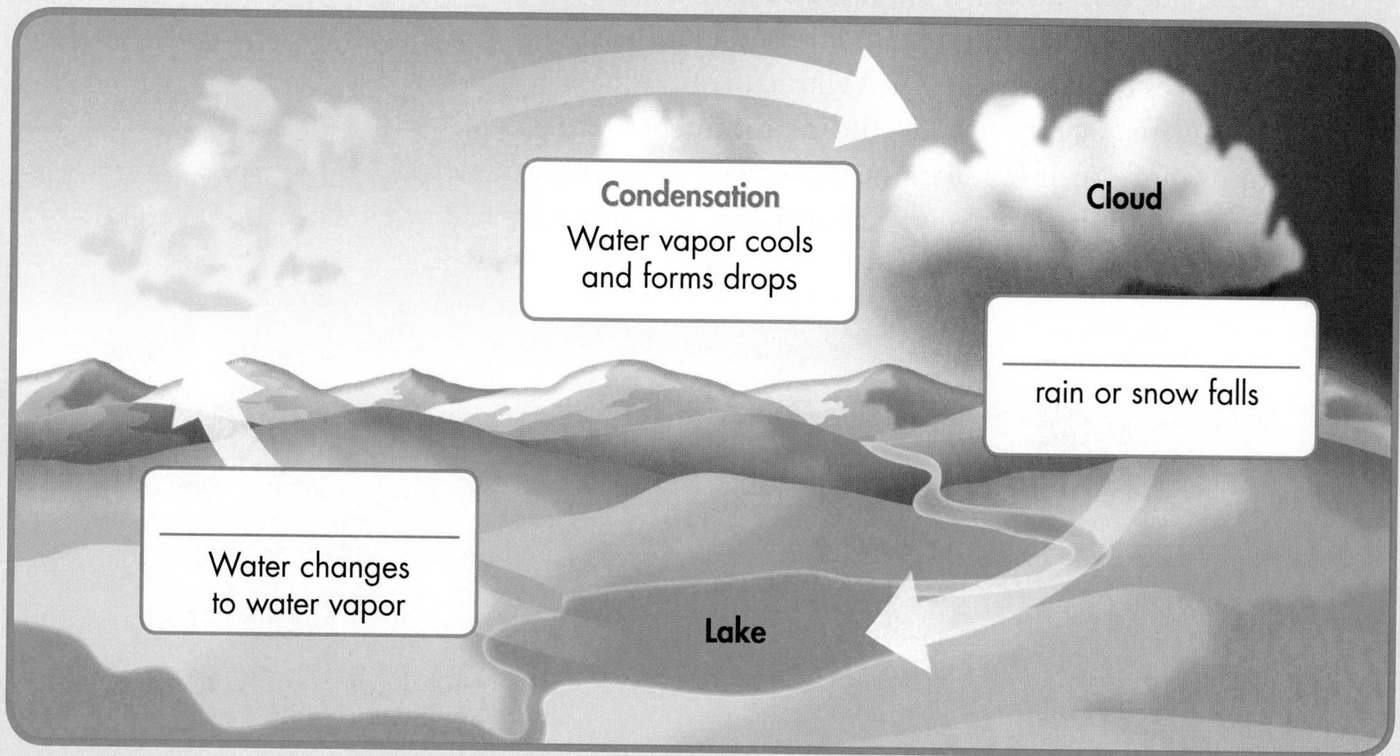

Plants and Animals in Indiana

Indiana's biosphere is as varied as its landforms and water features. The **biosphere** is all of the plants and animals living on Earth's surface. Wildflowers, such as goldenrod, violets, and clover, bloom in spring and summer throughout the state. Wild apples, persimmons, and cherries can also be found throughout Indiana.

Many less common plants can be found in the Indiana Dunes region. More than 1,100 kinds of plants and ferns grow there. These include prickly pear cactus, orchids, and prairie grasses. Still more types of plants, such as bluestem grasses, are found in Indiana's small prairie region.

In the early 1800s, more than 80 percent of Indiana was covered with forests. Over time, farmers cut down trees to make room for fields. Towns and cities grew. By 1917, only 7 percent of the state was forested. In the past 100 years, reforestation, or replanting trees, has led to 20 percent of the state being forested today, however. About half of this forested land is located in state parks and forests, including Hoosier National Forest. This forest in the hills of southern Indiana includes such trees as black walnut, hickory, oak, maple, and tulip.

Indiana is home to many animals, such as white-tailed deer, skunks, raccoons, rabbits, and moles. Mice, woodchucks, and squirrels are found throughout the state. Indiana's lakes and rivers are filled with catfish, trout, and bass, as well as rare fish like the lake sturgeon. Many water birds make their home in the state's wetlands. These include the sandhill crane, a type of bird that is in danger of dying out.

5. **Compare and Contrast** Look at the plant life in the pictures on this page and the next page. **Write** one way in which they are similar and one way in which they are different.

....

....

....

....

....

Hoosier National Forest

Years ago, other large mammals, such as black bears and elk, lived in Indiana. But they slowly disappeared. People hunted these animals. In addition, when people cleared land for farming and housing, they destroyed the places where the animals lived.

Now other animals could disappear from the state, such as sandhill cranes and Indiana bats. People work to protect these and other animals from dying out. Hoosiers have helped set aside more than 22,000 acres of land in nature preserves across the state.

Indiana grassland

Got it?

6. **Main Idea and Details** **Write** one detail that supports the main idea that glaciers shaped the landscape of Indiana.

....

....

....

7. **Describe** one way that people or businesses use Indiana's waterways.

my Story Ideas

....

....

....

Stop! I need help with ....

Wait! I have a question about ....

Go! Now I know ....

Lesson 2

Regions and Resources

Envision It!

Each picture shows a region of Indiana. Above is the Northern Lakes and Moraines region.

Geographers divide Indiana into regions. A **region** is an area that has common features. These features might be natural, based on the land, or cultural, based on language.

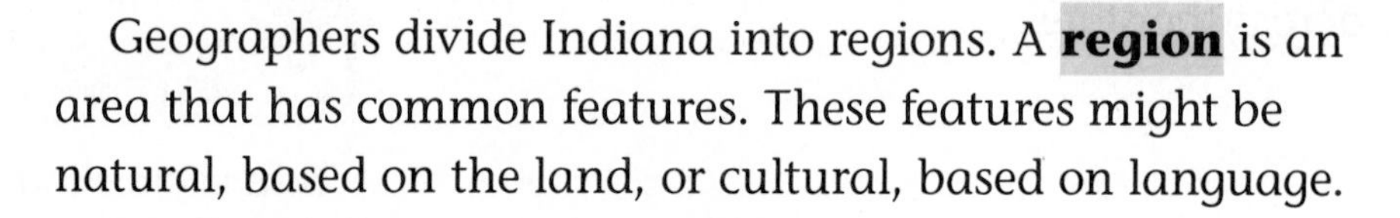

Indiana's Three Regions

Indiana is made up of three different regions. These are the Northern Lakes and Moraines, the Central Till Plain, and the Southern Lowlands. Each region has its own special characteristics. The northern region has several large cities and many lakes. Rich farmland covers much of the central region. In the southern region, there are limestone caves and rolling hills.

The landforms and natural resources found in Indiana's regions make them unique. A **natural resource** is something in the environment that people use. For example, water, trees, soil, and minerals are natural resources found in Indiana.

Natural resources include water, trees, and soil.

The Northern Lakes and Moraines

The Northern Lakes and Moraines region is mostly flat. A **moraine** is a mass of dirt and rocks left behind by glaciers. Moraines are among the only landforms that break up the flat appearance of this region. From a distance, they look like waves.

Hundreds of lakes and ponds are also in this region. The area along the shores of Lake Michigan is home to the Indiana Dunes National Lakeshore and Indiana Dunes State Park.

On the left is the Central Till Plain and on the right is the Southern Lowlands. Circle the photograph that is most similar to what the land looks like where you live.

UNLOCK THE BIG ?

I will know Indiana's land regions and their features.

Vocabulary

region
natural resource
moraine
till
weather
climate

IN Indiana Academic Standards

4.3.4 Map and describe the physical regions of Indiana and identify major natural resources and crop regions.

4.3.7 Explain the effect of the Earth/sun relationship on the climate of Indiana.

The area called the Calumet is located along Lake Michigan. In the late 1800s, large companies came to this area. The new industries depended on Lake Michigan for transportation. They used local resources, such as coal and limestone, to make steel. Oil companies also built factories there. Today, this area is an industrial center with cities such as Gary and Hammond. However, there is also farmland in the region. Major crops include soybeans, corn, and beef cattle.

1. **List** two natural resources found in the Northern Lakes and Moraines region. **Write** which one you think is most important and why.

Factories in Gary, Indiana, are located on the shores of Lake Michigan in the Northern Lakes and Moraines region.

Indiana's Regions

Lake Michigan
MI
Gary
South Bend
St. Joseph R.
Maumee R.
Kankakee R.
Fort Wayne
St. Marys R.
Wabash R.
OH
Muncie
Hoosier Hill (1,257 ft)
IL
Indianapolis
Terre Haute
White R.
Bloomington
N
W
E
S
Vincennes
East Fork White R.
New Albany
Wabash R.
0 50 mi
0 50 km
Evansville
Ohio R.
KY

KEY

- Northern Lakes and Moraines
- Central Till Plain
- Southern Lowlands
- ★ State capital
- ● Other city
- ▲ Highest point

2. Place an **X** on the map where you live. **Circle** the region in the map key.

The Central Till Plain

South of the Northern Lakes and Moraines region is the Central Till Plain. **Till** is the soil and rock that gets left behind after a glacier melts. The soil in the Central Till Plain is the most fertile in the state. Although most of this region is very flat, the highest point in Indiana, called Hoosier Hill, is located there.

The rich soil of this region makes it an ideal place for farming. The agriculture belt of the Central Till Plain is dotted with large farms, fields of crops, and fenced-in areas for hogs and cattle.

Indiana ranks fifth in the nation in corn production. Much of Indiana's corn is grown in this central region. Farmers here also grow soybeans, wheat, and hay. They raise hogs, cattle, and chickens. Milk and eggs are also important products of the region.

The state capital, Indianapolis, is located in this region. Leaders chose this region for the capital because of its central location. Indianapolis attracted industries in the late nineteenth century because of its nearby source of natural gas. Natural gas was a valuable resource. It was used to produce light and heat.

The automobile industry was one industry that grew in Indianapolis. The Ball brothers started their glass manufacturing company in nearby Muncie because of the availability of natural gas. Although the natural gas was soon used up, many industries stayed in the state.

The rich soil in the Central Till Plain is ideal for farming.

The Southern Lowlands

The landscape of the Southern Lowlands region looks quite different from the rest of the state. It has rounded hills, some forests, limestone caves, and rich, fertile lowlands. The land is not flat like the rest of the state because glaciers did not cross most of this region.

Coal and petroleum, or oil, are two of the natural resources found in the southwest corner of the region near the Wabash River. Farmers grow melons in the fertile soil found there. In the central area, a "limestone belt," or area of limestone deposits, runs from Bloomington to the East Fork White River. Limestone is a stone used for building. Towns like Bedford opened limestone quarries, or stone pits, more than 100 years ago.

Over time, water has worn huge underground holes in the limestone, forming caves. Wyandotte Cave, pictured in the last lesson, has 25 miles of passages. Historians believe that people lived there in prehistoric times.

In the southeast corner, there is a series of steep hills, called knobs. Artists like T.C. Steele and William Forsyth have been inspired by southern Indiana's natural beauty.

Cities in the Southern Lowlands include Evansville and Bloomington. Evansville is known as "Plastics Valley" because of the many plastics companies there. Bloomington has limestone quarries, electronics factories, and a large university.

3. **Compare and Contrast Fill in** the missing features, resources, and crops in the chart. **Circle** items that are unique to each region.

Indiana's Physical Regions

Region	Physical Features	Natural Resources	Major Crops
Northern Lakes and Moraines	flat land, moraines, lakes and ponds, dunes	water, coal, limestone, oil, soil	
Central Till Plain	flat land, Hoosier Hill, farmland		corn, soybeans, wheat, hay, hogs, cattle, chickens, eggs, milk
Southern Lowlands		coal, oil, limestone, fertile soil	melons

Climate and Precipitation

What is the weather like today? **Weather** is the condition of the air at a certain time and place. The weather may be different in different parts of Indiana. The weather affects what people wear and the activities they do.

Weather changes from day to day. The climate changes much more slowly. **Climate** is the pattern of weather in a place over a long period of time. Indiana has a temperate climate with four seasons. It is usually not extremely hot or extremely cold.

Indiana's distance from the equator is one reason for its temperate climate. Places close to the equator are warmest throughout the year because the sun shines strongest there. Places far from the equator, like the poles, are coldest. This is why Indiana has a warmer climate than many places to the north and a cooler climate than places to the south. The state has warm, humid summers and chilly, cloudy winters. Southern Indiana is slightly warmer than northern Indiana.

Lake Michigan affects the climate of northwest Indiana. In the fall, the lake's water remains warm from the summer. This warms the air above the lake and keeps temperatures mild. But in the spring, the water stays cold from the winter. This cools the air and keeps the temperature lower.

Indiana's Plant Hardiness Zones

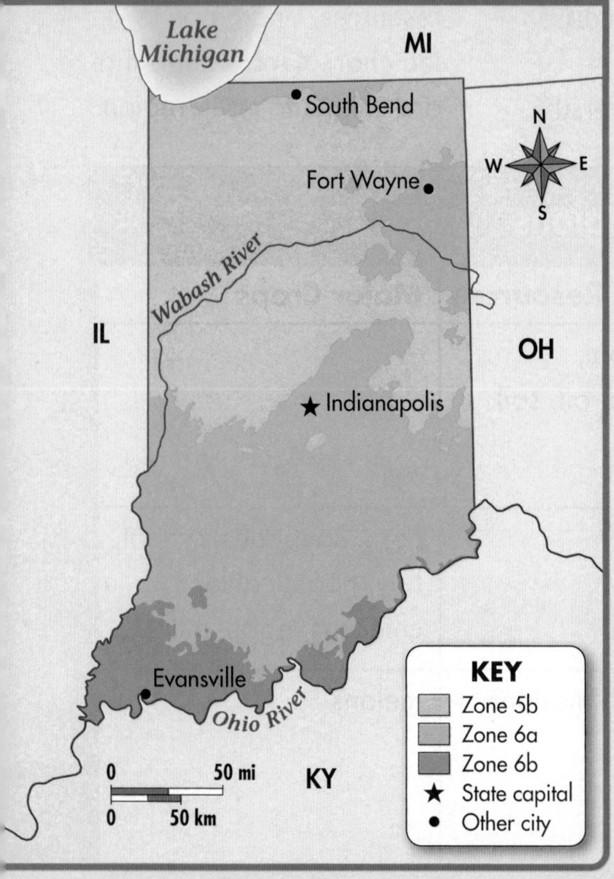

KEY
- Zone 5b
- Zone 6a
- Zone 6b
- ★ State capital
- • Other city

4. Look at the map. Gardeners and farmers use this USDA Plant Hardiness Zone Map to see what plants grow best where they live. **Circle** your zone in the key. Then **research** the plants and trees that grow well in that zone. **Write** the names of two plants or trees that could be used in a community park.

Lake Michigan also affects the precipitation in Indiana. Recall that precipitation is the amount of rain and snow that falls there. The average snowfall for Indiana is 20 inches a year. But the northern border near Lake Michigan often gets more than 100 inches a year! This is because cold air passing over the warmer lake produces very heavy precipitation.

The winds that blow across Lake Michigan cause heavy snowfall in places like Michigan City.

Got it?

5. **Main Idea and Details** The three land regions of Indiana have different physical features. **Write** three details to support this main idea.

....

....

....

6. **Describe** how the changing seasons affect how people in Indiana live.

my Story Ideas

....

....

....

Stop! I need help with ....

Wait! I have a question about ....

Go! Now I know ....

21C Map Skills

Use Latitude and Longitude

We use maps for many different purposes. They help us find physical features, such as lakes, rivers, dunes, and forests. Maps can also show features that were created by people. These human features of maps include cities, farms, highways, and railroad lines.

To find the exact location of physical and human features on maps, we use latitude and longitude. These imaginary lines form a grid system that identifies the location of features on maps. Lines of latitude are drawn east to west. The equator is the starting point for latitude. All locations north of the equator are marked with an N, and all locations south of the equator are marked with an S. Lines of longitude are drawn north to south. The prime meridian is the starting point for longitude. All locations east of the prime meridian are marked with an E, and all locations west of the prime meridian are marked with a W.

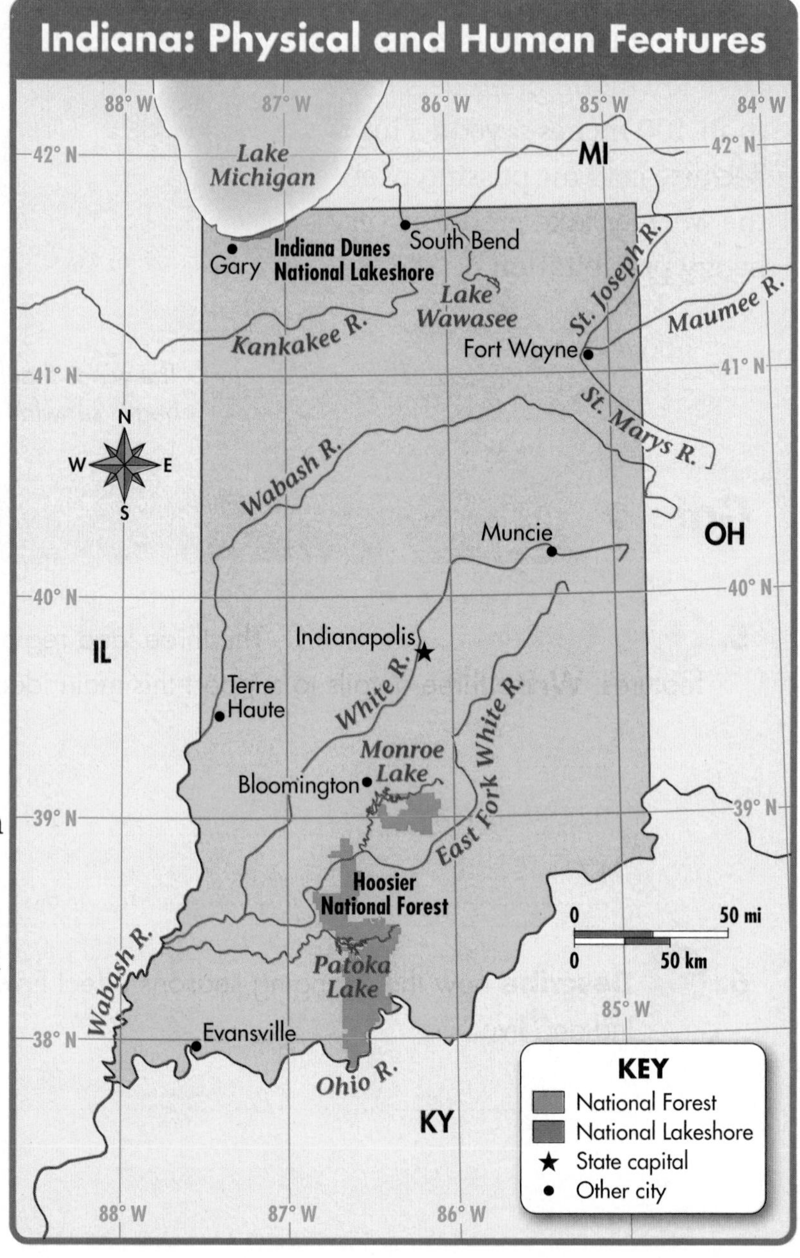

Study the blue grid on the map of Indiana at the right. To identify the latitude and longitude of Indianapolis, first find the capital city on the map. Next, find the line of latitude closest to the city. Use your finger to follow the line to the right or to the left to find the number. You will see that it is 40°N. Now find the line of longitude closest to the city. Use your finger to follow the line to the top or bottom of the map to find the number. It is 86°W. Now you know that Indianapolis is located close to latitude 40°N and longitude 86°W.

Learning Objective

I will know how to use latitude and longitude to identify features of Indiana.

IN **4.3.1** Use latitude and longitude to identify physical and human features of Indiana.

Use the map to answer the questions below.

1. **Find** Evansville on the map. What is the closest latitude line?

2. **Identify** the two lakes that are located between 87°W and 86°W.

3. The Ohio River forms the southern border of Indiana. What lines of longitude does the river cross in Indiana?

4. What two physical features are located near 42°N and 87°W?

5. **Apply** Suppose the state has decided to build a new railroad line (human feature) that will connect Gary and Indianapolis. **Draw** the railroad line on the map, as well as what its symbol would look like in the map key below. Then **write** the lines of latitude and longitude that the railroad will cross below.

Lesson 3

Indiana Connections

Envision It!

People celebrate their cultures in many ways. Here, Mongolian Buddhists dance at a festival in Bloomington, Indiana.

"The Crossroads of America" is Indiana's state motto, or saying. This motto describes the state's central location in the United States along roads, rivers, and train lines. Hoosiers are connected to the rest of the country by the interstate highways that crisscross the state.

Indiana, the United States, and the World

Indiana's location in the center of the country links it to other states. This allows businesses to easily ship goods to other places in the country. Fourteen interstate highways pass through Indiana, linking it to the rest of the nation. Indiana has more railroad lines than many other states. Trains carrying cargo, or goods, travel from Chicago, Illinois, and St. Louis, Missouri, through Indiana.

Waterways link Indiana not just to other states, but to the whole world. The Ohio River flows into the Mississippi River, which in turn flows into the Gulf of Mexico. From there, goods can be shipped all over the world. Southwind Maritime Center, in the town of Mount Vernon, is one of Indiana's ports on the Ohio River.

Portage, on the shores of Lake Michigan, is one of Indiana's largest port cities. It connects Indiana to Canada. Ships on the Great Lakes can reach the Atlantic Ocean through the St. Lawrence Seaway. From Portage, huge ships, called freighters, carry Indiana steel and other products to markets around the world.

1. **Look** at the picture of a barge on the Ohio River. Describe how Indiana is connected to other parts of the world.

....

....

....

Circle two items in the picture that represent this culture group.

UNLOCK THE BIG ?

I will know how Indiana is connected to other states and countries.

Vocabulary

trade
manufacturing
export
import
culture
cultural exchange

IN Indiana Academic Standards

4.3.11 Examine Indiana's international relationships.

4.4.3 Explain the benefits of trade and give examples of how people in Indiana have engaged in trade.

Benefits of Trade

Indiana is connected to the world through trade. **Trade** is the buying and selling of goods and services. Trade has many benefits. No single place can provide everything that the people who live there need. Each place depends on others to get the things they need and want. Trade benefits Indiana in other ways, too. It brings money into the state. It also creates jobs for workers.

Trade has existed for many thousands of years. Long ago, it took barges, wagons, and stagecoaches weeks or months to make a delivery. Today, a jet plane can cross those same distances in hours. And cargo ships can hold more goods than ever before. They can transport those goods far more cheaply, too. More goods are now shipped and received around the world than at any other time in history.

The Subaru of Indiana assembly plant in Lafayette makes goods that can be shipped all over the world.

2. Circle Indiana's top two trading partners. **Write** why you think these countries are top trading partners.

International Trade

Indiana trades goods with many countries. Indiana businesses ship more goods to Canada than anywhere else in the world. In 2013, the state shipped nearly $12 billion worth of goods to Canada.

Businesses in Indiana use the state's natural resources to make products that are needed in other regions of the world that might not have those resources. For example, Indiana's fertile soil is good for growing crops such as corn, soybeans, and mint. Farms ship crops to other areas where those crops do not grow well. In 2011, Indiana's agriculture industry earned $4.6 billion from selling crops to other countries.

Indiana's steel industry is centered in the northwestern part of the state. It produces 20 million tons of steel a year. Steel is used to make many products, such as stoves, televisions, and refrigerators. Indiana ships these products to other countries.

The industry in Indiana that ships the most goods to other countries is the vehicle manufacturing industry. **Manufacturing** is the making of goods by machines, usually in factories. Indiana companies make vehicles and parts for vehicles such as automobiles and aircraft. The steel that is produced in the state is used to make many of these products.

Top Exports and Imports

Indiana manufacturers make many different exports. **Exports** are goods that are shipped to another country to be sold there. The vehicle manufacturing industry in Indiana is the top exporter. The second highest exporter is the pharmaceutical industry. A pharmaceutical company exports medicine. One of the biggest pharmaceutical companies in the world is Eli Lilly and Company. It is located in the capital city, Indianapolis.

Indiana also relies on imports. **Imports** are goods that are brought in from another country to be sold here. Hoosiers cannot produce everything that people in the state need. Instead, they import goods from businesses overseas. Some of the top goods that Indiana imports are ingredients for medicine, cellular phones, and vehicle parts. Hoosiers import more goods from Canada than anywhere else. The state also buys many products from Ireland, China, Japan, and Mexico.

3. Look at the graph below that shows Indiana's top exports. About how much more money does Indiana earn through its export of industrial machinery than electric machinery?

....

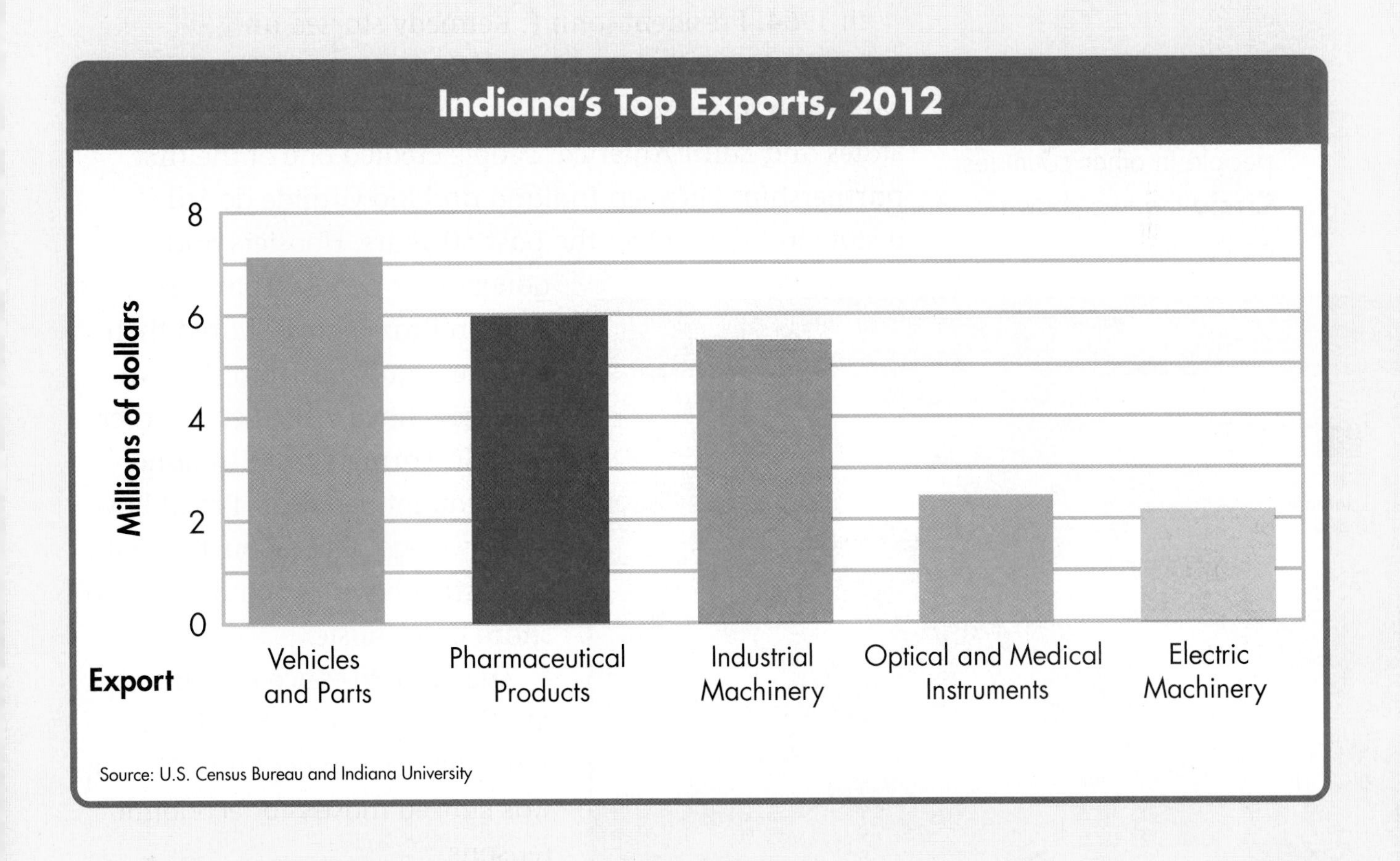

Cultural Exchanges

Indiana not only provides and receives products from other parts of the world, but the state and other countries also share their cultures. A **culture** is the way of life of a group of people. Indiana takes part in cultural exchanges with people in other countries. A **cultural exchange** happens when two different cultures share information with each other.

Indiana has sister cities and sister states in other countries. Sister cities and states work together as friends to understand the other's culture. These relationships also promote trade and tourism. Indianapolis alone has eight sister cities! These include cities in Taiwan, Germany, Italy, Slovenia, China, Brazil, the United Kingdom, and India. International relationships have many benefits to Hoosiers. They can learn about different cultures. They also create new volunteer and business opportunities. Each year, the city of Indianapolis celebrates its international relationships with the Indy Sister Cities Fest. Hoosiers enjoy music, games, world sports, and other cultural activities at this street fair.

In 1964, President John F. Kennedy started an organization called Partners of the Americas. Kennedy wanted to increase cultural exchanges between the United States and Latin America. People created one of the first partnerships between Indiana and Rio Grande do Sul, a state in Brazil. Over the past 50 years, Hoosiers and gauchos, or people from this state in Brazil, have shared their cultures. Students from the two countries have visited each other's schools. Farmers from Indiana have taught people in Brazil how to grow vegetables. Gaucho youth orchestras have visited Indiana to share their music.

Zhejiang Province in China is another sister state of Indiana. This partnership began in 1987. It was started mostly for economic reasons.

4. Indiana has partnerships with people in other countries. **Circle** the two shown on the map.

Indiana's exports to China have grown over the past decade. China uses more meat, coal, and steel than any other country in the world. Through this partnership, Indiana has increased trade with China. Schools in both countries have also started to work together.

Indiana students practice making Chinese characters in their Chinese class.

5. **Main Idea and Details**
Write what happens in a cultural exchange.

....

....

....

Got it?

6. **Main Idea and Details** **Write** two details to support the main idea that Indiana's waterways link the state to the rest of the world.

....

....

....

7. List three benefits of Indiana's relationships with its sister cities and states.

my Story Ideas

....

....

....

Stop! I need help with ....

Wait! I have a question about ....

Go! Now I know ....

Chapter 1
Study Guide

Lesson 1

Land and Water

- Indiana is located in the United States, in the Midwest region. Its capital, Indianapolis, is located in the center of the state.
- Long ago, glaciers shaped the landscape of Indiana.
- Indiana has varied landforms, water features, and plants and animals.
- The state's waterways include hundreds of lakes and two major rivers: the Wabash and Ohio rivers.

Lesson 2

Indiana's Regions and Resources

- Indiana has three land regions: the Northern Lakes and Moraines, the Central Till Plain, and the Southern Lowlands.
- Indiana's natural resources include water, trees, soil, and minerals.
- Indiana has a temperate climate that is affected by the state's distance from the equator.
- Lake Michigan affects the weather and precipitation in the state.

Lesson 3

Indiana Connections

- Indiana's central location in the United States makes it the "Crossroads of America."
- Trade benefits Hoosiers by allowing people to get things they need and want, bringing money into the state, and creating jobs.
- Indiana's top trading partner is Canada. Its top exports vehicles and vehicle parts.
- Hoosiers participate in cultural exchanges with other countries.

Review and Assessment

Lesson 1

Land and Water

1. **Describe** how glaciers shaped Indiana's landscape and environment long ago.

....

....

....

....

....

....

....

2. **Match** each waterway with its description.

_____	Lake Wawasee	a.	longest river in Indiana
_____	Monroe Lake	b.	largest reservoir
_____	Wabash River	c.	forms southern boundary of Indiana
_____	Ohio River	d.	largest natural lake

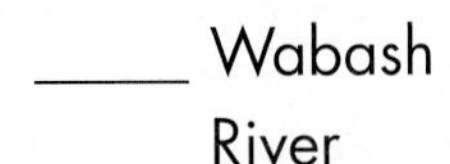

3. **Label** part of the hydrologic cycle.

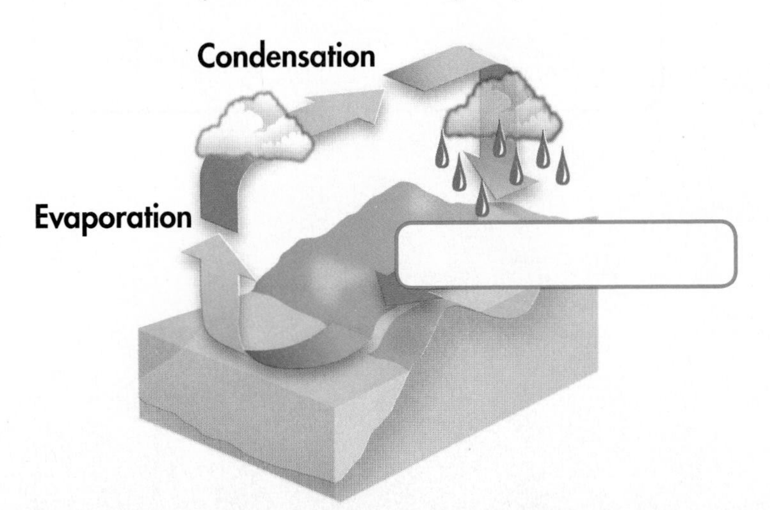

Lesson 2

Regions and Resources

4. Which region fits this description? The land is made up of rounded hills, some forests, limestone caves, and rich farmland.
   A. Northern Moraines and Lakes
   B. Central Till Plain
   C. Southern Lowlands
   D. Indiana Dunes

5. **Write** three natural resources found in the Northern Lakes and Moraines region.

....

....

....

6. **Fill in** the blanks.
   Indiana has a .... climate. The sun shines strongest in places .... to the equator. Places far from the equator have .... temperatures.

Review and Assessment

Lesson 3

Indiana Connections

7. **Main Idea and Details** **Write** two benefits of trade.

8. **Write** how the steel industry helps Indiana's trade business.

9. Which of the following best describes a cultural exchange?

   A. Two countries trade goods.

   B. Two countries share transportation.

   C. Two cultures share information.

   D. Two cultures build factories.

10. **How does geography affect the way we live?**

Look at the picture and **answer** the question.

How does Indiana's geography affect the work that people do there?

Go online to write and illustrate your own **myStory Book** using the **myStory Ideas** from this chapter.

How does geography affect the way we live?

IN **4.W.1** Write for discipline-specific tasks, purposes, and audiences.

Indiana has a variety of landforms, waterways, and resources, along with a temperate climate. This varied geography affects people in different ways, depending on where they live. Geography influences where we choose to live, what we wear, what we do for fun or work, and what our communities are like.

Think about where you live and what people in your community do for fun or work. **Write** how geography affects part of your life.

....

....

....

Now **draw** a picture to illustrate your writing.

While you're online, check out the **myStory Current Events** area where you can create your own book on a topic that's in the news.

Chapter 2

Indiana's Early History

my Story Spark

How do people adapt to where they live?

Long ago, people moved to the land that is now Indiana. They built homes from trees that they cut down on their land. They hunted in nearby forests. Think about your community. **Describe** ways people have adapted to where you live.

Early people in Indiana built earthen mounds, like these at Angel Mounds State Historic Site.

Robert de La Salle

Explorer (1643–1687)

Robert de La Salle decided in his early twenties that he wanted a life of adventure. In 1666, he traveled from his native France to the French territories in Canada. La Salle farmed in Canada and opened a trading post. There he learned several languages from the Native Americans who brought him furs to trade. In 1669, he was ready for bigger adventures.

La Salle began to travel south of what is today the Canadian border on the Great Lakes and the St. Joseph River, often by sailboat or canoe. By December 1679, he had reached the land that is now South Bend. His journey south was temporarily halted at this point, in part because of conflicts among the Native Americans living there.

La Salle explored lands in what is now Indiana in the late 1600s.

Two years later, La Salle returned to South Bend. He met with Native American leaders to discuss a peace treaty. The meeting happened near a huge oak tree, now known as the Council Oak, and was a great success. La Salle was now able to explore the region in peace.

La Salle then journeyed across Illinois, taking different rivers and streams to the Illinois River. He followed this river until he reached the Mississippi River, and eventually, the Gulf of Mexico. When he arrived at the Gulf in 1682, La Salle declared that the entire Mississippi basin belonged to France. He named it Louisiana for France's King Louis.

Think About It La Salle worked with the Native Americans he met. How do you think the story might have been different if he had not made peace with Native American leaders? As you read the chapter, think about how people adapt to where they live.

Lesson 1

First People

Archaeologists look for objects from early people. Objects from the past help us learn about the history of a culture.

What were the early people in Indiana like? Indiana's prehistoric people built houses. They created beautiful art. They made the things they needed from available resources. And they left behind artifacts that people wonder about today.

Early Cultures in Indiana

These early people were prehistoric, which means they lived before histories were written. Then how do we know so much about them? Historians work with archeologists to learn about the past. An **archaeologist** studies artifacts and sites to learn about ancient people. An **artifact** is an object made by humans. The artifacts tell a story about the first humans in the Americas.

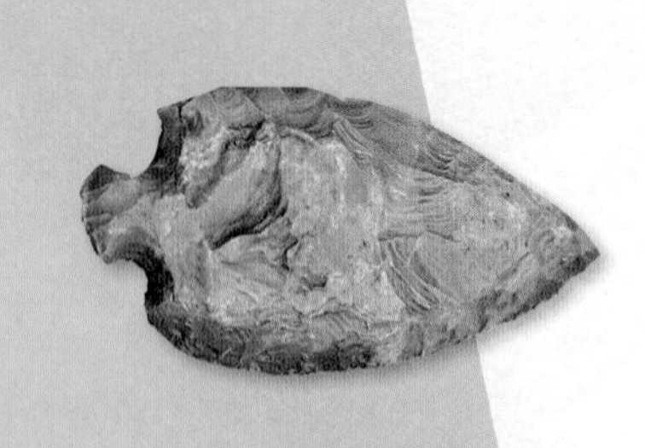

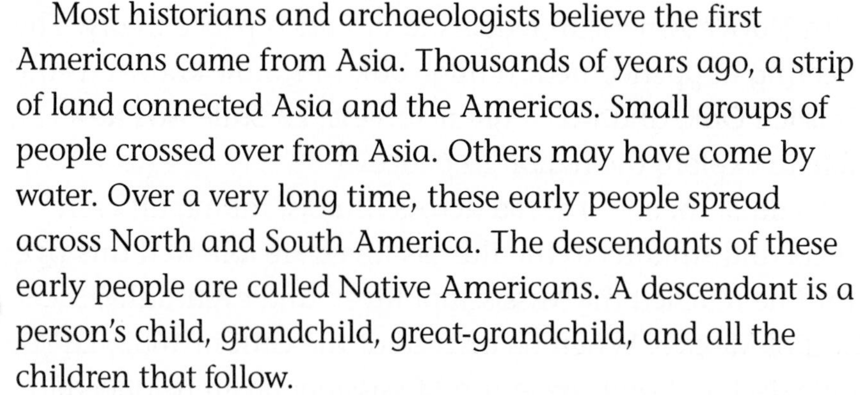

Most historians and archaeologists believe the first Americans came from Asia. Thousands of years ago, a strip of land connected Asia and the Americas. Small groups of people crossed over from Asia. Others may have come by water. Over a very long time, these early people spread across North and South America. The descendants of these early people are called Native Americans. A descendant is a person's child, grandchild, great-grandchild, and all the children that follow.

Native Americans hunted animals for food. These stone points would have been attached to a spear or a dart and used for hunting.

1. How did the first Americans come to America?

....

....

....

What can you learn from studying masks, stone tools, and clay pots discovered at sites such as these?

I will know how early cultures in Indiana were alike and different.

Vocabulary

archaeologist
artifact
adapt
mound
cultural group
agriculture

IN Indiana Academic Standards

4.1.1 Compare the early cultures that existed in the region that became Indiana prior to European contact.

The first people probably arrived in Indiana about 13,000 years ago. They lived by hunting animals and gathering plants to eat. As time went by, the people learned to adapt to their new homeland. When people **adapt,** they change to fit new situations. They farmed native plants, such as corn, squash, and sunflowers. They began making pottery to store their food. The pottery was heavy and thick and covered with elaborate decorations.

People built log tombs for their dead. The tombs were burned, and then covered with dirt. The result was a **mound**, or pile of earth. Mounds dotted the landscape, some reaching as high as 70 feet.

Cultures grew and changed over time. New cultural groups formed. A **cultural group** is a group of people connected by a common language, religion, and culture. About 2,500 years ago, a major Native American culture arose called the Adena. Next came the Hopewell culture and then the Mississippian culture.

2. Summarize What is a cultural group?

....

....

Early cultures adapted to their new homeland by growing plants that would survive there.

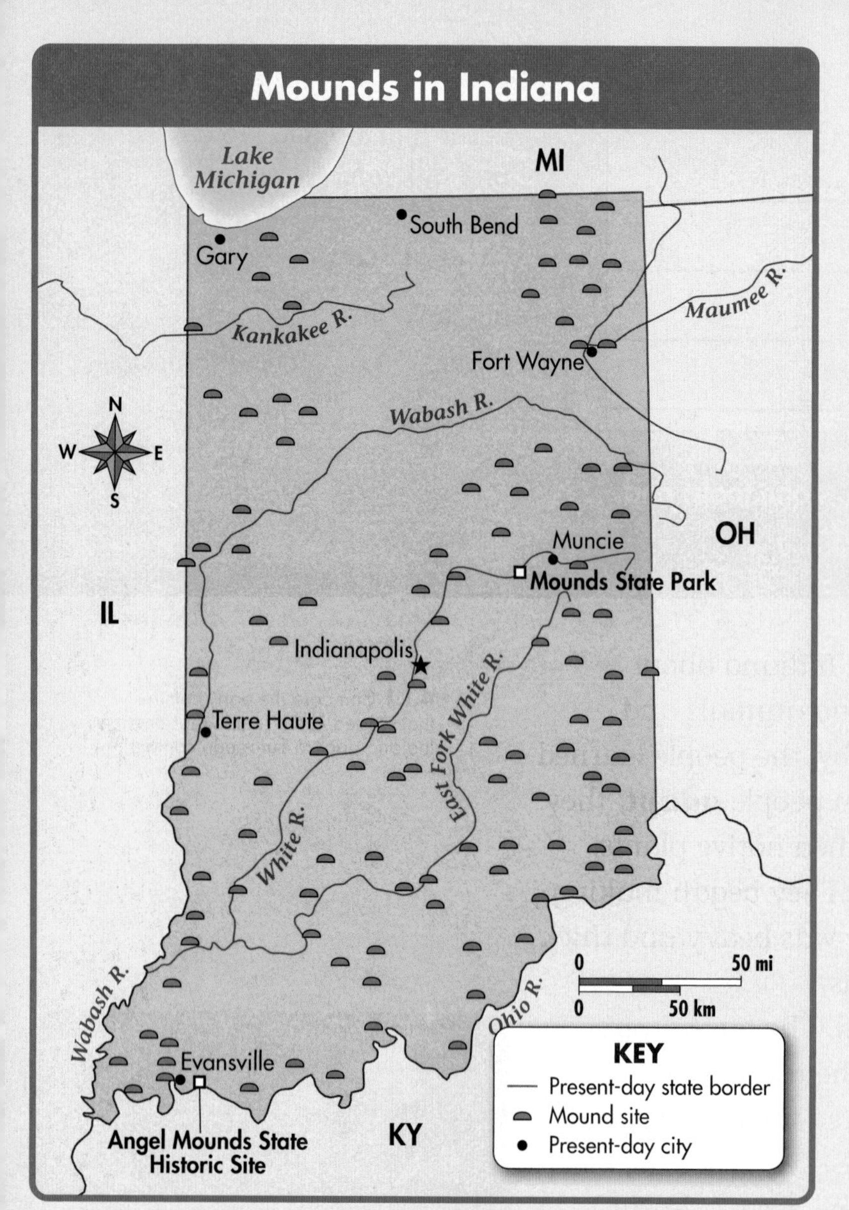

The Adena Culture

The Adena culture began about 2,500 years ago. The center of Adena culture was the region that is now the state of Ohio, but some Adena groups lived in the southeastern part of what would become Indiana.

Like many of the early cultures of the area, the Adena built mounds. Some were for burial, but others may have been for ceremonies. Historians are unsure of all of the purposes of the mounds.

The early Adena were hunter-gatherers. That means they got their food by hunting, fishing, and collecting wild plants that they could eat. However, sometime during the 600 years that the Adena culture existed, they began growing plants to eat. This was an early form of **agriculture**, or farming, in North America.

The Adena had circular houses and made them from the materials available to them. These included wood and tree bark. However, they often moved to follow the animals they hunted.

They used stone to make axes and knives. Once they started farming, the Adena also made hoes, a kind of farming tool, from stone. They made pottery from clay, which they then decorated. They created ornaments and jewelry from copper and seashells. These materials were not found locally, which shows that the Adena traded with people who lived far away.

3. Write what it means to be a hunter-gatherer.

....

....

The Hopewell Culture

When the Adena culture was about 600 years old, it had changed enough that it started to be known as the Hopewell culture. There were many ways in which the Hopewell were like the Adena. They still relied partly on hunting, fishing, and gathering wild foods they could eat. However, the Hopewell focused more on agriculture than the Adena.

Like the Adena, the Hopewell traded for goods from far away, such as copper and seashells. They also made things from local materials, including stone tools and clay pots. Their homes were built from local materials, but unlike the Adena's round houses, Hopewell houses were dome-shaped. They lived in villages or large towns.

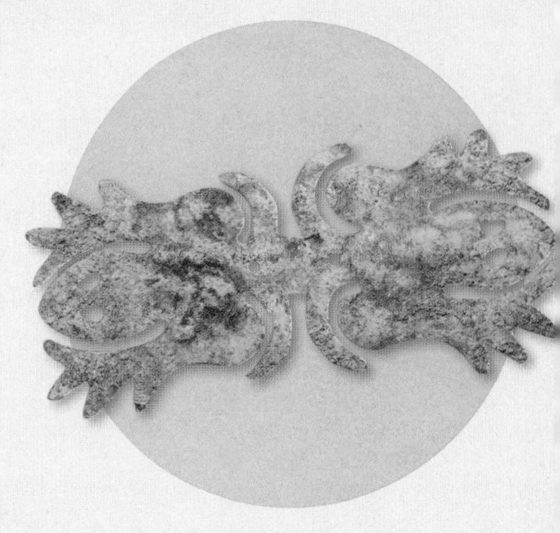

A copper artifact from the Hopewell culture

Though Hopewell culture also began in Ohio, it spread much farther than Adena culture. It spread across Indiana and even reached as far as what are now Nebraska and Minnesota.

Mound building was so important to the Hopewell that they were once called the Mound Builders. Their earthwork mounds were more complex than those of the Adena. They used mounds for ceremonies.

About 1,600 years ago, the introduction of the bow and arrow changed hunting and warfare. The bow and arrow allowed people to hit targets accurately from far away. Historians do not know what caused the end of Hopewell culture, but war may have been a factor.

4. Underline how the Hopewell were different from the Adena.

The Hopewell were known for the burial mounds they built.

The Mississippian Culture

The next important culture to develop in prehistoric North America was known as the Mississippian culture. It started about 1,300 years ago. The Mississippian culture was more sophisticated than the earlier cultures. People from this culture were still around when Europeans arrived, and there are still some people related to the Mississippians alive today.

The Mississippian culture covered a large area. The people lived along many of the main rivers of the region, especially the Mississippi River, from which the culture took its name. The Mississippian people in Indiana lived in the southwestern part of the state, along the Ohio River.

The Mississippian culture relied heavily on agriculture to feed the many people in its large towns. With larger groups of people, government became more complex. Larger towns controlled smaller ones.

Mississippian communities were much bigger than those of the Hopewell, and their houses were square or rectangular instead of dome-shaped. Every town had a central area for ceremonies. This area would have a large earth mound shaped like a pyramid or an oval. On top of the mound was a temple or the house of the chief.

A shell artifact from the Mississippian culture

Like other early people, the Mississippians traded with people far away. They did so to get the copper, seashells, and other items they needed and wanted.

In addition to beautiful clay pots and copper ornaments, the Mississippian people made complex headdresses. They crafted a wide variety of statues, showing people, snakes, and warriors. They also made weapons, both for ceremonies and for the frequent wars that they fought.

It is not known what happened to most of the Mississippian people. Some think they suffered from disease and warfare. Others suggest that the soil was no longer good for farming. Whatever the reason, they were gone from Indiana before the first Europeans arrived.

Comparing Early Cultures			
	Adena	**Hopewell**	**Mississippian**
How long ago?	2,500 years ago		1,300 years ago
How did they get food?		Hunting, gathering, more farming	Relied on farming
What did they build?	Mounds and circular houses		Large and small towns with large oval or pyramid-shaped mounds; square or rectangular houses

5. **Look** at the chart above. **Fill in** the missing details.

Got it?

6. Summarize **Write** what mounds are and what they tell us about early cultures.

....

....

....

7. **Describe** the way early people got their food. Then write how you get your food.

my Story Ideas

....

....

....

Stop! I need help with ....

Wait! I have a question about ....

Go! Now I know ....

myworldsocialstudies.com

Lesson 2

Native Americans of Indiana

Envision It!

Throughout history, people have used available resources to make things they needed. For example, they made canoes with light, wood frames covered with birch bark.

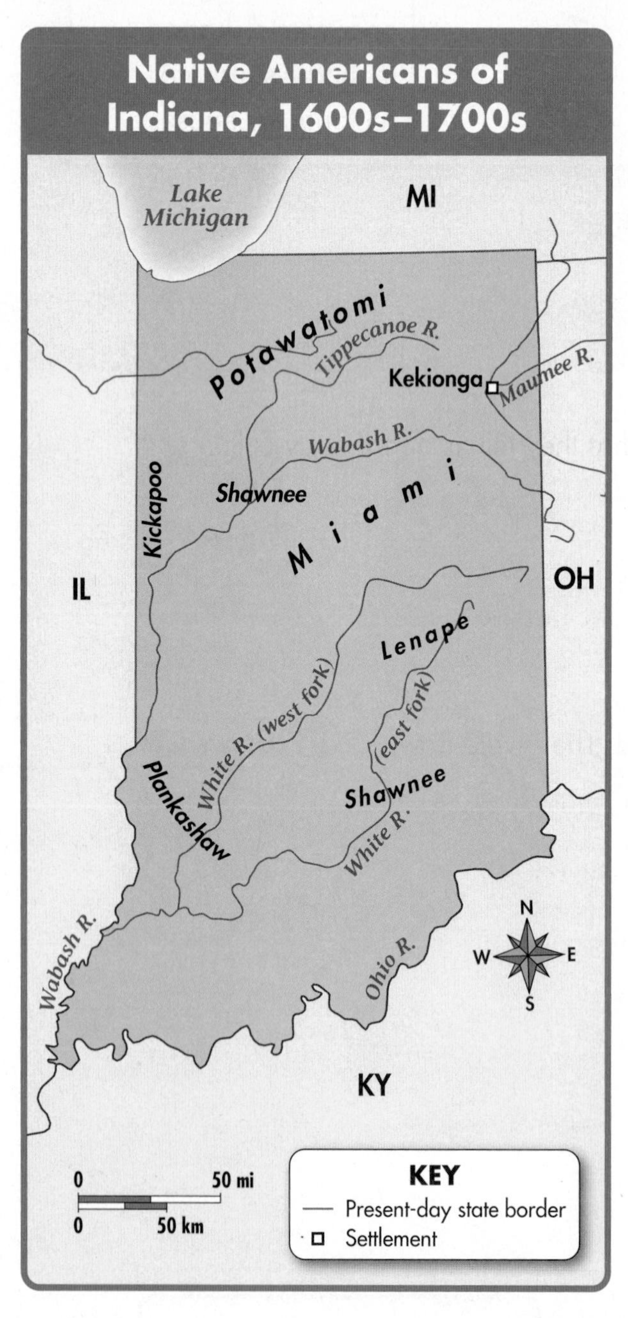

From the late 1600s to the early 1800s, Native American groups from other parts of North America moved to lands that would one day be part of Indiana. The Miami and the Potawatomi were the largest and most powerful of these groups. They settled in much of what is now central and northern Indiana. The Shawnee people also settled in this area, as well as in the southeastern corner of Indiana. The Lenape people lived near the White River, and the Kickapoo lived in lands along today's border with Illinois. All of the groups adapted to their new homelands in unique ways.

The Miami

The Miami and their **clans**, or related groups, came from the area that is now the states of Wisconsin, Illinois, and Iowa. Good hunting and fishing, as well as excellent farmland, drew the Miami to the region. The Miami called themselves "Twightwee," which was their word for the cry of the sandhill crane.

1. On the map, **circle** the name of the Native American group who lived closest to Lake Michigan. Then **write** the name of the river where the Lenape people lived.

....

Write about something in your home that is made from a resource available where you live.

I will know Indiana's Native American groups and how they adapted to their environments.

Vocabulary

clan
longhouse
wigwam

IN Indiana Academic Standards

4.1.2 Describe Native American groups in Indiana at the time of early European exploration.

4.1.3 Explain the importance of the Revolutionary War and other events and people that influenced Indiana's development as a state.

4.3.13 Read and interpret texts to answer geographic questions about Indiana in the past and present.

4.4.3 Explain the benefits of trade and give examples of how people in Indiana have engaged in trade.

4.4.6 List the functions of money and compare and contrast what was used as money in the past.

The Miami were farmers and hunters. Men and boys trapped and hunted animals. Women and girls gathered nuts and berries. They also planted and harvested crops. They stored foods, such as nuts and seeds, to eat during the long, cold winters. Women also preserved the skins of animals and used them to make clothing.

In the summer months, the Miami lived in villages. They built their villages near rivers and flat land that was good for farming. They built homes called wigwams. A **wigwam** is a round house built from young, flexible trees. This frame is covered with bark and animal skins. You can see a picture of a wigwam on the next page. After the harvest in the fall, families moved to smaller hunting camps in the prairies. The camps allowed small groups of people to live close to the animals they hunted. This movement from villages to camps was one way the Miami people adapted to the land and climate of Indiana.

Miami villages had councils and village leaders, or chiefs. The chief usually lived in a large structure that was also the village meeting place. The Miami believed that powerful spirits lived in humans, animals, and plants, and that these spirits protected people. Religious leaders, or shamans, were close to these spirits. They were also healers.

2. Write the names of the natural resources used to make wigwams.

A Miami chief

The Potawatomi

The Potawatomi came from the area that is now the states of Wisconsin and Michigan. They settled in the northern part of Indiana, near Lake Michigan. There, they found better soil for farming. They also found an abundance of fish in Lake Michigan and nearby rivers.

The Potawatomi built wigwams similar to those made by the Miami. However, they covered the wigwams with mats of woven reeds. Reeds were easily found near the Potawatomi lands. In the summer, the Potawatomi lived in longhouses. A **longhouse** is a large house where many people lived. Up to seven families could live in one longhouse. People made longhouses from poles cut from trees and covered with bark.

The Lenape

Unlike the Potawatomi and Miami people, the Lenape came to Indiana from lands to the east. European settlers and a more powerful Native American group forced the Lenape to leave their homeland in what is now the state of Delaware. They traveled west, eventually settling in Indiana.

There were three Lenape clans: Wolf, Turtle, and Turkey. Sons were expected to marry women from other clans, and children belonged to their mother's clan. Lenape villages could be large, with as many as 200 residents. Groups of relatives lived in longhouses in the summer. Like other Native Americans in Indiana, small family groups moved to camps in the winter to hunt.

The oldest woman in each longhouse chose the sachem, or chief. Each sachem was a member of the village council. Chiefs were expected to look out for the well-being of the whole community. They also led the people in religious ceremonies.

A Lenape wigwam

The Shawnee

The Shawnee, too, were forced to leave their original homelands in the east by a more powerful Native American group. They settled along the Maumee River and also lived in wigwams covered in bark, grasses, and reeds. Like the other Native Americans of this period, they farmed and hunted.

Every Shawnee person belonged to one of six clans: Turkey, Turtle, Rounded-feet, Horse, Raccoon, or Rabbit. Children were members of their father's clan. The title of chief passed from father to son. Each village had a large council house, which was used for meetings and celebrations. Their most important celebrations focused on food and farming.

The Kickapoo

The Kickapoo resisted when stronger Native American groups moved into their lands in the area that is now the states of Ohio, Michigan, and Wisconsin. However, despite their skill in battle, they too were forced to find new homelands. By the early 1700s, they settled in Indiana.

The Kickapoo worked hard to keep their culture from changing. Unlike many other groups, they did not want European traders bringing new things to their villages. Like other Native American groups, they lived in wigwams, raised crops, and hunted or fished. In summer, they lived in dome-shaped homes, near their fields. In winter, they moved to hunting camps, and built oval-shaped wigwams that were easy to move from place to place.

The Kickapoo were among the first Native Americans to ride horses when hunting. The Spanish had first brought horses to America in the 1500s, but some horses had run wild. The Kickapoo learned how to catch and ride the wild horses.

3. Compare and Contrast These Native American groups had much in common, but they also had differences. Beneath the name of each group, **write** one detail that was different, or unique, about each group.

Miami	Potawatomi	Lenape	Shawnee	Kickapoo
Named themselves after the cry of the sandhill crane				

Native Americans sometimes moved when seasons changed to hunt for food.

Adapting to the Land

Native Americans in Indiana relied on the land to provide for their needs. They adapted to life in the region in many ways. They adapt to situations, and adapted objects to meet their needs.

Seasons and the weather cause people to adapt. Native American groups lived in villages, but they moved with the seasons to have a reliable food source. As you read, many Native Americans farmed during the summer and then moved to a place for hunting in the winter. The homes of the different groups were similar. However, depending on the materials available locally, some wigwams were covered in bark, while others were covered in grasses, reeds, or animal skins.

The Need for Trade

Trade is the buying and selling of goods and services. Today, we use money when we trade. Money is easy to carry and people agree on its value. We use coins and bills. Other objects have been used for money in the past.

Some Native Americans used clamshells as money. However, not everyone wanted to trade for money. In the past, people traded for things they needed. For instance, someone might have traded dried corn for animal skins that could be made into clothing.

When Native Americans traded with each other, they often traded for things they could not get nearby. Groups in Indiana traded items with people as far away as the Gulf of Mexico. Once Europeans arrived, there were many new things to trade.

Some Native Americans, such as the Kickapoo, did not want these items to change their cultures. But many were eager to obtain the goods Europeans introduced. The Europeans wanted to obtain things that Native Americans could provide. In this way, both sides benefited from trade.

Some Europeans traded for services, such as being guided on the frontier. Most of them traded for goods, especially furs. Native Americans did not have metal pots or utensils for cooking. They made and used pots from clay and knives from stone. Therefore, European metal products were popular trade goods. Europeans also traded wool blankets and glass items for furs. Both groups were able to trade to get what they needed or wanted. By using European goods, the cultures of Native Americans slowly began to change.

Native Americans traded furs for metal, glass, and porcelain objects from Europeans.

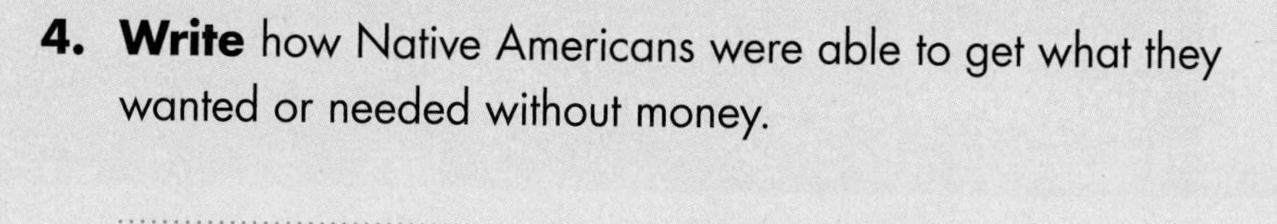

4. **Write** how Native Americans were able to get what they wanted or needed without money.

....

....

Got it?

5. **Summarize** **Write** two ways the Kickapoo were different from other Native American groups.

....

....

....

6. **Explain** one way Native Americans adapted to their physical environments.

my Story Ideas

....

....

Stop! I need help with ....

Wait! I have a question about ....

Go! Now I know ....

Lesson 3

Explorers and Settlers

Envision It!

Explorers and settlers depended on waterways to travel. These waterways were often challenging.

It was not easy to live in Europe in the 1500s and 1600s. There was not enough land. There were not enough jobs. Wars were frequent. Some people were treated badly because of their beliefs. Most people saw no way to improve their lives in Europe. But North America offered hope and a chance for a new life.

Europeans Arrive

Europeans came to North America with varying goals. Some wanted to get rich and return to Europe. Some wanted to build new lives in the new land.

The Spanish arrived first, landing in the southern part of North America. They named Florida and claimed it for Spain in 1513. A few years later, they claimed Mexico for Spain. The Spanish continued to claim land through the 1500s and 1600s.

Settlers arriving at Jamestown, Virginia

Look at the picture on the left. Then write why waterways could be challenging to explorers and settlers.

UNLOCK THE BIG ? I will know the challenges of early explorers and settlers in Indiana.

Vocabulary

colony
territory
ally
confederacy

Other European groups soon followed the Spanish. The British settled Jamestown, Virginia, in 1607. Then another group of British colonists called Pilgrims founded the Plymouth Colony in Massachusetts in 1620. A **colony** is a settlement in a new land where the people remain loyal to their home country. Colonists are people who settle a colony.

By 1608, the French settled in Canada, which was then called New France. The French settled there for financial reasons. They also wanted to increase the land they controlled. French explorers, such as La Salle, whom you read about at the beginning of the chapter, began to explore more of North America.

La Salle traveled from New France across the Great Lakes and down the Mississippi River. In 1682, he claimed the entire region on either side of the Mississippi River for France. That area included Indiana. It was a region of many rivers, dense forests, and rich farmland. It seemed a perfect place to travel, hunt, or settle.

1. Look at the map. **Circle** natural features that La Salle encountered during his travels. Why might these features have been challenging?

....

....

....

IN Indiana Academic Standards

4.3.8 Identify the challenges in the physical landscape of Indiana to early settlers.

4.3.9 Explain the importance of transportation routes in Indiana's exploration, settlement and growth.

4.4.1 Give examples of goods and services produced in Indiana.

La Salle's Explorations

L. Superior
L. Michigan
L. Huron
L. Ontario
L. Erie
St. Lawrence R.
Mississippi R.
St. Joseph R.
Kankakee R.
Illinois R.
Wabash R.
Ohio R.
ATLANTIC OCEAN
Gulf of Mexico
N
S
E
W
0 200 mi
0 200 km

KEY
La Salle's route
French fort

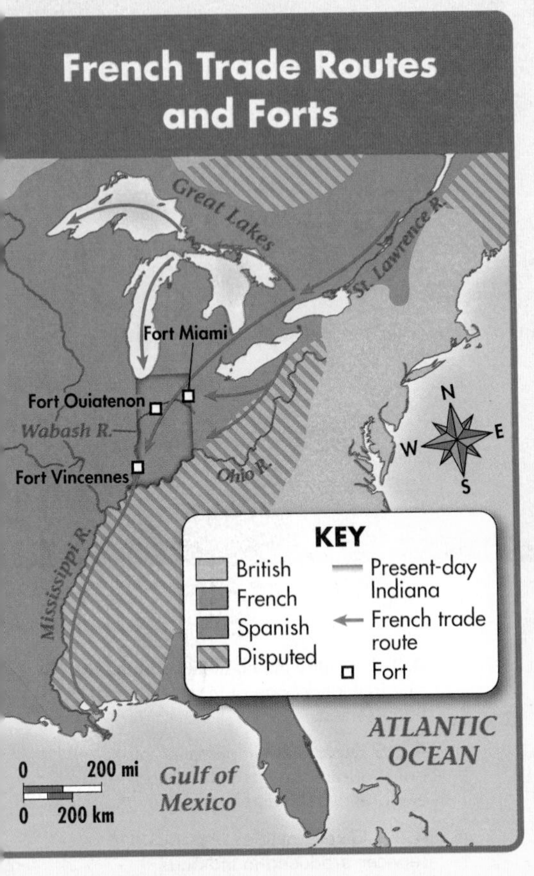

2. **Write** the main waterways that helped the French travel through French territory in Indiana.

....

....

The French in Indiana

During the 1700s, Indiana was part of the Louisiana Territory, which France claimed. A **territory** is an area of land that is controlled by an outside government.

Soon after the territory was claimed, French people began moving into the region. They mostly traveled by water since there were no roads. Trails could be long and difficult to follow. They began to settle along the rivers and lakes of the frontier. Most of the French who came to Indiana were trappers and traders. Trappers were people who caught animals for their fur. There were also soldiers who were there to protect French claims in the region.

The French built forts along the rivers. Forts were used for protection and also for trading posts. A fort is usually fortified, or strengthened, to offer protection. The French built their forts near rivers since most people traveled this way. This allowed the French to see and stop people more easily. Stockades surrounded some forts. A stockade is a defensive wall or fence built around a fort, usually made of wooden posts. In 1717, the French built Fort Ouiatenon (wee AHT uh nahn) by the Wabash River near present-day Lafayette, Indiana.

Such forts were needed because not all Native Americans were friendly. Also, some Native Americans were allies of the British. An **ally** is a partner or supporter who pledges friendship or help. Because the French and British were enemies at this time, an ally of the British would be an enemy of the French.

French forts and trading posts were supplied by the voyageurs (voy ah ZHERS). Voyageurs were Frenchmen from New France who traveled the rivers of the huge territory in large canoes. They brought trade goods from New France to people on the frontier.

Today, people recreate historic events at Fort Ouiatenon.

Trappers and Traders

French trappers and traders who came to Indiana faced many challenges. There were no maps for the dense forests that covered the territory. The forests were full of dangerous wild animals. However, many of those animals had fine fur. There were bears, wolves, badgers, foxes, raccoons, beavers, and more. The fur of these animals helped people dress warmly in the winter. They were important to both Native Americans and Europeans.

French traders got furs from both French trappers and Native American trappers. The British also began to trade with Native Americans for furs. The British had more goods that were usually cheaper and of higher quality than what the French traders brought to trade.

Many Native Americans remained allies of the French. However, many others liked British goods and wanted to trade with them. They signed treaties with the British. This made the French unhappy, because it threatened their control of the fur trade.

3. List two challenges the French trappers and traders faced in Indiana.

....

Native Americans offering fur to a trader

Growing Conflict

Conflict was not new to the territory. The Iroquois Confederacy was a long-time enemy of many less powerful Native American groups. A **confederacy** is a group of people or several smaller groups joined together for a common purpose. Iroquois warriors had fought the Shawnee, Lenape, and Kickapoo people and forced them to move west. When the French became allies of these smaller groups, they automatically became enemies of the Iroquois. As a result, the Iroquois led major attacks against the French in Canada in the 1600s.

The fact that the British were enemies of France made the Iroquois allies of the British. The Iroquois also traded with the British. They became dependent on British goods.

The British traded with other Native American groups as well. They traded with the Miami, who had once traded with the French. The Miami got along with the British and liked their trade goods. By 1747, the Shawnee and Delaware were also trading with the British. The French saw their control of the fur trade slipping away. They attacked the British and Miami in 1752, and they won.

The Potawatomi, which you learned were a powerful group, remained allies of the French. They had traded with the French for a long time. The French built more forts, hoping to regain control of their territory.

Settlers from Britain and other countries began to move westward into the Ohio River Valley. The French considered this their territory. In 1754, the conflict turned into a war. This war became known as the French and Indian War.

Iroquois warriors fought against French forces.

4. **Summarize** **Write** why Native Americans chose sides in the French and Indian War.

....

....

At first, it looked as though the French would win the war. The Potawatomi and French together won many victories during the first four years of the war. However, things began to change by the end of 1757. The French were running out of money and supplies. Some of the British joined their Native American allies to fight against the French and their allies. The French were also greatly outnumbered. The French and Indian War lasted for nine years. It ended in 1763, and the British had won. The British took control of French territories in Canada and all the French land east of the Mississippi River, including Indiana.

The French met with their Native American allies during the French and Indian War.

Got it?

5. **Summarize** **Write** why the French built forts near rivers.

....

....

....

6. Both waterways and forests offered challenges to the early settlers. How did they also offer opportunities?

my Story Ideas

....

....

....

Stop! I need help with ....

Wait! I have a question about ....

Go! Now I know ....

Map Skills

Interpret Maps

Different kinds of maps show different information. A **physical map** shows landforms, such as mountains, plains, and deserts. It also shows water features, such as lakes and rivers. A **political map** shows borders, capitals, and important cities. Other maps are known as special-purpose or thematic maps. These maps can show climate zones or population distribution, for example. They can also show events, such as historical battles or election results.

To make maps, a **cartographer,** or mapmaker, follows certain steps. A cartographer first thinks about what kind of map he or she wants to create. Will it be a political, physical, or special-purpose map? The map shown below is a special-purpose map.

Next, a cartographer will decide what to show on the map. For the map here, the cartographer decided to show an area covering much of the present-day eastern and midwestern United States. The cartographer chose to show the routes taken by Native American groups to reach Indiana. The cartographer included a key so that readers would know how to read the map. The key explains the meaning of symbols or colors on a map. Finally, the cartographer gave the map a title, so that readers would know the subject of the map.

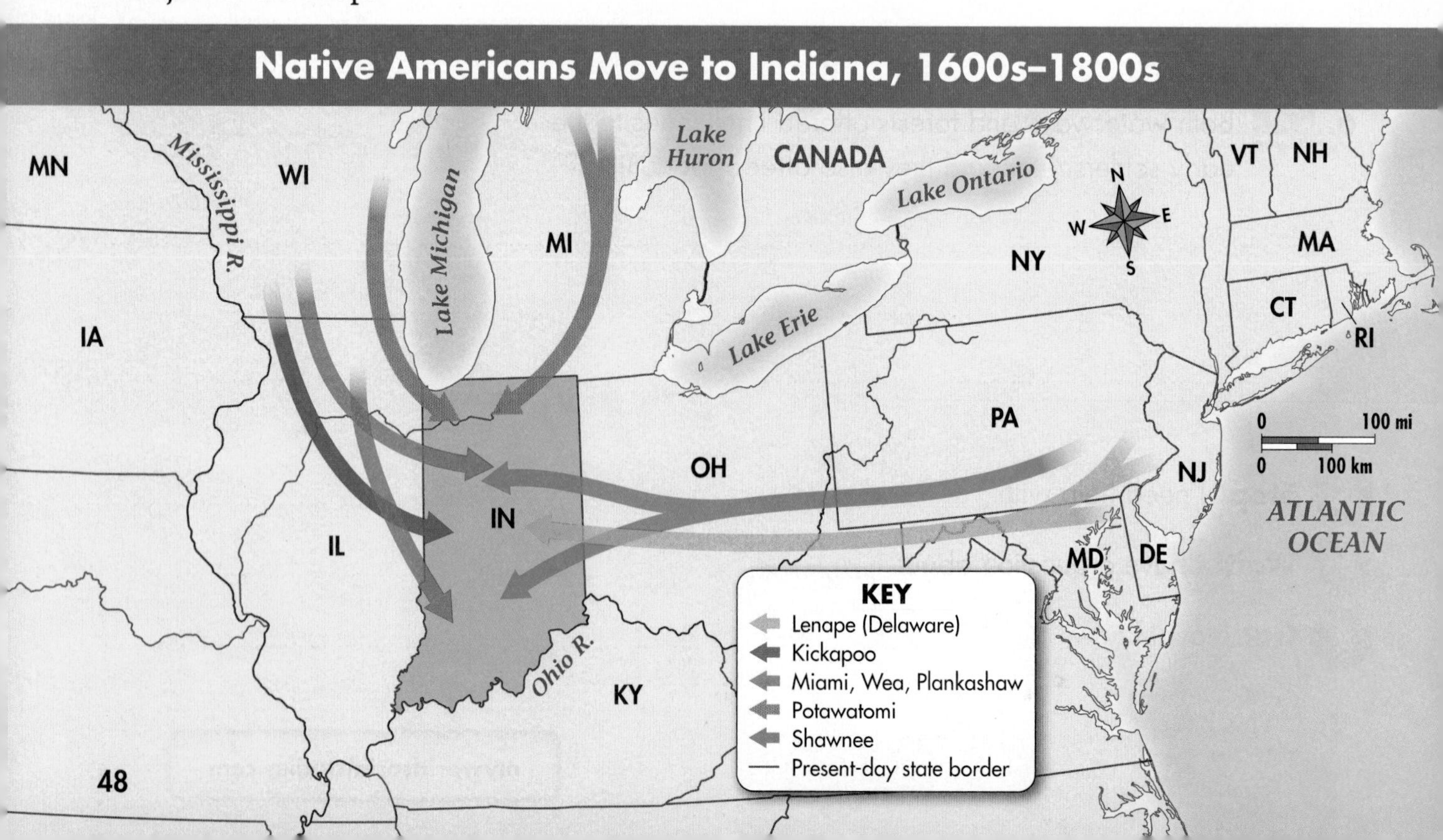

Learning Objective

I will know how to create and interpret maps.

IN **4.3.12** Create maps of Indiana showing regions and features; give examples of how people have modified their environment over time.

Suppose you are a cartographer. Follow the directions and answer the questions below to **create** your own map.

1. **Think** about what kind of map you want to create. **Describe** the map and its purpose.

2. What kind of map is it? **Circle** your response.

   Physical   Political   Special-Purpose

3. **Write** two or three features that will appear on your map.

4. **Apply** Now **draw** your map in the box below. **Write** a title for your map.

Chapter 2
Study Guide

Lesson 1

First People

- Early culture groups in Indiana included the Adena, the Hopewell, and the Mississippians.
- These culture groups lived in this area long before Europeans arrived.
- All groups built mounds, used stone tools, and traded for products they needed or wanted.

Lesson 2

Native Americans of Indiana

- Many Native American groups moved to Indiana in the late 1600s.
- Native Americans adapted things they found in their environment to meet their needs.
- Both Native Americans and Europeans relied on trade to get what they needed and wanted.

Lesson 3

Explorers and Settlers

- Many Europeans came to North America in the 1600s and 1700s.
- The French claimed the area now known as Indiana and built forts.
- The landscape presented challenges, but rivers helped people get from place to place.
- Conflicts arose among different groups, leading to the French and Indian War.

Chapter 2

Review and Assessment

Lesson 1

First People

1. **Write** a T for *true* and an F for *false* next to the following statements.

_____ a. Archaeologists use objects from the past to learn about early cultures.

_____ b. All three early cultural groups in Indiana built earthen mounds.

_____ c. The Mississippians were the first group known to live in Indiana.

_____ d. Hopewell villages were very large.

2. **Write** a brief definition of the term *artifact.*

....

....

....

3. **Match** each culture with its description.

_____ Adena	a. This group had towns with an area for ceremonies.
_____ Hopewell	b. This group was the first to develop agriculture.
_____ Mississippian	c. This group was the first to have bows and arrows.

4. **Write** two things that each culture gained through trade with people far away.

....

Lesson 2

Native Americans of Indiana

5. **Circle** the type of Native American home made from trees in which up to seven families could live.

A. dwelling

B. hut

C. wigwam

D. longhouse

6. **Summarize** How do both sides benefit from trade?

....

....

....

....

....

7. **Write** the name of an object that has been used for money in the past.

....

....

Review and Assessment

Lesson 3

Explorers and Settlers

8. Why did the Miami begin to trade with the British?

....

....

9. Write one reason why the French did not like the British trading with Native Americans.

....

....

....

10. Write why the French lost the French and Indian War.

....

....

....

11. Circle two features from the landscape of Indiana that might have been challenging for early settlers and explorers.

dense forests   rich farmland   waterways

12. Explain why people usually traveled by water through the Louisiana Territory.

....

....

....

13. How do people adapt to where they live?

Use the photograph and question below to think more about this chapter's Big Question.

What is one way people adapt to changing weather?

....

....

....

....

....

my Story Book

Go online to write and illustrate your own **myStory Book** using the **myStory Ideas** from this chapter.

How do people adapt to where they live?

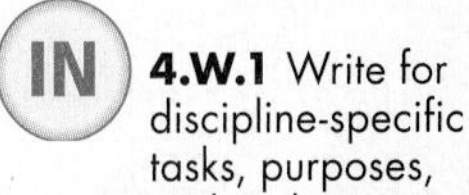

IN **4.W.1** Write for discipline-specific tasks, purposes, and audiences.

Changing seasons and geographic features, such as dense forests and rough rivers, were challenges for early cultures in Indiana. These challenges also presented opportunities. People adapted their ways of life and changed the land. For example, they farmed, built homes, wore furs, and moved to a better place to hunt for food in the winter.

Think about life in your community today. **Write** a challenge and how you and the people in your community could adapt to that challenge.

Now **draw** a picture that illustrates your writing.

While you're online, check out the **myStory Current Events** area where you can create your own book on a topic that's in the news.

Chapter 3

American Revolution to Civil War

my Story Spark

How does the past shape our present and future?

List two events that happened in your city, school, or family during the last year. **Choose** one and **describe** how that event affects you today.

Indiana Statehouse, Indianapolis

Lesson 1 American Revolution and Indiana
Lesson 2 Building and Expanding the Nation
Lesson 3 A New State
Lesson 4 Civil War and Indiana

Tecumseh

Leader, Warrior (1768–1813)

"Sell a country! Why not sell the air, the great sea, as well as the earth? Did not the Great Spirit make them all for the use of his children?" Tecumseh, a Shawnee leader, said these words in 1810. He opposed the sale of land by Native Americans. At the time, white settlers were occupying the land in the east and pushing Native Americans south and west. Tecumseh dreamed of uniting all Native Americans. He believed settlers would be forced to deal fairly with a large, powerful Native American confederation.

Tecumseh hoped to unite Native Americans.

Tecumseh grew up in the Ohio River Valley. Around 1808, Tecumseh and his followers settled Prophetstown, near present-day Lafayette, Indiana. The town's name came from his brother Tenskwatawa's nickname, The Prophet. Tenskwatawa was a Shawnee religious leader. The people of Prophetstown wanted to give up ways of life introduced by white settlers, such as using metal cooking tools. Tecumseh persuaded large numbers of Native Americans to join him.

He fought white settlers. But he also disagreed with some of the cruel fighting practices of the Shawnee. Tecumseh learned that words were powerful weapons. He became a respected speaker and leader.

In 1811, William Henry Harrison led an American army to Prophetstown. The battle that took place was known as the Battle of Tippecanoe. Tecumseh was not home, and when he returned, the town was destroyed. Tecumseh continued to resist white settlers until his death in battle in 1813. His death signaled the end of his dream and the end of Native American resistance to white settlement in the Ohio River Valley.

Think About It What lessons can we learn from Tecumseh? As you read the chapter, think about how Indiana's past affects life in Indiana today. How is Tecumseh's message important today?

Lesson 1

American Revolution and Indiana

Lady Liberty and the eagle were patriotic symbols during the American Revolution. They helped unite and define Americans.

It was July 1776. In Philadelphia, Pennsylvania, more than 50 men came together and said, "We . . . declare that these united colonies are . . . free and independent states." Each of the 13 colonies was governed by Britain. This made the colonists British subjects. Why were they declaring independence? **Independence** is freedom from being ruled by others.

The Road to Independence

Recall that 13 years earlier, in 1763, the British won the French and Indian War. This war had been very expensive. Britain needed money to pay its debts. A **debt** is money that is owed. The British government decided that it could pay its debts by creating new taxes. A **tax** is money that people pay to support the cost of government. The British created a tax on sugar. They also passed the Stamp Act. The Stamp Act was a tax on everything printed, from newspapers to playing cards. The colonists who were forced to pay these taxes grew angry.

King George III, the British ruler, did something else that angered the colonists. He issued the Proclamation of 1763, which drew an imaginary line along the Appalachian Mountains. He said that no colonists could live west of that line. The lands that were off limits included what is now Indiana.

The Stamp Act taxed printed products. These products were marked with stamps like these.

1. Write the difference between a debt and a tax.

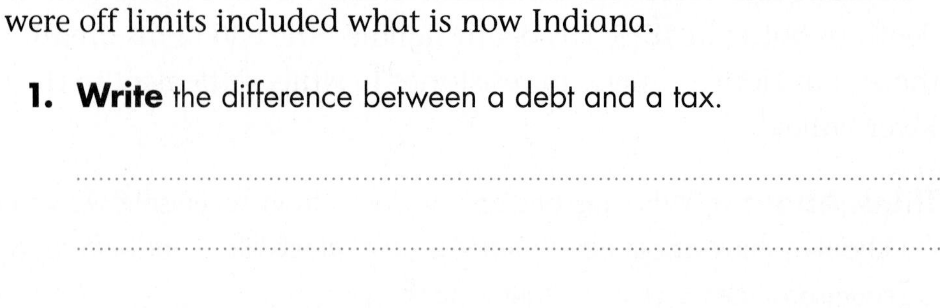

Draw a picture of an American symbol today. Write its name on the line.

UNLOCK THE BIG ? I will know about the American Revolution and how the war influenced Indiana.

Vocabulary

independence
debt
tax
strategy
surrender

IN Indiana Academic Standards

4.1.3 Explain the importance of the Revolutionary War and other events and people that influenced Indiana's development as a state.

Colonists wanted to be able to move west to find new land. As British citizens, they felt they should have a say in the laws that affected them. However, British lawmakers refused to listen. Many colonists feared that they were losing their right to self-government. So, in 1776, leaders from the different colonies met in Philadelphia. They asked Thomas Jefferson to write the Declaration of Independence. The Declaration marks the time when the colonies broke free from British rule and declared their independence. However, some Americans and most British disagreed and wanted the colonies to remain under the control of Britain's government.

2. The painting below shows our nation's early leaders signing the Declaration of Independence. Why was the Declaration of Independence important?

George Washington was a strong leader. He led the Americans to victory.

The American Revolution

The colonists began organizing and planning to fight for independence. They formed the Continental Army, led by General George Washington of Virginia. King George III was furious. He sent soldiers to the colonies. Their job was to stop the independence movement.

The colonists were successful in small, early battles. But they faced a strong British army and navy. Soon it looked as if the colonists might lose. After a defeat in New York, Washington won a battle at Trenton, New Jersey.

In 1777, the Continental Army won an important battle. The army defeated the British at Saratoga, New York. Seeing that the Americans could win, France agreed to help the colonists.

The following winter was a terrible time for the Americans. Washington and his army camped at Valley Forge in Pennsylvania. It was extremely cold. The soldiers did not have enough to eat.

The revolution continued for six long years. Across the colonies, more people became involved. About 5,000 African American colonists joined the Continental Army. Women worked at home to help. Some even fought on the battlefield. Finally, in 1781, George Washington led his soldiers to victory at Yorktown, Virginia. The long war was over.

3. **Sequence** On the timeline, **circle** the battle that came first: the Battle of Yorktown or the Battle of Saratoga.

War for Independence

April 1775
Fighting at Lexington and Concord

June 1775
Battle of Bunker Hill

July 1776
Declaration of Independence

December 1776
Battle of Trenton

October 1777
Battle of Saratoga

October 1781
Battle of Yorktown; war ends.

1774 | 1775 | 1776 | 1777 | 1778 | 1779 | 1780 | 1781 | 1782

The Revolution in Indiana

While most of the fighting during the Revolution was in the colonies on the east coast, there was also some action in the territory to the west. The British knew that this territory was not defended well. However, they needed Native Americans there to help, such as the Shawnee.

The British had a base at Fort Detroit, in what is now Michigan. Fort Detroit became a major supply center for British troops in this region. The British commander at the fort was Henry Hamilton. Hamilton met with the Miami and Potawatomi people. He dressed in clothing similar to what they wore. He was friendly, and gave the people food, supplies, and weapons. He then convinced them to use their new weapons against the colonists.

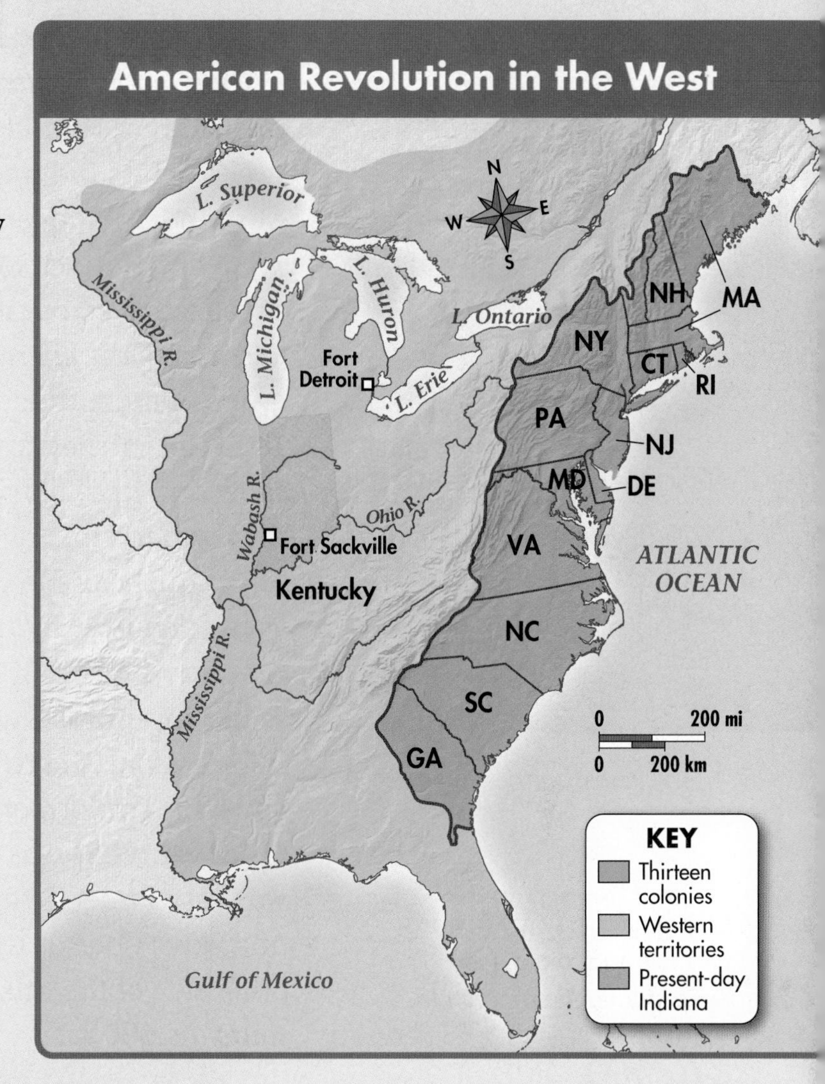

The Native Americans raided settlements in Kentucky, along the Ohio River. George Rogers Clark wanted to stop these attacks. He gathered a group of about 175 men. His plan was to capture forts located along the Wabash and Mississippi rivers. Clark and his men planned to use the forts to stop the Native American attacks.

Clark and his troops were successful. Clark was even able to convince the Native Americans in the area to stop helping the British. Eventually, the British commander, Henry Hamilton, left Fort Detroit with his troops. They followed the Wabash River across Indiana toward Fort Sackville in Vincennes. In December 1778, the large British force easily defeated the small group of American soldiers Clark had ordered to guard Fort Sackville.

4. Look at the map. **Write** why Fort Sackville might have been built where it was located.

Ending the Fight in Indiana

Clark soon heard about the loss of Fort Sackville. He also learned that Hamilton was planning an attack that would sweep across Indiana and capture Kentucky. Clark did not want that to happen.

A winter attack would be difficult due to the challenges of the weather, but it would be unexpected. Clark wanted to surprise the enemy. So on February 5, 1779, Clark and a group of more than 100 men set off from Kaskaskia for the 180-mile journey to Vincennes. Clark's men encountered snow and ice. Cold rain caused rivers to flood. Sometimes they had to cross rivers, wading waist deep in the icy water. They came close to running out of food. The Americans were exhausted by the time they reached Vincennes on February 23.

In Vincennes, Clark's strategy started with gathering information. A **strategy** is a careful plan. A French hunter gave Clark information about how the fort was defended. Clark's strategy was to convince the British that his force was very large. He told his men to wait behind a small hill and wave flags as they marched around. The British, on the other side of the hill, saw only the flags. They thought as many as 600 men were attacking!

George Rogers Clark and his men had to cross icy rivers during their march to Vincennes.

The Piankashaw (part of the Miami) and Kickapoo sided with the Americans. Even with this help, Clark's force was greatly outnumbered. But the British did not know that. Fighting began on the night of February 23. The Americans fought so well that Hamilton **surrendered**, or gave up and agreed to stop fighting, on February 25. Hamilton and his officers were amazed when they left the fort to meet Clark and realized how few men had defeated them.

5. Write why Clark attacked during the winter.

....

....

....

Got it?

6. Sequence **Write** the correct number next to the following events in the order that they happened.

.... The American Revolution ended.

.... The Continental Army defeated the British at Saratoga.

.... George Rogers Clark led more than 100 men from Kaskaskia to Vincennes.

7. Explain how life in Indiana and the United States might be different if the American Revolution had not happened.

my Story Ideas

....

....

....

Stop! I need help with ....

Wait! I have a question about ....

Go! Now I know ....

Lesson 2

Building and Expanding the Nation

Envision It!

George Washington helped make rules for the United States. Your teacher has rules about what is allowed in class.

The American Revolution was over. A new country had been born: the United States of America. Now, the new nation had a lot of work to do.

Building a New Nation

The 13 new states were not united in the way our country is today. They were not used to working together. In 1781, the states signed the Articles of Confederation to govern the country. A **confederation** is a union of states that agree to cooperate.

Leaders from the states met in a congress. A **congress** is a group of people responsible for making a country's laws. The states agreed the nation would be a republic, a form of government where everyone is represented. But soon they were arguing. They disagreed about money, so soon each state was printing its own money. They also disagreed about who owned land in the west.

Delegates from each state met in 1787 in Philadelphia to help solve these problems. A **delegate** is someone who represents a group of people. The delegates planned to revise the Articles of Confederation. Instead, they created an entirely new government. The delegates spent the summer of 1787 working out the details of this new plan of government, or **constitution.** The delegates still did not agree on everything. They compromised on many issues. Most delegates agreed to sign the U.S. Constitution in September 1787. One by one, each state then ratified the new constitution. To **ratify** means to approve. The states ratified the U.S. Constitution in June 1788.

1. **Fill in** one effect.

The new country's government under the Articles of Confederation has weaknesses.

↓

( )

Why do you think both schools and countries need rules? Write some reasons.

I will know that the United States grew and how Indiana became a state.

Vocabulary

confederation
congress
delegate
constitution
ratify
ordinance
slavery

The New Nation Grows

One of the accomplishments of the Articles of Confederation was the plan for settling lands west of Pennsylvania. The government passed several ordinances to help organize settlement, especially in the Northwest Territory. An **ordinance** is a law. The Northwest Territory consisted of the present-day states of Ohio, Indiana, Illinois, Michigan, Wisconsin, and part of Minnesota. The Land Ordinance of 1784 served as the basis for future ordinances. It called for the land to be divided into districts that would become states.

Under the Land Ordinance of 1785, surveyors divided the Northwest Territory using a grid of squares. Each square represented a township and was six square miles. Each township was then divided into 36 sections that were one square mile each.

Indiana Academic Standards

4.1.3 Explain how the Revolutionary War and other events and people influenced Indiana's development as a state.

4.1.4 Explain key documents in Indiana's development to statehood.

4.1.6 Explain how key individuals and events influenced the early growth and development of Indiana.

2. **Write** the purpose of the Land Ordinance of 1785.

The Land Ordinance of 1785

The Land Ordinance of 1785 set forth how the government would measure, divide, and distribute land. The grid established is still visible today in the lands that were part of the Northwest Territory.

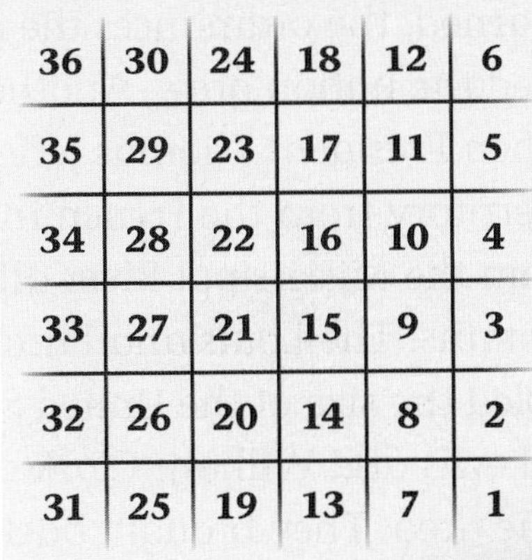

Settlers in the Northwest Territory cut down trees and planted crops on the land they had purchased.

The Northwest Ordinance of 1787 set up rules for creating states from the Northwest Territory. It stated that the territory be divided into not less than three, nor more than five, states. An individual territory could become a state when its population reached 60,000. The ordinance also said slavery was forever outlawed in the Northwest Territory. **Slavery** is the act of owning people and forcing them to work without pay.

The Northwest Territory was an area rich with resources, such as water, fertile soil, and wood. People had begun moving into the region as early as the 1770s. These early settlers came from the east. They settled along the Ohio River Valley. This valley forms the southern border of the present-day states of Ohio and Indiana.

Some of the land in the region was set aside for soldiers who had never been paid for their service during the American Revolution. The rest of the land was sold to people who wanted to farm or build new towns.

In the early 1800s, pioneers began coming to the Northwest Territory by the thousands. The government encouraged people to farm. They knew the nation could only grow if many people were raising and growing food. The government sold the land at very low prices, so many people could afford farms.

As you learned, the ordinances the government passed helped the nation grow. Another way the nation grew was when President Thomas Jefferson bought the Louisiana Territory from the French in 1803. This territory stretched from the Mississippi River all the way to the Rocky Mountains. The Louisiana Purchase, as it was called, doubled the size of the United States. Jefferson sent Meriwether Lewis and William Clark on a two-year journey to explore the area. They brought back much information about the land and people of the west.

3. **Sequence** **Circle** which came first: Land Ordinance of 1785 or Louisiana Purchase.

Conflicts With Native Americans

Native Americans still lived in many parts of the Northwest Territory. As new settlers continued to arrive, conflict arose between the groups. The British in Canada encouraged Native Americans to attack the settlers. Chief Little Turtle, a Miami leader, gathered warriors from many groups and began attacking settlers near the Maumee River. In 1790 and 1791, he defeated American forces sent to stop him.

Promises of help from the British brought more Native Americans together. More than 2,000 warriors gathered near Fort Miami on the Maumee River in 1794. General Anthony Wayne, from the Legion of the United States, went with his troops to stop the Native Americans. The Native Americans were gathered behind a cluster of fallen trees, so the battle became known as the Battle of Fallen Timbers. The battle lasted less than two hours. This was an important victory because it resulted in U.S. occupation of the Northwest Territory.

4. **Study** the map. Then **write** which was larger: the Northwest Territory or the lands acquired by the Louisiana Purchase.

....

....

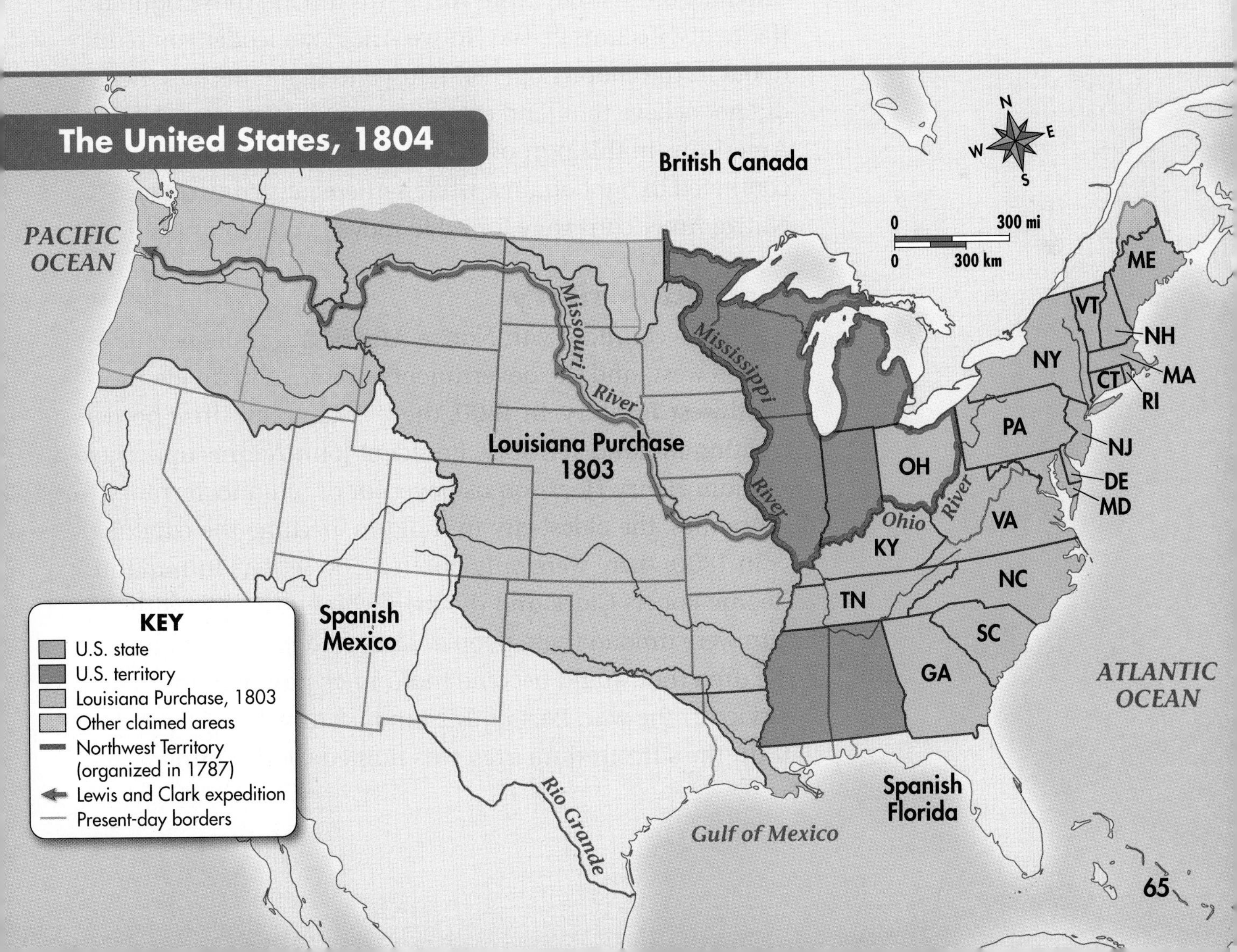

The Treaty of Greenville offered money to Native Americans in exchange for land and an end to fighting.

Next, General Wayne built Fort Wayne at the head of the Maumee River. He then headed for Fort Greenville, where Native American leaders signed a treaty called the Treaty of Greenville. The treaty gave the United States most of Ohio and part of Indiana. Little Turtle was among those signing the treaty. Tecumseh, the Native American leader you read about in the chapter opener, refused to sign it because he did not believe that land could be owned. Like many Native Americans in this part of the United States, Tecumseh continued to fight against white settlement. Many other Native Americans were forced to move to other lands.

Indiana Territory

Despite conflicts with Native Americans, more people moved west, and the government continued to divide the Northwest Territory. In 1800, the U.S. Congress drew borders, creating Indiana Territory. President John Adams appointed William Henry Harrison as governor of Indiana Territory. Vincennes, the oldest city in Indiana, became the capital.

In 1800, there were only about 5,600 settlers in Indiana. George Rogers Clark and the men who had fought with him were among these people. They had been given land in the area that would become Indiana as payment for their service in the war. Part of this land became Clarksville. In 1801, the surrounding area was named Clark County.

Governor Harrison wanted to make it easier for people to buy farms in the Northwest Territory. The Land Ordinance of 1785 had created properties that were 640 acres each. In 1800, Harrison convinced the U.S. Congress to pass a law known as the Harrison Land Act. This allowed people to buy smaller plots of land at 320 acres.

Ohio became a state in 1803. Then, in 1809, Illinois Territory was created. This created the borders that Indiana still has today.

In 1813, the Indiana legislature moved the territory capital from Vincennes to Corydon. By 1815, the population of Indiana had grown to 63,000. New farms and new towns began to spread along all the territory's waterways. The new territory was ready to become a state.

5. Recall the rules of the Northwest Ordinance of 1787. **Write** why Indiana Territory was ready to become a state.

....

Got it?

6. **Sequence** **Write** an event in Indiana's history that happened after the first two events listed here.

1. The Land Ordinance of 1785 divides territories into townships.
2. Chief Little Turtle attacks settlers.
3. ....

....

7. **Write** the effects of the Land Ordinance of 1785 and the Northwest Ordinance of 1787 on Indiana.

my Story Ideas

....

....

Stop! I need help with ....

Wait! I have a question about ....

Go! Now I know ....

Lesson 3

A New State

Envision It!

People in Indiana dug canals, like the Wabash and Erie Canal shown here, to connect rivers and lakes.

Indiana's Path to Statehood

1815

1816

December 1815 Jennings asks Congress to allow Indiana to become a state

May 1816 Congress allows Indiana statehood process to begin.

June 1816 Delegates write Indiana Constitution.

December 1816 Congress admits Indiana into the Union as the 19th state.

By early 1816, nearly 64,000 people lived in Indiana, and many eagerly anticipated statehood. In December 1815, a lawyer and politician from Indiana named Jonathan Jennings requested that Congress let Indiana become a state. By May 1816, Congress had agreed to begin the process.

Indiana Becomes a State

Before Indiana could become a state, it needed a state constitution. In June 1816, 43 delegates from different parts of Indiana met in Corydon. Led by Jonathan Jennings, they wrote the new constitution in just 18 days. Many of their ideas came from the United States Constitution, including the protection of people's rights. The delegates discussed whether slavery should be allowed in Indiana. They decided they would not allow it. The new constitution went into effect on June 29, 1816.

On December 11, 1816, Congress admitted Indiana into the Union as the 19th state. Indiana elected its first state officials. Jennings became the state's first governor. The new state government continued to meet in Corydon, the capital of the territory. However, people thought the state capital should be near the center of the state. So, in 1820, they started to build a new capital—what would become Indianapolis. In 1825, the government moved to its new home.

1. **Sequence** On the timeline, **circle** the event that occurred before Indiana was admitted to the Union.

Based on what you know about the importance of waterways, why do you think people built canals?

UNLOCK THE BIG ? I will know how Indiana developed in the early 1800s.

Vocabulary

immigrant
canal
supply
demand
utopia
reservation

IN **Indiana Academic Standards**

4.1.5 Explain the causes of Native American groups' removal and their resettlement during the 1830s

4.1.6 Explain how key individuals and events influenced the early growth and development of Indiana.

4.3.9 Explain the importance of transportation routes in the exploration, settlement and growth of Indiana

4.4.3 Explain the benefits of trade and give examples of how people in Indiana have engaged in trade.

Indiana Grows

Many of the people coming to Indiana arrived from New England, but others came from southern states, such as Virginia and Kentucky. They came for land. In the more settled areas of the United States, there was not enough land available for people who wanted to farm. So people moved to Indiana where land was plentiful.

One settler who came to Indiana from Kentucky was Tom Lincoln. He came in 1816 to farm the land. Lincoln arrived with his wife and his seven-year-old son, Abraham—a boy who would grow up to become president one day.

The crowded cities of the eastern states also caused people to move west. In the first half of the 1800s, more and more immigrants arrived in the United States. An **immigrant** is a person who moves from one country to another. As immigrants settled in eastern cities, others moved west.

Some immigrants came straight to Indiana from countries in Europe. Europeans left their homes to escape war and poverty. They came to Indiana because it offered them the opportunity to be free and to own land.

Soon, people in Indiana needed more land. They wanted lands used by Native Americans. In 1818, Governor Jennings told the Miami Indians that the government wanted their land, which covered much of central Indiana. The Miami were given money, salt, and tools in exchange for the land. This agreement was known as the New Purchase. It would not be the last time Native Americans would be forced to leave Indiana.

Abraham Lincoln's Indiana boyhood home in Lincoln City

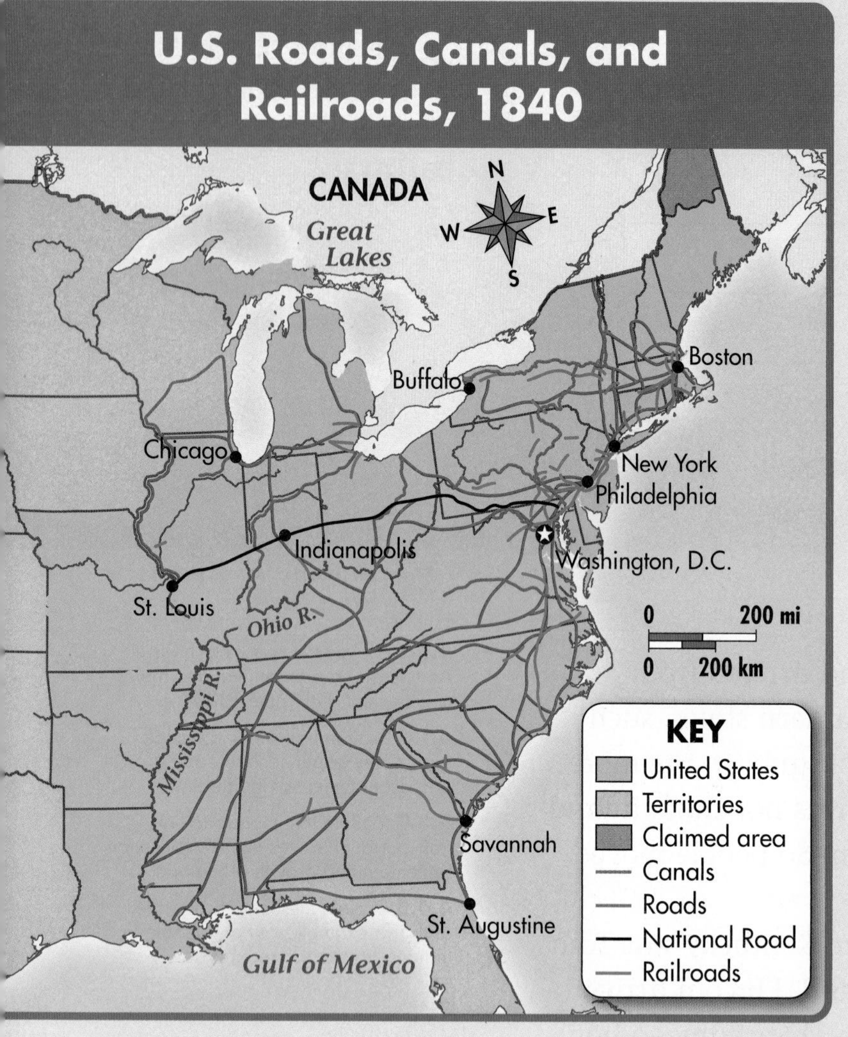

Transportation Improves

In Indiana in the early 1800s, the most common method of transportation was by river. Settlers traveled down the Ohio River on slow, flat-bottomed boats. They faced dangers, such as robbers who attacked the boats to steal cargo. The U.S. government knew that it needed to improve transportation in order to encourage more people to move west.

In 1811, the U.S. government began building the National Road. This wide, paved road started in Maryland. Construction was slow. The National Road reached Indiana in 1827. By 1839, it stretched all the way to Vandalia, Illinois. The success of the National Road inspired people in Indiana to build other roads. Soon, roads stretched across the state, connecting towns and cities.

Canals were another new means of transportation that improved life in the new state. A **canal** is a human-made waterway dug across land. Canals connected rivers and lakes. They made it possible to travel by water in places without rivers or roads.

Some Hoosiers thought canals would help Indiana's farmers. Canals would allow farmers to move their crops to markets faster. They would allow more settlers to reach areas of the state with low populations. In 1832, the people of Indiana began work on the Wabash and Erie Canal. This canal made it possible for boats to travel from the Great Lakes all the way across Indiana to the Ohio River.

By the 1850s, an even more significant improvement in transportation reached Indiana—the railroad. Train engines were powerful, and they could move faster than barges on canals. It was also much easier to lay tracks than to dig canals. By 1855, seven railroad lines passed through Indianapolis. This was one of the reasons Indiana became known as the "Crossroads of America."

2. **Predict** the impact of the National Road on the future of Indiana.

....

....

....

....

....

....

....

The Impact of Improved Transportation

Better transportation had a huge impact on Indiana. People and manufactured goods could reach Indiana from the eastern states more easily. Farmers could earn money by selling crops in distant places and use the money to buy manufactured goods. The sale of crops in Indiana was based on supply and demand. **Supply** was the amount of crops farmers had to sell. **Demand** was the amount of crops people were willing to buy. Roads, canals, and railroads allowed farmers to move their crops to where demand was greatest and supply was lowest. Higher demand and lower supply meant higher prices paid to the farmers.

Most settlers came to Indiana to farm. However, people needed goods and services, as well, and towns developed to provide these. Towns built post offices. Doctors arrived. People opened shops to sell farmers the things they needed.

Towns grew up along the National Road. Since it became the main street of so many towns, the National Road became known as the Main Street of America.

To build the canals and railroads, thousands of new workers came to Indiana. Many were immigrants who came from Germany and Ireland. Thanks to the newcomers, Indiana had the fifth largest population in the United States in 1860.

Some people came to Indiana hoping to create a utopia. A **utopia** is an imagined place where everything is perfect. A group called the Harmonists moved from Pennsylvania to Indiana in 1814. They settled near the Wabash River. In 1825, the Harmonists sold their land to a man named Robert Owen. He renamed the community New Harmony. Owen hoped to create a utopia for writers, scientists, and thinkers. However, quarrels broke out often. New Harmony was not utopia. Owen gave up in 1828 and returned home to Britain.

New Harmony, Owen's utopian dream in Indiana

In 1837, U.S. government officials told Potawatomi leaders that their people were going to be moved to reservations in Kansas.

Growth Leads to Conflict

The New Purchase of 1818, an agreement between the Potawatomi and the United States, opened up a lot of land for the many settlers flooding into Indiana. However, settlers kept coming, so even more land was needed. The government asked Native American groups to sell their land in the northern part of Indiana. Some groups left on their own because their way of life was disappearing. But some decided to stay.

When the U.S. government passed the Indian Removal Act of 1830, it gave President Andrew Jackson the authority to force Native Americans to move to reservations farther west. A **reservation** is an area of land that the United States set aside for Native Americans.

When Native Americans did not want to sign treaties or move to reservations, the U.S. military forced them to move. In 1838, soldiers marched 800 Potawatomi from their homes in northern Indiana to new land in Kansas. More than forty of the Potawatomi died as they traveled. The march became known as the Trail of Death.

The Miami stayed in Indiana until 1846. Then, many of them were also forced to move to reservations in Kansas. However, about a hundred Miami returned and asked the government of Indiana to let them stay. By 1850, there were only about 250 Miami still living in Indiana.

3. Underline in the text why the government asked Native American groups to move from their lands.

A New Constitution

Even as Native Americans left the state, Indiana's population was growing rapidly. The state government was trying to keep up with the growth. In 1836, the state passed laws to improve transportation further by digging more canals, building new roads, and laying tracks for new railways. The plan was to connect all cities in the state. These improvements cost about $10 million, money the state had to borrow from banks outside the state.

Then in 1837, a financial crisis struck. People lost jobs. The prices of crops dropped. This crisis lasted until the mid-1840s. Indiana was not able to pay its huge debt. Work stopped on the canals, roads, and railways.

The people of Indiana knew changes needed to be made to the state constitution to prevent another financial crisis. Delegates gathered in Indianapolis in 1850 to work on the new constitution. In 1851, voters approved it. This constitution said the state would no longer be allowed to borrow money. Although it has been amended several times, this is still Indiana's constitution today.

4. **Fill in** the missing cause on the chart.

Cause

Effect

Indiana needed new roads and railroads.

Got it?

5. **Sequence** **Explain** what happened after the U.S. government passed the Indian Removal Act of 1830.

6. The National Road connected Indiana to states in the east. **Write** how this major transportation route shaped Indiana.

my Story Ideas

Stop! I need help with

Wait! I have a question about

Go! Now I know

Lesson 4

Civil War and Indiana

Envision It!

Many Americans, including Hoosiers, fought in the Civil War. This is a company of African American soldiers from the war.

1. **Write** one effect of the Missouri Compromise of 1820.

As you learned, Indiana became a state in 1816. At this time, difficult issues divided the country. Many people in the North had different beliefs than people in the South. The most important difference was about slavery. These differences grew into a major conflict.

The North and the South

Indiana was a free state in the North. This meant that it did not allow slavery. Other states, located in the South, were slave states. They did allow slavery. Some Northerners were in favor of **abolition**, or the ending of slavery. Many Northerners did not want new western territories to allow slavery. Southerners disagreed. They wanted enslaved workers to work in the fields.

In 1820, Congress passed the Missouri Compromise. This bill drew an imaginary line through the Louisiana Purchase territory. Slavery was outlawed north of the line but was allowed south of it. After the Missouri Compromise was signed, there were 12 slave states and 12 free states.

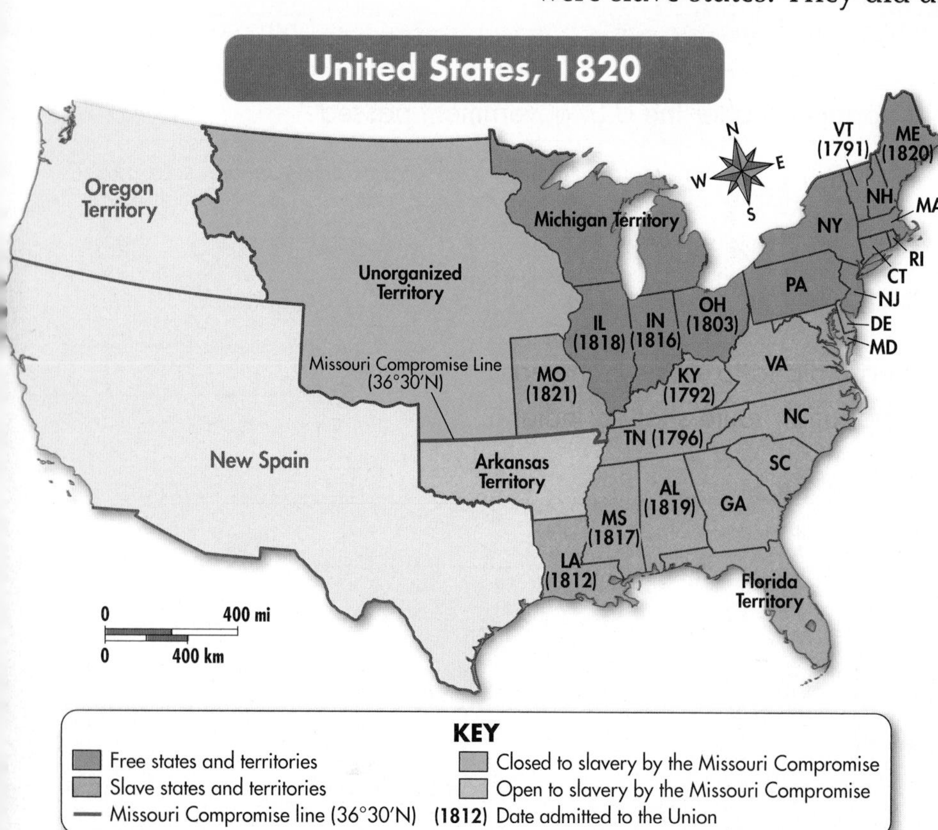

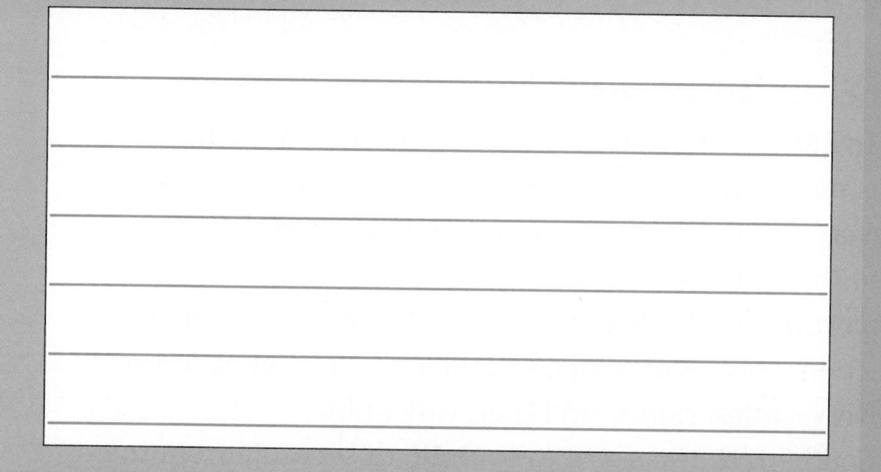

What does this picture tell you about the people who fought in the Civil War?

UNLOCK THE BIG ?

I will know what led to the Civil War, the impact of Lincoln's presidency, and Indiana's participation in the war.

Vocabulary

abolition
states' rights
secede
civil war
regiment
militia

IN Indiana Academic Standards

4.1.7 Explain the roles of various individuals, groups, and movements in the social conflicts that led to the Civil War.

4.1.8 Summarize the impact of Lincoln's presidency on Indiana and describe how Indiana citizens participated in the Civil War.

4.1.16 Identify different opinions and the central questions in historical documents and resources.

Abolitionists, or people who thought slavery was wrong, looked for ways to help people escape slavery. In the 1790s, some of them had started the Underground Railroad. This was a secret network that helped enslaved people escape to free states and Canada. Information about routes was passed along through hidden messages in songs. Between 40,000 and 100,000 people used the system to gain their freedom.

Many escape routes passed through Indiana. Thousands of people escaped slavery by traveling through Newport, a town in western Indiana. For 20 years, Levi and Catharine Coffin helped enslaved people gain freedom here.

Once African Americans were free, some people worried they would not receive justice in the United States. They came up with a plan to move them to Africa. This movement, known as the colonization movement, started in 1816. The government and states set aside money and, in a few years, founded Liberia on Africa's west coast. By 1867, more than 13,000 emigrants had been sent there. Many opposed the movement, however, and it eventually came to an end.

This painting shows Hoosiers Levi and Catharine Coffin helping enslaved people escape to freedom on the Underground Railroad.

Lincoln Becomes President

In 1860, Abraham Lincoln was elected president. He was part of the new Republican Party, which was against slavery. Southern states argued for **states' rights**, the idea that the states had the power and the right to decide important matters for themselves. Following Lincoln's election, Southerners viewed Lincoln's election as a threat to slavery, states' rights, and their way of life.

Southern states began to **secede**, or separate from the United States. Soon, 11 southern states formed the Confederate States of America, or the Confederacy. Recall that a confederacy is a loose union of groups or states.

President Lincoln did not accept the states seceding. He said the Confederate states were still part of the United States. He would do everything he could to keep the country united. He used the term Union to describe a country he envisioned with liberty for all and no slavery.

On April 12, 1861, not long after Lincoln was sworn in to office, Confederates fired shots on Fort Sumter in South Carolina. These first shots marked the beginning of the Civil War. A **civil war** is a war between different groups of people in the same country.

Abraham Lincoln became the 16th president of the United States in 1860.

2. Underline what caused Southerners to secede.

Confederate battle flag

Union flag

The War Begins

Posters encouraged Hoosier men to join the army.

Both the Union and the Confederacy had strengths and weaknesses. The Union had a larger population and more factories. This meant more people could make supplies for the army. But most Civil War battles took place in the South. Union soldiers did not know the land as well as the Confederates did. The Union also had many railroads for moving troops and supplies, but the Confederacy did not have as many.

Soon after the first shots were fired on Fort Sumter, the president called for 75,000 volunteers to fight for the Union. Hoosiers remained loyal to the Union and played important roles in the war. Oliver P. Morton was the governor of Indiana at the start of the Civil War. He strongly supported President Lincoln and the Union. When other states were trying to compromise in order to avoid a war, Morton told Lincoln he had 6,000 soldiers to help defend the Union.

Within two weeks after the war began, 12,000 Indiana men volunteered to fight. Indiana formed six regiments. A **regiment** is a military unit usually made of several groups of soldiers. Governor Morton needed officers to lead the volunteers. He selected Lew Wallace and Benjamin Harrison, both lawyers in Indiana, to lead the volunteers into battle.

Important Civil War Battles

Most people thought the war would end quickly, but they were wrong. Fighting lasted for four years and spread across 23 states. In all, soldiers fought as many as 10,000 battles.

Union troops cried, "On to Richmond!" as they advanced on Confederate forces in July 1861. The Confederate soldiers were camped in Virginia, close to the country's capital in Washington, D.C. Lincoln and many other Northerners believed this would be an easy win for the Union army. They also thought it would clear the path to Richmond, where Union troops could capture the Confederate capital and quickly end the war. However, the inexperienced Union soldiers were no match for the determined group of Confederate soldiers. The First Battle of Bull Run was a major victory for the South.

Important Civil War Battles

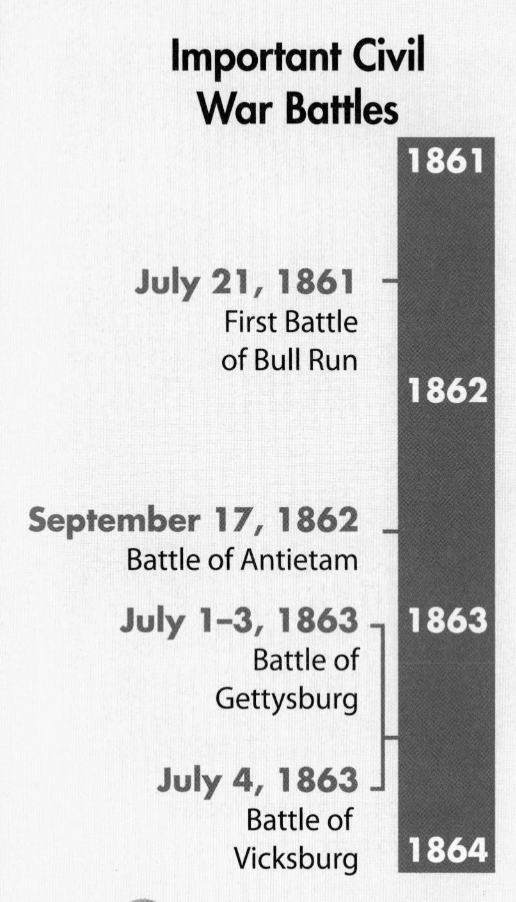

3. **Sequence** **Circle** which occurred first: the Battle of Gettsyburg or the Emancipation Proclamation.

The Battle of Antietam, on September 17, 1862, was the single bloodiest day of the war. The Confederate army had decided it was time to invade the North. They attacked Union troops near Sharpsburg, Maryland. Thousands of soldiers on both sides were killed and wounded during this battle. The Union army successfully forced the Confederate army to retreat from Maryland and go back to the South.

President Lincoln used the Union's success at Antietam as an opportunity to announce the Emancipation Proclamation on January 1, 1863. This document promised to free all the slaves once the Union took back control of the South.

Later in 1863, the U.S. Congress passed a law that allowed African Americans to serve in the Union army. Thousands of men eagerly enlisted. Many of them joined the 28th Regiment, United States Colored Troops, which formed in Indiana in November of 1863. Soldiers of the 28th Regiment fought in some of the war's most important battles. More than 200 men of the 28th died in the war.

The most significant battle of the war was fought in Gettysburg, Pennsylvania, from July 1 to 3, 1863. This battle was the turning point of the war. The Union victory there ended Confederate General Robert E. Lee's hopes that he could win the war. Far to the south, on July 4, Union forces captured Vicksburg, Mississippi, which gave them control of the Mississippi River. Fighting continued for two more years, but Vicksburg and Gettysburg were the beginning of the end for the Confederacy.

The Battle of Antietam

The War in Indiana

Although Indiana fought for the North, some Hoosiers agreed with the South. Governor Morton worried they might rebel. He also feared that Southerners across the Ohio River might invade Indiana. So, early in the war, in May 1861, the Indiana General Assembly organized the Indiana Legion. This was a militia group. A **militia** is a group of people who are not in the military but are still trained as soldiers. A militia handles emergencies at home. One job of the Indiana Legion was guarding Confederate prisoners at Camp Morton. But this was not their only job.

On July 8, 1863, John Hunt Morgan, a Confederate general, led troops on horseback across the Ohio River into Indiana. He hoped to steal horses and supplies. He also hoped to find people in southern Indiana who supported the Confederate cause. His actions became known as Morgan's Raid.

John Hunt Morgan

The next day, on July 9, about 450 members of the Indiana Legion faced Morgan and his 2,400 men about a mile south of Corydon. The Battle of Corydon was the only Civil War battle fought on Indiana soil. The Indiana Legion fought bravely, but they had no battle experience and were outnumbered. They were quickly defeated. Morgan continued his raid, moving into Corydon that night and then north to Salem the next day.

Morgan next swept across eastern Indiana and into Ohio, where he was eventually captured. He escaped from prison but was killed in battle in Tennessee in 1864.

4. Underline the reason Governor Morton organized the Indiana Legion.

John Hunt Morgan led his men through Indiana during his raid.

The Home Front

When the men of Indiana marched off to war, they left behind their wives and children. Women at home suddenly faced new responsibilities and tasks. They managed both their homes and their farms by themselves. Some worked as nurses. Some turned their work and social clubs into groups that helped the war effort. Organized by Governor Morton, who supported the troops, many women sewed clothing and knitted socks for soldiers. They rolled bandages and helped make ammunition. Some women even took jobs in the state arsenal that Governor Morton had set up in Indianapolis. An arsenal is a place where weapons are kept. These women worked to supply Indiana soldiers with weapons and ammunition.

The Civil War Ends

By April 1865, the Confederate army was hopelessly outnumbered by the Union army. The war ended on April 9, 1865, when the Confederates surrendered to the Union. General Lee and General Grant met in Virginia at Appomattox Court House to officially end the fighting.

Confederate General Lee surrenders to Union General Grant at Appomattox Court House.

When the war ended, the divided country had to begin reuniting. The cost of the war had been high. About 600,000 Americans from the North and South had died. Indiana regiments had seen action in 308 battles. More than 197,000 Hoosiers had fought in the war. Of those, more than 25,000 died in battle or from wounds or disease.

President Lincoln had plans for rebuilding the country and reuniting the people. But he was shot and killed before he had a chance to put his plans into action. Rebuilding the nation had to begin without him.

Abraham Lincoln is considered one of our nation's greatest presidents. He is remembered for preserving the Union and for his role in ending slavery. In Indiana, Lincoln's supporter, Morton, is remembered as the "Great War Governor" for his efforts during the Civil War. After the war, Morton became a U.S. senator and also championed African Americans' rights.

5. Write one impact of Lincoln's presidency.

....

....

Got it?

6. Sequence Read each pair of events. **Circle** the event that happened first within each pair.

A. Lincoln's election

The South's secession

B. Morgan's Raid

The creation of the Indiana Legion

7. Explain how Indiana might be different today if the Civil War had not been fought.

....

....

Stop! I need help with ....

Wait! I have a question about ....

Go! Now I know ....

Critical Thinking Skills

Compare Viewpoints

Historical documents might be based on fact or on opinion. A **fact** can be checked and proven to be true or false. An **opinion** is what someone believes or thinks, and it cannot be proven.

We can better understand history by learning about people's opinions or viewpoints. A person's viewpoint shapes the way he or she looks at events, issues, and the world. By identifying and comparing viewpoints, we can see more than one side of historical events.

To recognize viewpoints or opinions in historical documents, look for signal words. Words such as *think, believe, feel, best, most,* and *worst* usually tell that a statement is an opinion. For example, stating "I think the 1860 election was the most important election in American history" is an opinion. "Abraham Lincoln was elected President in 1860" is a fact.

In addition to identifying viewpoints or opinions, finding the central questions, or main ideas, is important when we read historical documents. To identify the central question, first read the text. Then look for important details. These will help you identify the main idea. Finally, restate this main idea, or central question, in your own words.

Both of the documents below were written during the Civil War. The first was written by a Boston lawyer after the battle of Fredericksburg. Union forces suffered heavy casualties and lost this battle. The second is from an Indiana newspaper, the *Madison Daily Courier,* written later in the war.

> "My confidence is terribly shaken. So is everybody's. Things have never looked so black to me as at this moment."
>
> —Boston lawyer, December 1862

> "We are confident that Gen[eral] Sheridan will win [praise] as chief of cavalry of the Army of the Potomac; and that Gen[eral] Grant has done well in placing him in that responsible position."
>
> —*Madison Daily Courier,* April 8, 1864

Learning Objective

I will know how to identify different opinions in historical documents and compare viewpoints.

IN **4.1.16** Identify different opinions and the central questions in historical documents and resources.

Use the historical documents on the previous page to answer the following questions.

1. What is the viewpoint of the author of the first document? What phrases indicate this viewpoint?

2. What is the central question or main idea in the first document?

3. What is the viewpoint of the author of the second document? What phrases indicate this viewpoint?

4. What is the central question or main idea in the second document?

5. **Apply** **Compare** the viewpoints of the two documents. **Write** one way that they are different.

Study Guide

Lesson 1

American Revolution and Indiana

- Following the French and Indian War, Great Britain forced new taxes on American colonists.
- In 1776, American colonists declared their independence.
- George Washington led the American army against the British and led them to victory in 1781.
- George Rogers Clark fought the British in Indiana.

Lesson 2

Building and Expanding the Nation

- The United States set forth its plan of government in the U.S. Constitution.
- Settlers began to move into the Northwest Territory. The government passed several ordinances to organize the settlement.
- Native Americans in Indiana came into conflict with settlers who wanted their land.

Lesson 3

A New State

- Indiana became the country's 19th state in 1816.
- New roads, canals, and railroads made travel easier.
- Improved transportation helped farmers bring crops to market and led to the growth of towns.
- As more settlers arrived, Native Americans left or were forced off their land.

Lesson 4

Civil War and Indiana

- Northern and southern states disagreed over issues of slavery and states' rights.
- The election of Abraham Lincoln caused southern states to secede.
- Thousands of Hoosiers fought in the Civil War, which lasted four years.
- The Battle of Corydon was the only battle fought on Indiana soil.

Chapter 3

Review and Assessment

Lesson 1

American Revolution and Indiana

1. **Match** each word with its meaning.

_____	debt	a. careful plan
_____	independence	b. money that is owed
_____	strategy	c. give up and stop fighting
_____	surrender	d. freedom from being controlled

2. **Explain** why American colonists wanted independence.

....

....

....

....

....

3. **Describe** how George Rogers Clark helped colonists in Indiana during the American Revolution.

....

....

....

....

....

....

Lesson 2

Building and Expanding the Nation

4. **Circle** the reason delegates from each state gathered in Philadelphia in 1787.
   A. to pass the Northwest Ordinance
   B. to make a plan for settling lands in the west
   C. to create the U.S. Constitution
   D. to write the Articles of Confederation

5. **Explain** why both the United States and Indiana needed constitutions.

....

....

....

....

....

6. **Sequence** On the line below, **list** these events in the order that they occurred.
   a. States ratify the U.S. Constitution.
   b. Indiana becomes a territory.
   c. The Battle of Fallen Timbers occurs.
   d. The Northwest Ordinance of 1787 sets up rules for creating new states.

....

Review and Assessment

Lesson 3

A New State

7. **Write** the correct answers in the blanks.
   The success of the ....
   inspired people in Indiana to build more roads. To connect rivers and lakes, people dug .... that ran across the state.

8. **Describe** how building canals helped increase trade in Indiana.

9. What was the Indian Removal Act of 1830?

Lesson 4

Civil War and Indiana

10. What role did Hoosiers Levi and Catharine Coffin play in the Underground Railroad?

11. How did the citizens of Indiana contribute to the Civil War?

12. **How does the past shape our present and future?**

    Use the photograph and question below to think more about this chapter's Big Question.

How did the Civil War affect the people of Indiana?

my Story Book

Go online to write and illustrate your own **myStory Book** using the **myStory Ideas** from this chapter.

How does the past shape our present and future?

4.W.1 Write for discipline-specific tasks, purposes, and audiences.

The decisions people in a country make shape the country's future. When George Rogers Clark captured British forts in the Ohio and Mississippi river valleys during the American Revolution, he changed Indiana's future. He helped bring Indiana into the United States.

Think about Indiana joining the United States. **Write** how life in Indiana would be different if Indiana had not become a state.

Now **draw** a picture or a map that shows how the United States might look today if Indiana had not become a state.

While you're online, check out the **myStory Current Events** area where you can create your own book on a topic that's in the news.

Chapter 4

A Growing State

my Story Spark

How does change bring opportunity?

Describe a time when you tried a new activity. **Explain** how it affected you.

This painting of a busy street in Indianapolis shows some of the changes Indiana experienced, such as improvements to transportation.

Lesson 1 Economic Changes
Lesson 2 New People, New Jobs
Lesson 3 Growth and Development

Gene Stratton-Porter

Naturalist, Photographer, Author (1863–1924)

At an early age, Gene (Geneva) Stratton-Porter discovered her love for nature. She took walks around her family farm in Wabash County, Indiana. She watched the birds and even fed them in their nests.

Stratton-Porter and her husband built a large home near Limberlost Swamp in northeastern Indiana. Stratton-Porter liked to explore the swamp. She took photographs of birds and animals and sent the photographs to a nature magazine. She also began to write fiction. Most of her books were set in or near Limberlost Swamp. Her books, such as *A Girl of the Limberlost*, became very popular. During her life, Stratton-Porter wrote twelve novels, seven nature study books, and three books of poetry.

Gene Stratton-Porter's books have sold more than 8 million copies, making her one of the most widely read authors in the world.

In the early 1900s, some people in Indiana looked at swampland as wasteful and dangerous. Businesses drained Limberlost Swamp to create more farmland and drill for oil. Stratton-Porter wrote that people should try to preserve nature:

> "Certainly to plant trees and preserve trees, to preserve water, and to do all in our power to save every natural resource . . . is a work that every man and woman should give immediate . . . attention."
>
> – Gene Stratton-Porter, *Let Us Highly Resolve,* 1927

Stratton-Porter moved and built a cabin on Sylvan Lake. Her property there included woods, fields, and gardens. People can visit the cabin today and see the wildflowers and trees that inspired her.

Think About It How does Stratton-Porter's story show that change can bring new opportunities? As you read this chapter, think about the changes that Hoosiers went through.

Lesson 1

Economic Changes

Envision It!

In the late 1800s, Washington Street in Indianapolis was filled with people and traffic.

After the Civil War, Indiana experienced important changes. Hoosiers discovered new resources and invented new machines. These helped the state's economy grow. An **economy** is the way a place uses its resources to produce goods and services. Railroads also had an impact on the economy. They helped connect Indiana to other parts of the country so that farms and businesses could ship goods faster.

Good Times for Farmers

In the 1870s, most people in Indiana lived and worked on farms. Many others worked in industries connected to farms. The farms and industries supplied food and other products for Indiana and the country. Indiana farmers grew grain, vegetables, and fruit. Every county in the state had mills for making flour from grain. Farmers also raised livestock for meat. Meat-packing plants were located along the Wabash, White, and Ohio rivers.

The growth of farm industries created a need for new types of machines and tools. Soon inventors and business leaders in the state started companies to help meet those needs.

Wellington Mills, a flour mill in Indiana

Study the picture. Circle parts that show that Indianapolis was going through good economic times.

UNLOCK THE BIG ? I will know that new machines and railroads helped Indiana's economy grow.

Vocabulary

economy	regulate
productivity	entrepreneur
profit	oil refinery

The Impact of New Machines

Indiana's farmers used new machines to help them do their work. James Oliver from South Bend, Indiana, invented a new type of steel plow in the mid-1800s. It had a stronger blade and kept its sharp edge longer than older plows. Oliver's plow was very popular. Soon his company became the largest maker of plows in the world.

Oliver's plow and other new machines increased productivity on Indiana farms. **Productivity** is the amount of goods or services workers can make or provide in a set amount of time. With new machines, farmers could do their work more quickly and make better use of resources. They produced more food and farm products than before. However, having more products available caused prices to go down. Farmers made less profit on their products. A **profit** is the money a business earns after all its expenses are paid.

IN Indiana Academic Standards

4.1.9 Give examples of Indiana's increasing agricultural, industrial, political and business development in the nineteenth century.

4.1.12 Describe the transformation of Indiana through immigration and through developments in agriculture, industry and transportation.

4.4.1 Give examples of goods and services produced in Indiana in different historical periods.

4.4.2 Define productivity and provide examples of how productivity has changed in Indiana during the past century.

4.4.7 Identify entrepreneurs who have influenced Indiana and the local community.

1. **Explain** productivity in your own words.

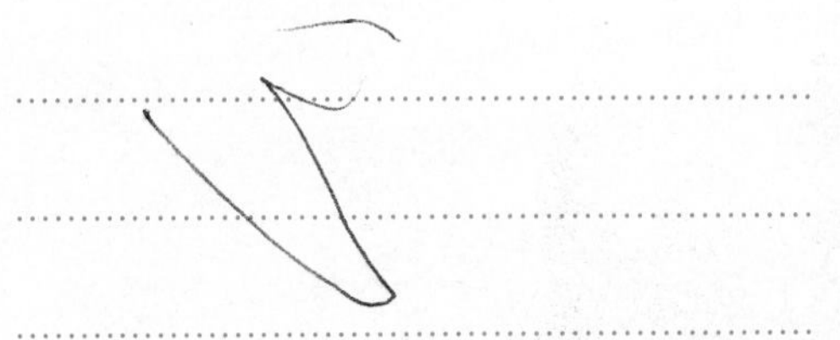

The Oliver Chilled Plow increased productivity of Indiana farms in the late 1800s.

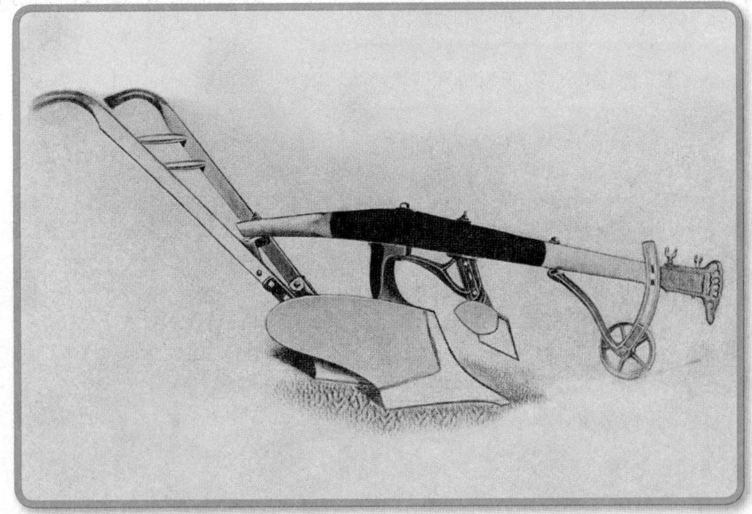

The Indiana Railroad Boom

Not all Hoosiers worked in the farming industry. Some planted or cut down trees to use for lumber. Workers at sawmills cut the wood into boards. Railroads made it possible to ship products such as these across the country.

The first railroads in Indiana were built in the 1840s. By 1854, Indiana had about 1,400 miles of track. Railroads had a major impact on Indiana's economy in the late 1800s. The railroads brought positive, or good, changes. They helped Indiana farmers and businesses ship products quickly and easily. Farmers sold their products all over the country. As a result, many Hoosier farms and companies became busier and more profitable than before. Trains also brought new people to Indiana. Some newcomers found jobs on farms. Most settled in towns and cities, where they worked in stores and factories.

The railroads also brought negative, or bad, changes. As farmers and businesses used the railroads more, the demand for shipping services increased. In response, train companies charged more for their services. This meant less profit for farmers and business owners. Many farmers made less money than before. But they paid higher prices for shipping their goods. As a result, many farmers went into debt.

2. **Compare and Contrast** **Write** how farms and businesses were better off after railroads were built.

....

....

....

Michigan Central Depot in Michigan City, Indiana

Farmers Push for Change

The Grange hoped to unite farmers.

Indiana farmers and railroad owners disagreed over prices. The farmers wanted the railroads to lower their rates. High prices allowed the railroads to make larger profits. However, they decreased the farmers' profits. The railroads found ways to keep their prices high. For example, railroad companies often made agreements with each other to all charge the same high prices. This meant that customers were unable to shop for better deals.

Many farmers decided to work together to get railroads to reduce prices. They joined a new organization called the Grange. The Grange was formed in 1867 by Oliver Hudson Kelley. Kelley had two goals. He hoped to educate farmers about good farming practices. He also wanted to unite farmers so that they could stand against the railroads' price increases. By the mid-1870s, there were Grange groups in every state in the Midwest. More than 800,000 men and women joined up. Indiana and the state of Missouri had the most members.

Indiana farmers who belonged to the Grange put pressure on state and national political leaders. They demanded that officials find ways to regulate shipping prices. To **regulate** means to control or maintain with rules and regulations. The farmers said they would vote only for those political leaders who agreed to regulate the railroads. The Grange's efforts were partly successful. State leaders did pass some laws to regulate prices. However, the railroads fought back, and most of the laws were soon changed.

3. Write why Indiana farmers and railroad owners disagreed about railroad prices.

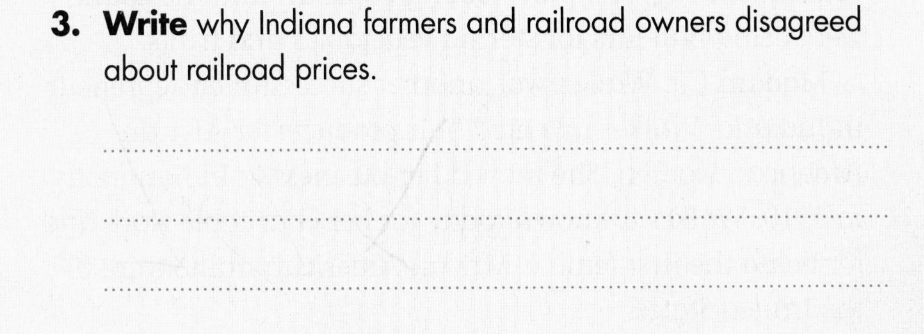

Mineral Resources in the Midwest

KEY
Coal
Natural gas
Oil

4. Circle cities on the map where business owners might start new companies. **Explain** why.

....

New Industries and Goods

Indiana's natural resources helped bring other industries to the state. For example, there were large deposits of coal along the Wabash River. As the railroads grew, companies began mining coal to help power the trains. Soon, trains carried coal from Terre Haute to other parts of the country.

Natural gas was discovered in east central Indiana in 1867. Engineers and scientists thought that natural gas could be a good source of power for lighting towns, homes, and businesses. They began testing ways to get the gas out of the ground. The first gas wells were drilled in Eaton and Portland in 1886. They provided huge supplies of natural gas. Nearby cities such as Muncie, Marion, and Anderson offered free natural gas to attract new businesses to the area.

The chance to build new businesses attracted many entrepreneurs to Indiana. An **entrepreneur** is a person who risks money and time to start a new business. In 1876, Eli Lilly started a company in Indianapolis to manufacture medicines. It remains a major company today. In 1887, five brothers moved from New York to Muncie to take advantage of the natural gas there. These entrepreneurs built a successful company called the Ball Brothers Glass Manufacturing Company. Soon people around the country were using Ball jars for storing vegetables and fruits.

Madam C.J. Walker was another successful entrepreneur in Indiana. Walker invented hair products for African American women. She moved her business to Indianapolis in 1910. Walker is known today for her charitable work and for being the first female African American millionaire in the United States.

Ball jars are still used for storing food today.

Indiana and Oil

Many people in Indiana believed that the state's supply of natural gas would last forever. At the time, gas lights were the main source of indoor lighting. People and businesses often left them burning all day. By 1898, the state's gas resources were almost all used up. Indiana needed a new source of power.

That source turned out to be oil. In 1889, oil was found in southwest Indiana. At the time, scientists were testing new ways to refine, or clean, crude oil to produce useful fuels such as gasoline and kerosene. That same year, Standard Oil began building a huge oil refinery in Whiting, on Lake Michigan. An **oil refinery** is a factory where oil is processed into gasoline and other products. The oil wells and refinery provided hundreds of new jobs, which helped the economy of northwestern Indiana to grow.

The Standard Oil refinery in Whiting

Got it?

5. **Compare and Contrast** **Write** one way the businesses set up by the Ball brothers and Madam C.J. Walker were similar and one way they were different.

....

....

....

6. **Explain** how the discovery of oil and gas brought new businesses to Indiana in the late 1800s.

....

....

Stop! I need help with ....

Wait! I have a question about ....

Go! Now I know ....

Lesson 2

New People, New Jobs

Immigrant children from different cultures attended Indiana schools together in the early 1900s.

In the late 1800s, people looking for work knew that Indiana was a great place to live. Business owners had built new factories and needed workers. The state's railroads, coal mines, gas and oil wells, and oil refineries were also hiring. Indiana was moving ahead.

1. **Look** at the graph. Between which years did Indiana's population increase the most?

Changes in Indiana's Population

Between 1860 and 1910, Indiana's population doubled. More than one million more people lived in Indiana than before. Also, more Hoosiers lived in towns and cities. Before the Civil War, most Indiana residents lived in **rural**, or country, areas. They lived and worked on or near farms. Only a small number of Hoosiers lived in **urban**, or city areas.

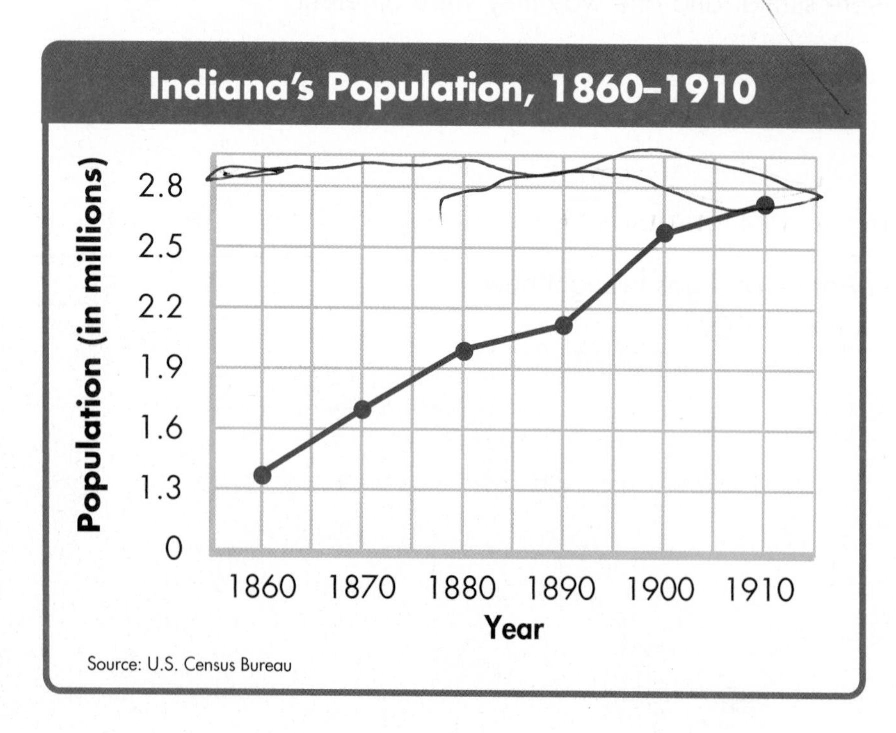

That began to change. Starting in the 1870s, many Hoosiers left farms to take jobs in factories located in cities. They were joined by thousands of immigrants who arrived looking for work. In addition, many African American and white families from the South migrated to Indiana cities for jobs. To **migrate** means to move from one place to another.

Write one reason why immigrants may have chosen to make Indiana their new home in the late 1800s.

I will know that new jobs and immigrants helped Indiana grow.

Vocabulary

rural
urban
migrate
public education
literacy

Immigrants in Indiana

Immigrants came to Indiana in two different waves, or periods of time. The first groups arrived before the Civil War. They came mostly from England, Scotland, Ireland, and Germany. Some immigrants came for political reasons. The leaders of their countries were harsh. They did not have religious freedom. Others came for economic reasons. Many Irish and German farm families left Europe when their crops failed. In America, they could find cheap land and jobs. Other Irish and German immigrants came to help build canals and railroads in Indiana.

A second wave of immigration began in the 1870s and 1880s. Many newcomers arrived from southern and eastern European countries such as Italy, Russia, Greece, and Poland. Some fled religious or political persecution. Like the first wave, many came for jobs and for better lives. Immigrants helped Indiana's economy by taking on jobs in some of the toughest workplaces. These included coal mines near Terre Haute, steel mills in northwest Indiana, and natural gas and oil wells in east-central Indiana. They contributed to Indiana's culture with their native foods, clothing, and songs.

Most immigrants settled in urban areas near other people from their homelands and created their own organizations and churches. While many worked in factories, some immigrants opened businesses, such as grocery and clothing stores.

IN Indiana Academic Standards

4.1.9 Give examples of Indiana's increasing agricultural, industrial, political and business development in the nineteenth century.

4.1.11 Describe important events and movements that changed life in Indiana in the early 1900s.

4.1.12 Describe the transformation of Indiana through immigration and through developments in agriculture, industry, and transportation.

4.3.10 Identify immigration patterns and describe the impact of diverse groups on Indiana.

2. Write two jobs that immigrants had in Indiana.

Teenage boys work in an Indiana coal mine.

Streetcars connected Indiana cities with nearby towns.

Challenges in the Cities

At the end of the nineteenth century, Indiana's cities grew quickly. Many factory owners moved to the state to take advantage of cheap and abundant fuel. The cities where these factories were located filled with new people. Cities in north and central Indiana grew the fastest. Those areas had the most railroad lines. In addition, a new type of electricity-powered streetcar connected Indiana cities with nearby towns. These streetcars made it possible for people to live in a town and work in a city. As a result, both the cities and nearby towns grew.

Life in Indiana's growing cities could be exciting. It could also be hectic and even dangerous. In some city neighborhoods, people lived together in crowded buildings. Improving city life and solving problems required careful planning, hard work, and money. Residents looked to their city government leaders for help and agreed to pay taxes to fund new programs.

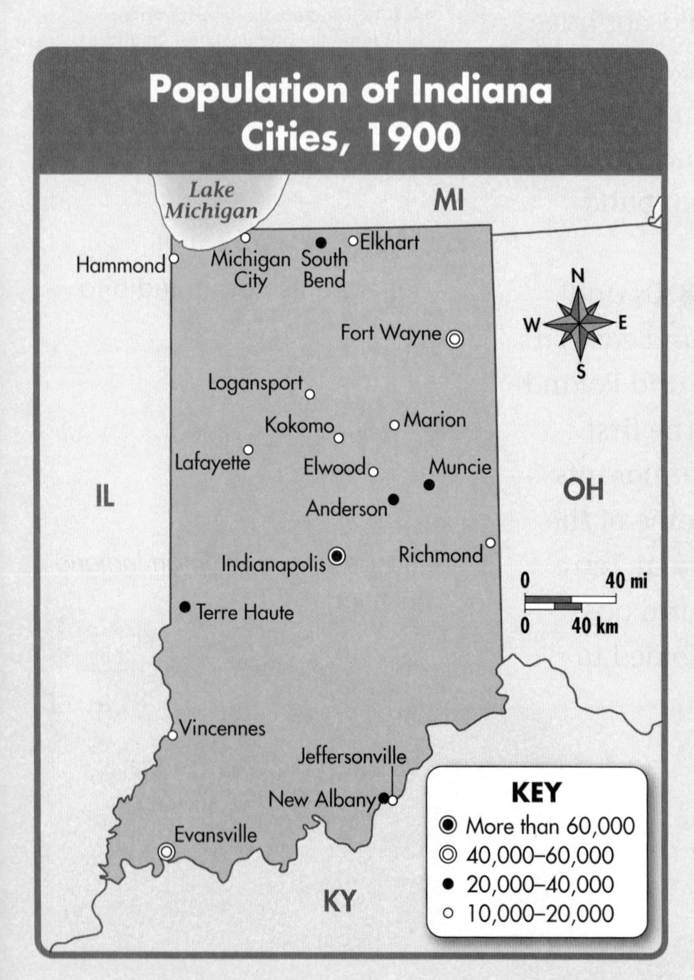

3. Look at the map. **Circle** the cities with the second highest populations in 1900.

One of the first challenges cities had to tackle was how to deal with fires. Most city buildings were made of wood. Fires spread quickly from one building to another. Early fire companies were made up of volunteers. Later, many cities hired and trained professional firefighters. Indianapolis started its paid fire department in 1859. The city soon purchased its first steam fire engine that shook and puffed as it raced toward a fire. The city also built a high tower on top of a building in the center of town. They paid a watchman to stand in the tower. When he spotted a fire, he would ring a bell to alert the fire department.

Getting water to the cities was another challenge. At first, people hauled their own water from streams, wells, or canals. They often had to carry the water long distances. As cities grew, more people needed water closer to home. Cities and towns began hiring companies to pump water into cities. Unfortunately, the water was sometimes pumped from rivers into which sewers had drained. People often got sick from drinking dirty water.

Cities also improved by paving muddy streets to make travel easier and safer. Cities hired people to sweep the streets and collect garbage. This greatly improved the health of those who lived in cities.

Lighting city streets at night also improved safety. In 1880, Wabash installed four electric lamps in the dome of its courthouse. It became the first city in the world to be lighted by electricity.

Electric lights improved safety in cities.

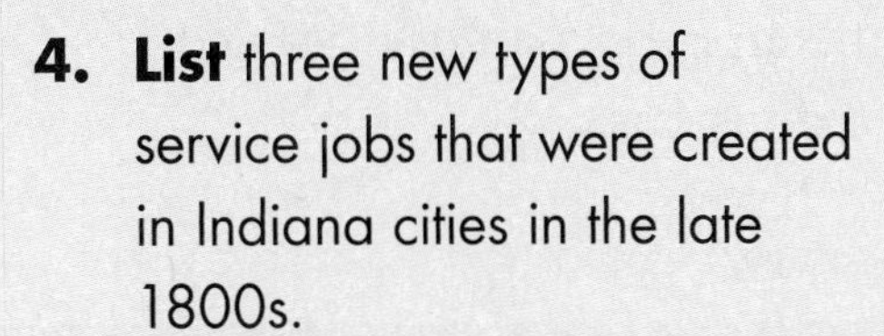

4. List three new types of service jobs that were created in Indiana cities in the late 1800s.

A horse-drawn fire engine races through city streets.

Caleb Mills worked to improve Indiana's school system.

5. **Compare and Contrast Write** one way that rural schools differed from urban ones.

....

....

....

....

....

....

....

Improvements in Education

As Indiana's population increased, state and local leaders began pushing for a system of public education. **Public education** means that a government provides schooling for all children. Indiana's first constitution in 1816 had called for creating public education in the state. However, no system had been developed.

Some private schools did exist, but parents had to pay for their children to attend. Religious groups created and supported these schools. Some towns also had Sunday schools that focused especially on the poor. These schools provided instruction in both regular subjects and religious topics one day a week for a few hours.

In 1833, a New England teacher named Caleb Mills came to Indiana and established a school. Mills was a good teacher and a persuasive writer. Mills believed that Indiana needed to raise taxes to pay for more schools, teachers, and books. He wrote a series of letters in 1846 to Indiana lawmakers. Mills pointed out that, according to census figures, Indiana children ranked lower in literacy than children in many others states. **Literacy** is the ability to read and write. Mills's letters convinced many people that Indiana needed a better school system. However, it would take another 20 years before the state established a full-time public school system. Not all public schools were alike. The type of school a student went to often depended on where he or she lived. Students in rural areas usually attended a one-room school with all grades taught by one teacher. Students in urban areas attended schools divided into grades or divisions.

One-room schoolhouse, early 1900s

Public education in Indiana continued to improve at the beginning of the twentieth century. William Wirt was the driving force behind many advancements. He served as superintendent of Gary schools between 1907 and 1938. Gary was one of the state's fastest-growing cities. To accommodate more students, Wirt set up a system where he divided students into groups and had them move from room to room. They kept their books and papers in lockers. While some students attended classes in school subjects, others went to labs for science and gyms for physical education. Wirt also made sure that Gary schools offered classes and activities in music and art. Soon Wirt's ideas spread to other schools in Indiana and around the country.

Madam C.J. Walker donated money to improve Indiana schools.

Indiana's schools got a boost from several of the state's entrepreneurs whom you read about in Lesson 1. The Ball brothers provided the state with land and buildings for a teachers' college in Muncie. That college is now called Ball State University. Madam C.J. Walker also made generous donations to improve education in the state.

Got it?

6. **Compare and Contrast** **Write** how the two waves of immigration to Indiana were similar and different.

....

....

7. **Describe** how the growth of cities in Indiana provided opportunities for people.

....

....

Stop! I need help with ....

Wait! I have a question about ....

Go! Now I know ....

Lesson 3

Envision It!

Growth and Development

This giant motor provided electric power for Inland Steel's factory in the Calumet.

People living in Indiana have always been hard-working. By the late 1800s, many Hoosiers had jobs in industries new to the state. Some made iron and steel in factories. Others would eventually build cars and make automobile parts with that iron and steel.

1. **Look** at the map. **Write** one reason industries built factories in the Calumet.

....

New Century, New Industries

Before the 1890s, few people lived in the northwestern corner of Indiana along Lake Michigan. The Grand Calumet River ran through the area, so the region became known as the Calumet. The Calumet was covered with swamps and marshland. It was not a place where most Hoosiers wanted to live or work. Within 20 years, that all changed.

Starting in 1889, several major industries built factories in the Calumet. The land was inexpensive to buy. There was also good transportation available by ship and railroad.

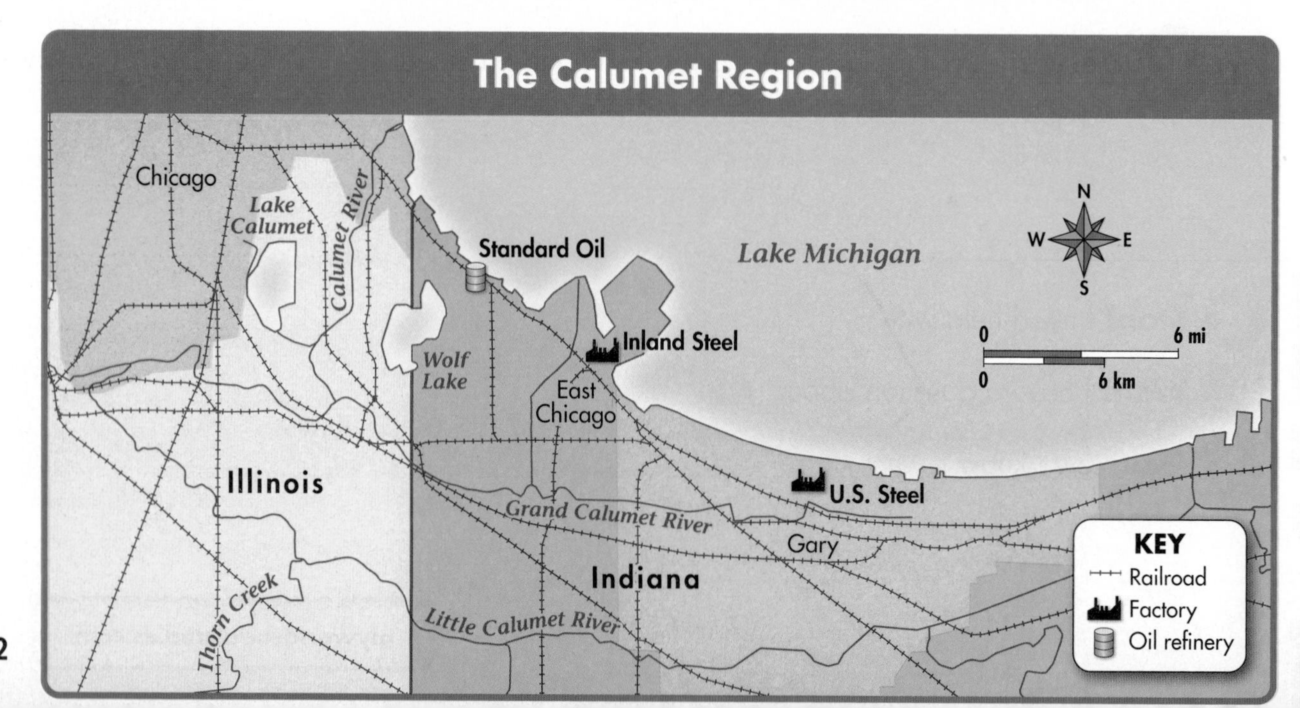

Write how building a factory like the one in the picture might impact people who live nearby.

UNLOCK THE BIG ?

I will know the impact of new industries in Indiana in the early 1900s.

Vocabulary

corporation
steelworks
labor union
strike

The first industry to arrive was the oil industry. As you read, Standard Oil built a huge oil refinery at Whiting. The iron and steel industries soon followed. Inland Steel built the first steel mill in East Chicago, Indiana, in 1901. Many Hoosier men and women came to work in Calumet factories. Some had started out as farmers. However, falling prices forced them to sell their land and move to the Calumet to find jobs. Immigrant laborers also joined the workforce in the region.

IN Indiana Academic Standards

4.1.9 Give examples of Indiana's increasing agricultural, industrial, political and business development in the nineteenth century.

4.1.12 Describe the transformation of Indiana through immigration and through developments in agriculture, industry and transportation.

4.3.10 Identify immigration patterns, and describe the impact of diverse groups on Indiana.

2. **Write** why many Hoosiers came to work in the Calumet.

By 1910, railroads and factories could be found across much of the Calumet.

3. **Compare and Contrast** How did the area that became Gary change once U.S. Steel started building its steelworks?

Building a Factory and a City

Gary, one of the largest cities in the Calumet today, did not exist in 1900. The idea for the city came from the chairman of U.S. Steel, Judge Elbert S. Gary. The city was eventually named after him.

In 1906, the U.S. Steel Corporation bought 9,000 acres of land in Lake County. A **corporation** is a company or organization designed for a specific purpose. There, it built an even larger steelworks than Inland Steel's. A **steelworks** is a factory where steel is made. Since the company was building in an area of the state that was undeveloped, U.S. Steel built both a factory and a city in which factory workers could live. The initial project took three years to complete. In 1909, the factory opened. The giant complex contained 47 furnaces for melting steel.

While the factory was under construction, the company laid out streets and began building homes for thousands of workers. The homes made jobs at U.S. Steel even more desirable. Workers flooded to northern Indiana. When the census was taken in 1910, the new city already had nearly 17,000 inhabitants.

U.S. Steel was more than just a workplace for new Gary residents. The company also organized social events and educational programs for employees and their families. It offered programs to immigrants to help them learn English and adjust to American life.

U.S. Steel executives walk through the empty streets of Gary in 1908.

Women worked in the steel mills during World War II.

Over the next decade, the city of Gary more than tripled in size. At first, the steel mill attracted mostly immigrants from European countries such as England, Ireland, Italy, Germany, Greece, Poland, and Russia. By 1920, there were more than 55,000 people living in the city. In the 1920s, African Americans began moving to Gary from southern states. During the same period, the company encouraged workers to move to Gary from Mexico. The city's population reached more than 100,000 by 1930.

Immigrants and their American-born children made up nearly half of Gary's population in 1930. Nearly one in five were African Americans. All of these workers helped the city and factory to prosper.

Unfortunately, living conditions were not equal for everyone. African American workers were often forced to live in separate housing from white families, and their homes were in the worst part of the city. Their schools were also separate.

Mostly men worked at the factory in Gary in its early years. But in the 1940s, U.S. Steel employed many women to fill in for men who were away fighting in World War II.

4. **Write** two sentences from the point of view of a worker in the picture. What is it like to work in the steel mill?

Haynes's gasoline-powered automobile

Indiana and Automobiles

In the last years of the 1800s, as the first factories were being built in the Calumet, a teacher from Portland worked on an invention that would dramatically change transportation and industry. On July 4, 1894, Elwood Haynes tested out his new invention on a road near Kokomo. The invention was a gasoline-powered automobile. Haynes was only the second inventor to build an automobile that actually worked. On his test drive, Haynes's car reached what was an amazing speed at the time—seven miles per hour!

Haynes quickly joined with two partners to start his own automobile company. In 1898, the Haynes-Apperson Automobile Company produced five handmade cars. By 1916, Haynes had sold more than 7,000 cars built by workers in his factory in Kokomo.

In the early 1900s, 375 automobile companies in 40 cities in Indiana were manufacturing cars. Why was Indiana such a popular location for automobile manufacturing? The reasons were similar to those that attracted steelmakers to the state. The state had good transportation systems, an abundance of coal, and lots of steel made in the Calumet.

For many years, Indiana was one of America's top auto-producing states. In the 1920s, Indiana-built cars, such as the Stutz Bearcat and Duesenberg, became famous around the world. Then, slowly, most of Indiana's carmakers went out of business as they went bankrupt. The company that remained in Indiana the longest was the Studebaker Corporation.

Studebaker was started by a group of brothers in South Bend. In the 1880s, the company was one of the largest makers of horse-drawn wagons in the world. Studebaker introduced an electric car in 1902 and its first gasoline-powered car in 1904. In the 1920s, Studebaker was the fifth-largest automaker in the country. It continued manufacturing cars in Indiana until 1963.

Today, there are no Indiana-owned automobile companies left in the state. But the auto industry is still very important to the state's economy. Several Japanese car companies have plants in Indiana. In addition, Indiana companies make more mobile homes, motor homes, campers, and car carriers than any other state.

5. **Circle** in the text why automobile companies started in Indiana.

Growth of Sporting Events in Indiana

In 1908, an Indiana auto parts maker and businessman named Carl Fisher decided to build a racetrack in Indianapolis. He thought the racetrack would be a good place for Indiana car makers to test their new automobiles. Fisher called it the Indianapolis Motor Speedway. It soon gained a new name: the Brickyard. That was because Fisher decided to pave the track with bricks in order to provide a safe, smooth surface. Workmen used more than 3 million bricks to cover the track. The bricks are still there today, but most are covered with a smooth surface called asphalt.

Starting in May 1911, the Brickyard began hosting a 500-mile car race each year. The Indianapolis 500 soon became one of the world's most famous sporting events. More than 400,000 fans come to Indianapolis each year to view the race.

At one time, Indy race drivers were all men. Then, in 1977, Janet Guthrie became the first woman to earn a spot in the race. She raced again in 1978 and came in ninth. In 2005, Danica Patrick finished fourth and even led the race for several laps. That is the best performance so far by a female driver at Indy.

Less than 10 years after construction started on Indianapolis Motor Speedway, Bosse Field was opened in Evansville. Today, this baseball stadium is the third oldest professional ballpark in the country. The project was approved and funded by the Evansville School Board, and the entire project cost the city $65,000. On opening day in 1915, bleacher seats cost fans just a quarter! In 1992, scenes from the movie "A League of Their Own" were filmed at Bosse Field. The stadium seats more than 7,000 people, and today, fans go there to support the Evansville Otters.

Danica Patrick is the only woman who has taken the lead during the Indianapolis 500.

About 400,000 people can attend events at the Indianapolis Motor Speedway. It seats more fans than any other sports venue in the world.

These teenage boys are working at midnight in an Indiana glass factory in the early 1900s.

The Labor Movement

Workers in Indiana's factories had a difficult life. Making steel, glass, and automobiles was hard work. Most people worked ten hours a day, six days a week. People in steel mills often worked even longer hours. Women and children earned less than men and had to work the same hours.

Working conditions in factories were also dangerous. Many people got hurt on the job. When workers could not work because they were injured, the companies were not required to pay them.

Indiana workers hoped to improve their pay and working conditions. Many of them decided to join labor unions. A **labor union** is a group of workers who have joined together to demand better wages and working conditions. Union leaders would meet with business owners. The two sides would discuss how to improve work conditions. If they could not reach an agreement, the workers in the union might decide to go on strike. A **strike** is a protest in which workers refuse to work until their demands are met.

Indiana has seen many union strikes. One of the first occurred in 1877. Railroad owners announced they were cutting workers' wages, so the workers went on strike. The railroad soon brought in non-union workers to replace the men who were on strike. As a result, the union was forced to stop the strike.

A more violent strike occurred in Gary in 1919. Steel mill owners refused to reduce the length of workers' workdays from twelve to eight hours per day. The workers went on strike, and the owners brought in non-union replacement workers. Fights broke out when angry strikers attacked the replacement workers. The governor had to call in troops to restore order. When the strike ended, the union had lost. As a result, union membership went down for many years.

6. Describe why labor unions started.

....

....

Political Leaders From Indiana

Political leaders from Indiana played important roles in American government in the late 1800s and early 1900s. In 1888, Benjamin Harrison from Indianapolis was elected president. In 1892, Harrison oversaw the opening of Ellis Island in New York. Millions of immigrants came into the United States through the inspection station there.

Two Hoosiers served as U.S. vice presidents at the beginning of the twentieth century. Charles W. Fairbanks served under President Theodore Roosevelt from 1905 to 1909. Then Thomas R. Marshall was elected to two terms with President Woodrow Wilson from 1913 to 1921.

In all, five Hoosiers have been elected vice president. The others include Schuyler Colfax, Thomas Hendricks, and Dan Quayle. In addition, several other Hoosiers have been nominated as vice president but failed to win. That is why Indiana is sometimes called the "Mother of Vice Presidents."

Benjamin Harrison

Got it?

7. **Compare and Contrast** **Describe** how the Calumet looked before and after Standard Oil, Inland Steel, and U.S. Steel built factories there.

....

....

....

8. **Write** to explain how buying a car in 1910 may have changed the way families lived.

my Story Ideas

....

....

Stop! I need help with ....

Wait! I have a question about ....

Go! Now I know ....

21C Graph Skills

Interpret Timelines

How can you keep track of all the dates and events in history? One way is with a timeline. A **timeline** is a chart that shows important events and the dates they occurred. The events are placed in the order in which they happened. This can help you understand connections between events. You can also see how one event leads to another.

Look at the timeline below. It is horizontal, or one that you read from left to right. Other timelines are vertical and read from top to bottom. This timeline shows important events in the development of industries in the Calumet region of Indiana. The earliest date on the timeline is on the left. The most recent date is on the right. A timeline is divided into equal units of time. On this timeline, each unit equals a decade, which is 10 years. By studying and interpreting, or understanding, a timeline, you can understand how events progressed during that period.

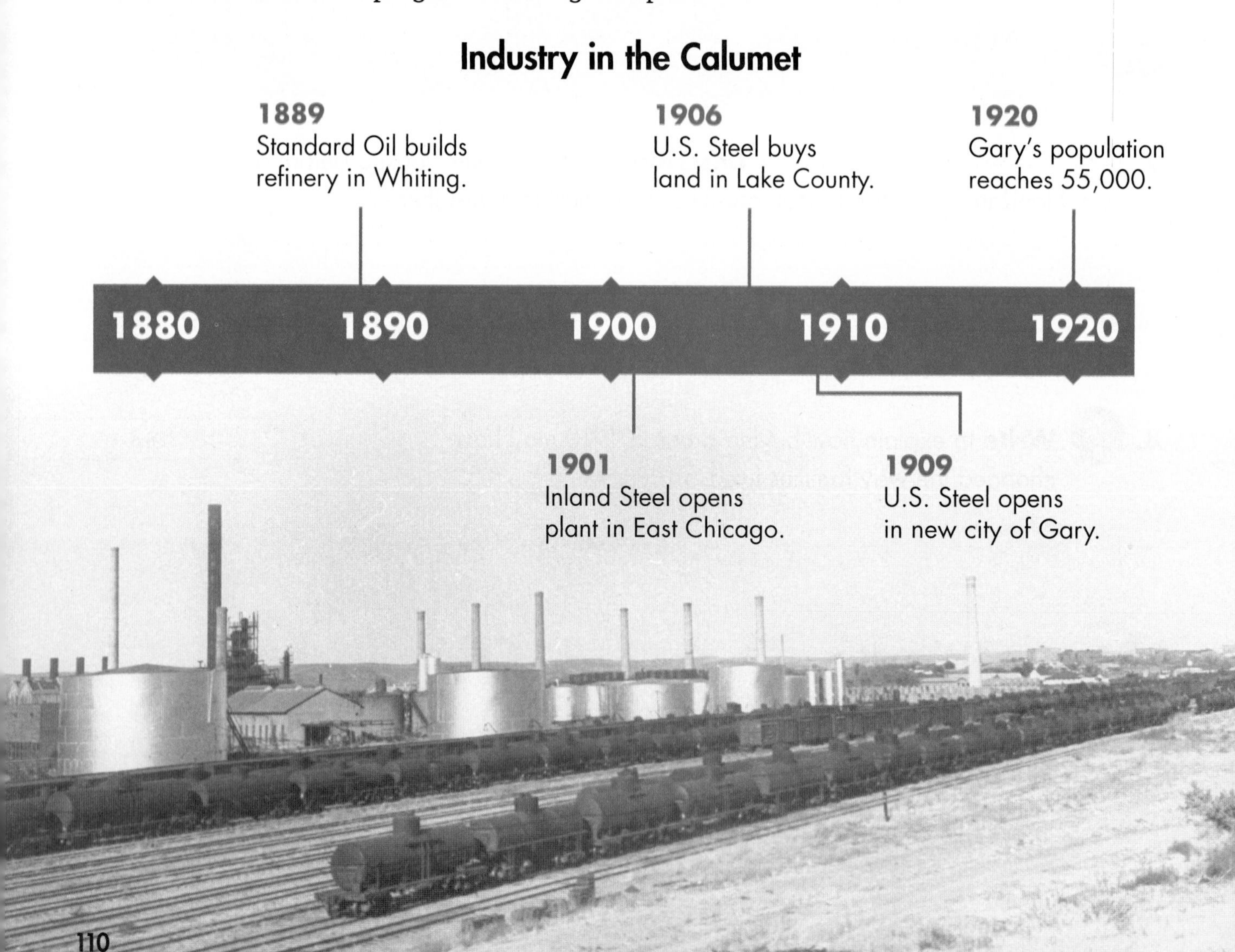

Learning Objective

I will know how to create and interpret timelines.

IN 4.1.15 Create and interpret timelines about the history of Indiana.

Use the timeline to answer the following questions.

1. What time period does the timeline cover?

   ....

2. Which company was the first in the Calumet?

   ....

3. Which two companies opened plants in the same decade, or 10-year period?

   ....

4. Which company opened in the new city of Gary?

   ....

5. **Create** a timeline of your own. Reread pages 106–107. **Fill in** three dates and events important to the history of automobiles in Indiana in the boxes. Then draw lines that connect the events to their correct place on the timeline.

Haynes invents first gasoline-powered automobile.

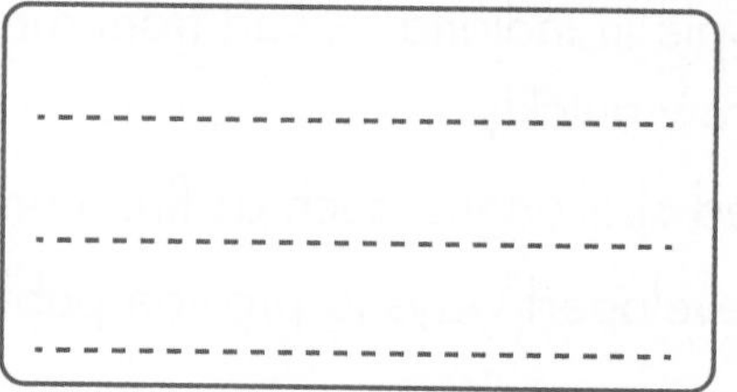

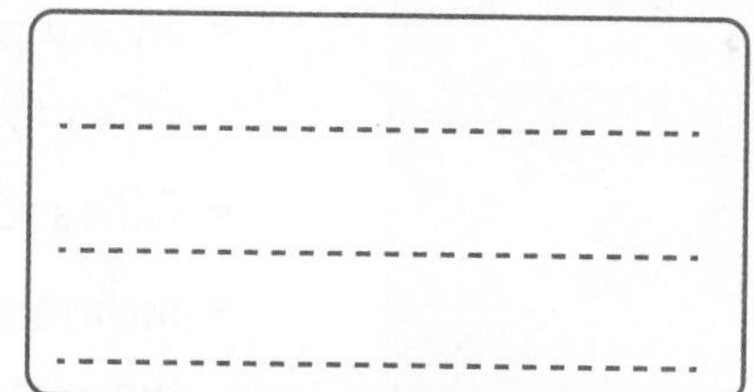

1880 | 1890 | 1900 | 1910 | 1920

myworldsocialstudies.com ▶ Experience ▶ Skills

Chapter 4
Study Guide

Lesson 1

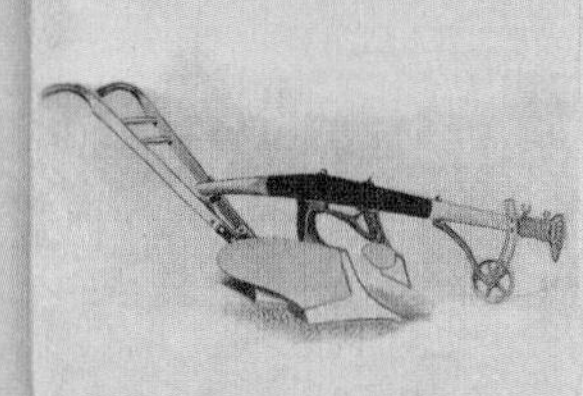

Economic Changes

- In the mid-1800s, new machines increased the productivity, or the amount of goods produced, of Indiana farms.
- Railroads helped Indiana farmers and businesses ship products quickly and easily, and brought goods and people to Indiana.
- Many farmers joined an organization called the Grange to try to push railroads to lower their rates.
- The discovery of coal, natural gas, and oil in Indiana helped bring other industries to the state.
- The chance to build new businesses attracted many entrepreneurs to Indiana.

Lesson 2

New People, New Jobs

- In the late 1800s, Indiana's population increased as immigrants arrived from Europe, and African American and white families from the South moved to the state.
- Immigrants came to Indiana for different reasons. They contributed to Indiana's culture and economic growth.
- Many people in Indiana moved from rural areas to urban ones, causing cities to grow quickly.
- Cities faced challenges, such as fire, crime, water, and cleanliness.
- Indiana developed ways to provide public education for all children in the state.

Lesson 3

Growth and Development

- New oil refineries and steel mills in the Calumet provided work for thousands of Indiana men, women, and children.
- U.S. Steel created the city of Gary, where most of its workers lived.
- The automobile industry started in Indiana and became an important part of the state's economy.
- Many workers joined labor unions to try to improve their pay and working conditions in Indiana factories.

Chapter 4
Review and Assessment

Lesson 1

Economic Changes

1. **Write** two goods that Indiana industries related to farms produced in the 1800s.

....

2. **Fill in** the blanks.
In the late 1800s, new machines increased the .... of Indiana farmers. As more farm products became available, farmers earned less ....

3. **Match** the entrepreneurs with the products they developed.

_____ Ball brothers   a. steel plow

_____ James Oliver   b. hair products

_____ Madam C.J. Walker   c. glass jars

4. **Explain** why many Indiana farmers joined the Grange.

....

....

....

....

....

....

....

5. **Describe** one negative impact of railroads on farmers and business owners.

....

....

....

....

Lesson 2

New People, New Jobs

6. **Name** one reason Indiana's population doubled from 1860 to 1910.

....

....

7. **Write** two contributions that immigrants made to Indiana's culture.

....

....

....

8. **Circle** the letter of the item that describes a problem that Indiana's growing cities faced.

A. Not enough volunteer firefighters

B. Not enough clean water

C. Not enough land for houses

D. Not enough streetlights

Chapter 4

Review and Assessment

Lesson 3

Growth and Development

9. **Compare and Contrast** How was the railroad workers' strike in 1877 similar to the steel workers' strike in 1919? How was it different?

....

....

....

....

....

....

10. **Number** the following events in the order that they occurred.

.... Race car drivers race in the first Indianapolis 500.

.... Elwood Haynes test drives his first gas-powered car.

.... Steel mill strike occurs in Gary, Indiana.

.... Benjamin Harrison is elected U.S. president.

11. **Describe** how the steel and automobile industries in Indiana relied on each other.

....

....

....

....

....

....

12. **How does economic growth provide opportunity?**

Use the photograph and question to think about this chapter's Big Question.

How did the building of new industries in Indiana change the state?

....

....

....

....

....

Go online to write and illustrate your own **myStory Book** using the **myStory Ideas** from this chapter.

my Story Book

How does economic growth provide opportunity?

4.W.1 Write for discipline-specific tasks, purposes, and audiences.

When an economy grows, more people work and earn money. Indiana's economy grew in the late 1800s and early 1900s. This growth meant many new opportunities for people in Indiana. People moved from farms to cities. Railroads shipped more goods. People opened shops. Immigrants and African American and white families from the South arrived and built new lives. Factories and cities grew. People took advantage of these opportunities to improve their lives.

Think about the reasons people moved to the United States and Indiana in the late 1800s. **Write** one reason people moved to Indiana. What opportunities did people find?

....

....

....

Now **draw** a picture to illustrate your writing.

While you're online, check out the **myStory Current Events** area where you can create your own book on a topic that's in the news.

myworldsocialstudies.com ▶ Understand ▶ myStory Book

Challenging Times

my Story Spark

What causes are worth fighting for?

Describe a cause, or something that you support, and **explain** how you might support that cause.

During World War II, U.S. Army soldiers drove Studebaker trucks built in Indiana.

Lesson 1 World War I and the 1920s
Lesson 2 The Great Depression and World War II
Lesson 3 A Changing State

Ernie Pyle

Journalist and War Reporter (1900–1945)

Journalist and war reporter Ernie Pyle wrote about soldiers' lives on the battlefront in World War II. Pyle's reporting provided a special view of the war since he was so close to the action.

Pyle was born in 1900 near the small western Indiana town of Dana. He studied journalism at Indiana University, but he left school early to work as a reporter in La Porte, Indiana. A few months later, he moved to Washington, D.C., to work on a newspaper there called the *Washington Daily News*. He traveled around the country, writing columns about the places he visited.

When Americans went to war in Europe in 1942, Pyle began traveling with the troops. He wrote from battlefields in North Africa, Italy, and France. He also reported from the Pacific. The American soldiers respected Pyle. They felt that he shared their true experiences. Whether they were homesick, tired, or telling funny stories, Pyle shared the soldiers' viewpoints with the world. Pyle won a Pulitzer Prize for his reporting in 1944.

Hoosier Ernie Pyle was one of the most famous war reporters in history. His reporting gave people a real picture of World War II.

Pyle was killed in an ambush on a small island in Japan. At the time he died, his column appeared in several hundred newspapers. As word of Pyle's death spread, Americans around the world felt great sadness. President Harry Truman said about Pyle:

> "[A]ll Americans understand now how wisely, how warm heartedly, how honestly he served his country and his profession."

Think About It How do you think Pyle felt about those who fought for the cause of World War II? As you read this chapter, think about the causes and events that touched the lives of people in Indiana in the 1900s.

Lesson 1

World War I and the 1920s

Envision It!

During World War I, Americans, including people from Indiana, served both away from home (above) and at home (right).

In the early 1900s, people in Indiana and the entire country faced challenges. A major war broke out in Europe. Should the United States join the war? Many women in America wanted the right to vote in elections. Would they gain that right at last? Both the country and Indiana would go through many changes during this time period.

World War I

When World War I started in Europe in 1914, the United States was not involved. Many Americans believed the country should stay **neutral**, or not choose a side. Then German ships attacked U.S. ships that were carrying supplies to Germany's enemies. As a result, Congress declared war on Germany in 1917. There were two sides in the war. The United States joined the Allies, which included Great Britain, France, and Russia. President Woodrow Wilson selected General John Pershing to command the American forces in Europe. The opposing side was the Central Powers and included Germany, Austria-Hungary, and Turkey.

Many soldiers from Indiana fought in the 84th Infantry Division during World War I.

Based on each picture, write one way people might serve during a war.

I will know about events that changed life in the United States and in Indiana in the early 1900s.

Vocabulary

neutral	amendment
draft	ratify
suffrage	prosperity

IN Indiana Academic Standards

4.1.10 Describe how Indiana citizens participated in World Wars I and II.

4.1.11 Describe important events and movements that changed life in Indiana in the early 1900s.

The United States needed soldiers to fight in the war. In May 1917, Congress passed a law creating a draft. A **draft** is a system in which men of certain ages are required to join the armed forces for a certain period of time. About 130,000 Hoosiers served in the armed forces in the war. Most were drafted. Others volunteered for the military. Samuel Woodfill of Jefferson County, Indiana, was a first lieutenant in the U.S. Army during the war. He earned the Medal of Honor for his bravery. His commander, General Pershing, called him the most outstanding soldier of World War I.

Most of Indiana's soldiers were sent to fight overseas. It was a tough war to fight, especially due to strategies used such as trench warfare. This meant that soldiers fought from trenches, or long, narrow ditches. Soldiers lived in these trenches day and night. Some women also volunteered for war service. They were sent to France where they served as nurses and telephone operators.

1. What jobs did women have overseas during World War I?

Hoosier Samuel Woodfill earned the country's highest military medal for his bravery in World War I.

The Home Front in Indiana

2. Write one way Indiana citizens participated in World War I at home.

Indiana's people and industries geared up for the war. Many Hoosiers moved from farms to cities to work in factories producing goods for the war effort. Workers in some Indiana factories made trucks that carried army supplies in Europe. Others helped make parts for saddles for cavalry soldiers, who are soldiers that fight on horseback. Those who remained on the farms worked even harder growing food for those overseas or at home.

People moved to Indiana to work during the war years. Many newcomers were African Americans who migrated from the South, found work, and stayed. The African American population grew in cities that had factories such as Gary, Hammond, and South Bend. African Americans helped keep factories running as other workers left to fight in the war. In some companies, such as Gary's steel mills, African Americans received promotions to better jobs. However, most companies continued to employ them in low-paying, unskilled jobs.

After many men left jobs to fight in the war, some Indiana women took jobs in factories. Others helped the war effort from home. They sewed clothing and blankets for soldiers.

Life in Indiana during the war was hard for many Hoosiers. Families cut back on meat, sugar, and bread to save food for soldiers. Much of America's coal was also kept for war use. This meant that Indiana's steel factories and railroads had less coal to use. World War I ended on November 11, 1918. About 3,370 Hoosier servicemen died in the war.

During World War I, women took on factory jobs. These women are making parts for automobiles.

Women Gain the Right to Vote

As you read, women played important roles during World War I at home and on the job. Yet in most states, including Indiana, women were still not allowed to vote.

The campaign for women's **suffrage**, or the right to vote, had started before the Civil War. Several Indiana women actively worked in the suffrage movement. May Wright Sewall was a teacher from Indianapolis. She helped found a school for young women. In the 1880s, Sewall led a drive to grant women the right to vote in Indiana. Her efforts gained support, but they failed in the end.

Ida Husted Harper, a journalist from Terre Haute, worked with Sewall and other suffrage leaders. She wrote many articles designed to educate the public about why women wanted the right to vote.

Helen M. Gougar, a lawyer from Lafayette, sued Tippecanoe County leaders when she was turned away from the voting polls in 1894. She lost in court but continued to fight for women's suffrage. Gougar died in 1907, 14 years before women won the right to vote in Indiana. Many women still consider her a hero today.

In 1919, Congress passed an amendment to the Constitution recognizing women's right to vote. An **amendment** is a change or improvement. Thirty-six states needed to **ratify**, or approve, the Nineteenth Amendment before it became law. On January 16, 1920, the Indiana legislature voted to ratify the amendment. Several months later, Tennessee became the thirty-sixth state to vote yes. The Nineteenth Amendment was officially added to the Constitution. In 1921, Indiana also made a women's suffrage amendment part of its state constitution.

The achievement of women's suffrage changed politics in Indiana. Women were now active voters in the state. People running for office needed to seek women's support in order to get elected. Women also began seeking office themselves. In 1923, Elizabeth Rainey became the first woman elected to the Indiana House of Representatives. In 1933, Virginia E. Jenckes became the first Indiana woman to serve in the U.S. House of Representatives.

3. **Cause and Effect** **Fill in** the missing effects in the graphic organizer at right.

Ida Husted Harper

Women's Suffrage in Indiana

Cause

Women earn the right to vote.

Effects

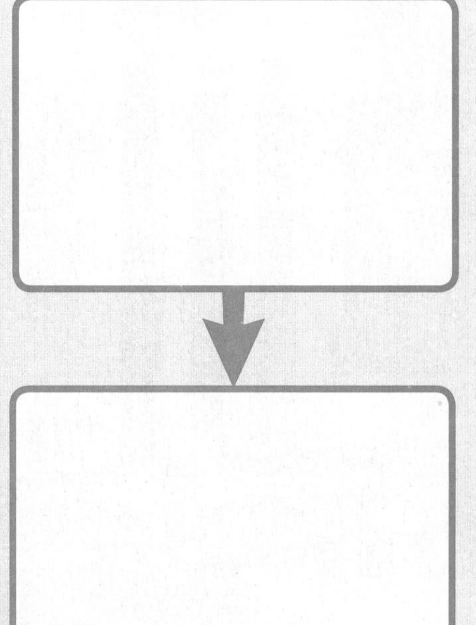

Life Changes in the 1920s

The period after World War I was a time of prosperity for many Hoosiers and Americans in other states. **Prosperity** means success or good fortune. This time period was known as the "Roaring Twenties." Indiana's steel and auto industries were booming. Factories were hiring more workers. Many people had more money to spend.

Automobiles had a major impact on the lives of Indiana residents. Many Hoosiers throughout the state worked in factories making cars. Then they used some of their earnings to buy cars for their families. The state built new roads to make driving easier. It also opened a network of state parks where families drove to play, swim, or picnic.

Daily life for many Indiana residents improved. More homes had indoor plumbing and electricity. People bought new home appliances to make their lives easier. These included washing machines, refrigerators, irons, and toasters.

The Indiana Theater in downtown Indianapolis was popular in the 1920s for movies and dancing.

Many Hoosiers also had more free time because they worked fewer hours. There were new forms of entertainment available. People could go to movies, theaters, dances, or sporting events. The radio was a new invention, and people enjoyed listening to popular music. They often sang along to tunes by Indiana songwriters Cole Porter from Peru and Hoagy Carmichael from Bloomington.

Close to 140,000 racing fans watched as Jimmy Murphy won the Indianapolis 500 in 1922.

4. Describe two ways life improved for many Hoosiers during the Roaring Twenties.

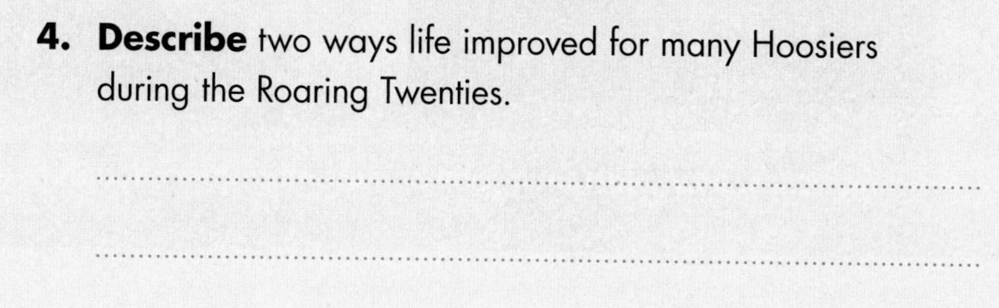

Got it?

5. Cause and Effect Explain two effects of World War I on women in Indiana.

6. Write how women gaining the right to vote changed the lives of people in Indiana.

my Story Ideas

Stop! I need help with

Wait! I have a question about

Go! Now I know

Lesson 2

The Great Depression and World War II

Envision It!

The Great Depression was a challenging time for Hoosiers and Americans. Many lost their jobs and did not have enough to eat.

Indiana's economy was strong in the 1920s. Factory workers were busy making steel, building cars and trucks, and manufacturing other products. Farmers were producing more food with the help of modern tools. The future looked bright, but bad times were just ahead.

The End of the Roaring Twenties

Recall that for most people in Indiana and the rest of the country, the 1920s were a time of prosperity. People earned money at their jobs. Then they spent money on their households and on leisure, or free-time, activities. Sometimes they spent more than they made by buying products on credit. By using credit, they borrowed money with the promise to pay it back later.

Indiana's farmers were also doing well, but they began to have problems. They produced so much food that there were not enough buyers to purchase it all. Prices began to drop, and farmers lost money. Some farmers went into debt to buy equipment.

During the Roaring Twenties, some Americans bought **stocks**, which are shares or portions of ownership in companies. When the price of a stock goes up, the person who owns the stock can make a profit if he or she sells the stock at the higher price. These investors placed their savings in the stock market, hoping to get rich. The **stock market** is a place where people buy and sell stocks.

By the late 1920s, the price of stocks began to go down. Investors worried that if stock prices kept going down, their stocks would become worthless. They rushed to sell stocks. The prices fell even more. In October 1929, stock prices dropped so much that a "crash" occurred.

n the box above, write short captions for each picture on the
pposite page.

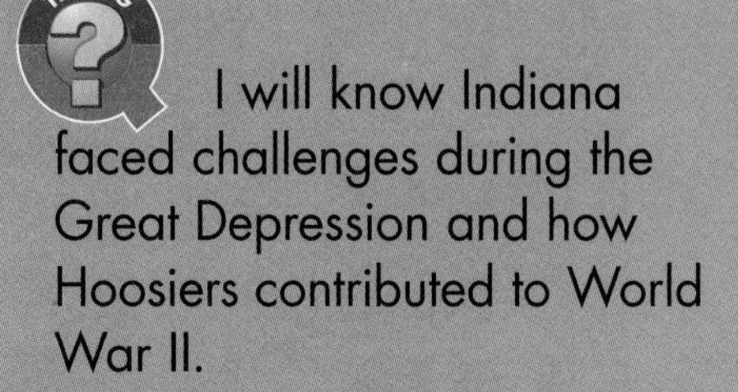

I will know Indiana faced challenges during the Great Depression and how Hoosiers contributed to World War II.

Vocabulary

stocks
stock market
loan
unemployed
depression
New Deal
ration

IN Indiana Academic Standards

4.1.10 Describe how Indiana citizens participated in World Wars I and II.

4.1.11 Describe important events and movements that changed life in Indiana in the early 1900s.

4.1.12 Describe the transformation of Indiana through immigration and through developments in agriculture, industry and transportation.

The Great Depression

The stock market crash caused other businesses to fail. Some Americans had borrowed money to buy stocks. Money that is lent to someone, often from a bank, is called a **loan.** When the stock market crashed, they were unable to repay their loans. This meant that people and businesses that gave out loans were not repaid and lost the money.

When people lose money, they spend less. They may stop buying goods they want so they can afford the goods they need. This meant that companies that sold goods had fewer customers.

To avoid going out of business, some companies began to fire workers. This meant that many people were suddenly **unemployed,** or out of work. Other businesses shut down completely.

The country had entered a **depression,** or time when business activity is slow and many people are out of work. This depression lasted about 10 years and became known as the Great Depression.

1. Look at the bar graph. **Circle** the year that had the highest rate of unemployment. **Underline** the year that had the lowest rate of unemployment.

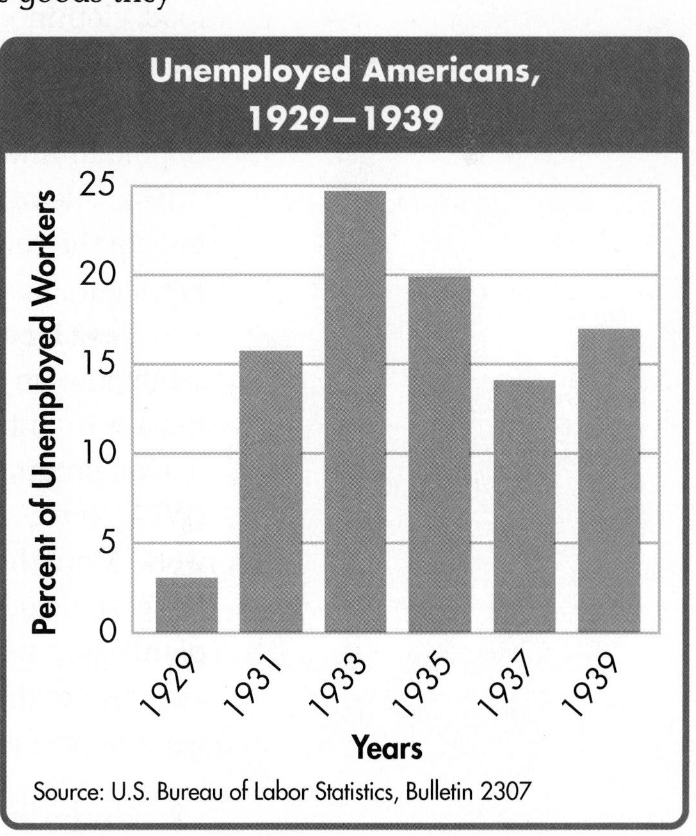

Artist William Dolwick painted a mural on the wall of the post office in Hobart in 1938 as part of a WPA program.

The New Deal and Other Programs

The Great Depression hit the country and Indiana very hard. Sales of coal and limestone dropped to almost nothing. Nearly half of the people in southern Indiana lost their jobs. The steel and automobile industries in northern Indiana also suffered. Many families did not have enough money to pay for food or other necessities.

Local and national government leaders stepped forward to help. In Indiana, Governor Paul McNutt started public relief programs to assist people. These programs provided food, clothing, and medicine to those in need. Often, people stood in long lines to receive soup or bread provided by the government to feed their families. They also lined up hoping to find jobs on state projects.

The federal government also established programs to help the country recover from the Great Depression. President Roosevelt's plan to help was called the New Deal. The **New Deal** was a federal program that created jobs and set up laws to help protect the banking system and the stock market from future crashes. It also created relief programs.

One program was the Works Progress Administration (WPA). It was designed to provide jobs for people able to work. More than 75,000 Hoosiers worked on WPA projects. Projects included building roads, bridges, water treatment plants, and inexpensive houses. Even Indiana artists found work under the WPA. Some artists painted murals on the walls of post offices around the state.

2. Underline in the text the description of Indiana's public relief programs.

World War II

After losing World War I, many Germans were angry. Some followed a leader named Adolf Hitler. Hitler led the Nazi Party, which gained control in Germany in 1933. Hitler promised Germans wealth and power. Soon, the Nazis were invading European countries and by 1939, Europe was at war again. Soon, Great Britain, France, and the Soviet Union joined forces and became the Allied Powers. They fought against Germany, Italy, and Japan, or the Axis Powers.

At first, the United States did not join the war. Then on December 7, 1941, Japanese planes attacked Pearl Harbor, an American naval base in Hawaii. Japan was fighting with Germany in the war. The next day, the United States entered the war and joined the Allied Powers.

Millions of American men and women fought in World War II in Europe, Africa, Asia, and the Pacific. It was a horrible conflict. More people were killed in World War II than in any other war. Many cities in Europe and Asia were bombed and destroyed.

One of Hitler's most horrible acts was his attack on Jewish people. Jewish people were taken from their homes and killed. About 6 million Jewish people died in what is called the Holocaust.

The war came to an end when two powerful atomic bombs were dropped on Japan in 1945. The cities of Hiroshima (heer uh SHEE muh) and Nagasaki (nah guh SAH kee) were destroyed. The worst war in human history was finally over.

Soldiers train at a U.S. Army base in Indiana during World War II.

Men and women work together building cars for Studebaker during the war years.

Indiana and World War II

More than 338,000 Hoosier men and 118,000 Hoosier women served in the military during the war. Of that number, more than 13,000 lost their lives.

World War II had a major impact on Indiana's economy. Steel mills, which had slowed during the Great Depression, went back into full production. Steelworks in the Calumet began running 24 hours a day, seven days a week. The state's oil refineries produced fuel needed for the war effort. Automobile factories in Indiana, such as the Studebaker plant in South Bend, began manufacturing trucks and other vehicles to be used in the fighting. In fact, so many Studebaker trucks were used in the Soviet Union during the war that the people there began calling all trucks *Studebakers*.

The increased activity in the state led to the creation of many new jobs. Women went to work in record numbers to help fill these jobs. More African Americans also found work in Indiana factories.

Indiana produced many heroes during the war. Eight soldiers from Indiana received the Congressional Medal of Honor, America's highest military award. They showed exceptional bravery in the face of great danger. Three of the medal winners died saving the lives of their fellow soldiers.

One of the most famous Hoosiers during the war was a newspaper reporter named Ernie Pyle. You read about him in the chapter opener. He won several awards for his articles about the day-to-day lives of ordinary soldiers.

Life on the Home Front

People worked together to help the war effort. Many bought war bonds and stamps. This was a system of lending the government money for the war. Adults and children collected metal, rubber, and paper to be recycled into war supplies.

Millions of Americans also planted gardens called Victory Gardens. This home-grown food helped feed their families. People also hoped to grow enough extra food to ship food overseas. They grew vegetables, such as tomatoes, carrots, lettuce, beets, and peas. Americans at home planted more than 20 million Victory Gardens during the war years.

Life on the home front was sometimes difficult. Rationing became common. To **ration** means to allow each person to have only a fixed amount of food or supplies.

Americans also learned what to do in case enemy planes made an attack on the country. Schools held practice drills, similar to fire drills today. At the sound of a siren, students and teachers headed to areas used as shelters.

3. **Main Idea and Details** **List** three ways that Americans on the home front supported the war effort.

During World War II, thousands of Hoosiers planted Victory Gardens to raise food for themselves and for the soldiers fighting abroad.

4. Explain how the growth of highways in the years after World War II affected life in Indiana.

....

....

....

....

....

....

Indiana After the War

After World War II, thousands of soldiers returned to Indiana. They took jobs in factories, returned to farms, or established new businesses. Some went to college with the help of the GI Bill, a government education program. Many of the women who had worked in factories during the war decided to stay home to raise families. The population of the state grew quickly.

There was a lot of movement inside the state. The population of urban areas increased, while the population in rural areas decreased. Many young people left farms to find work and higher wages in cities. In addition, there was a steady migration of workers from the South, mostly African Americans, who came to Indiana cities to work in factories.

Indiana's industries began producing more. That meant that more jobs were available in cities around the state. Fort Wayne grew following the war when big businesses such as General Electric and International Harvester expanded their factories there. Indianapolis, a center of medicine and machinery industries, also attracted large numbers of workers. Evansville's factories began turning out so many refrigerators that the city was often called the "refrigerator capital of the world."

Many miles of highways were built in the 1950s and 1960s, as shown on the map at left. They connected Indiana towns and cities. Cities and nearby suburban areas grew. With better cars and improved roads, more Hoosiers decided to live in the suburbs and drive into cities to work. Business people built new shopping centers, theaters, and restaurants in the suburbs. These provided jobs and entertainment.

Indiana Highways, 1960

Lake Michigan
MI
South Bend
Elkhart
Fort Wayne
N
W
E
S
Marion
Lafayette
IL
OH
Anderson
Indianapolis
Terre Haute
Bloomington
New Albany
Evansville
KY
0
50 mi
0
50 km
KEY
Federal highways
State highways
State capital
Other city

Urban Changes

As Indiana's suburbs grew, many white people left cities to live there. Meanwhile, African Americans continued moving into cities. In cities such as Indianapolis, Gary, East Chicago, and South Bend, the population of African Americans grew rapidly. In Indianapolis, their numbers rose from 15 percent in 1950 to 24 percent in 1965. In Gary, African Americans became the majority by 1965.

African Americans in Indiana's cities faced challenges. Many lived in neighborhoods that were run-down, or neglected. Their houses and schools were not as good as those in neighborhoods where more white residents lived. This sometimes led to tensions and protest. The need for fairness and equality for all Americans would become an important issue in the coming years.

5. **Underline** in the text challenges African Americans faced in Indiana's cities.

Got it?

6. **Cause and Effect** **Explain** what caused Indiana and the federal government to create public relief problems during the Great Depression.

7. **Write** how Indiana's steel mills contributed to the war effort.

my Story Ideas

Stop! I need help with

Wait! I have a question about

Go! Now I know

Lesson 3

Envision It!

A Changing State

In 1954, the Supreme Court ruled that separation of races in public schools was illegal.

As you learned, Hoosiers began to notice that not everyone was being treated fairly and equally. Many people wanted change, but change can be challenging. It often requires fight and persistence.

1. This picture shows two people carrying signs in a civil rights protest. **Write** what you think their signs might say.

The Civil Rights Movement

In the 1950s, a social movement known as the Civil Rights Movement swept the country. **Civil rights** are rights guaranteed to citizens of the United States. The U.S. Constitution spells out these rights. Yet, for centuries, some of those rights were denied to African Americans who faced discrimination. **Discrimination** is unfair treatment based on a person's gender, religious beliefs, or race.

The Civil Rights Movement began in the South but soon spread to northern states, including Indiana. African Americans, joined by many white people, began to demand civil rights. People took part in marches and other types of protests. They wanted changes in state and local laws.

In Indiana, many African American children were forced to attend different schools from those that white children attended. The enforced separation of different races is known as **segregation.** On March 8, 1949, Indiana's state legislature passed a law banning segregation. Indiana's schools were integrated. To **integrate** means to bring together people of all races. In 1954, an important Supreme Court case challenged school segregation. That year, the U.S. Supreme Court ordered every state in the country to integrate its schools.

In the box above, write about a change that has happened in your school. How did it affect you and other students?

UNLOCK THE BIG ? I will know how and why Indiana changed during the last half of the twentieth century.

Vocabulary

civil rights
discrimination
segregation
integrate

IN Indiana Academic Standards

4.1.12 Describe the transformation of Indiana through immigration and through developments in agriculture, industry and transportation.

4.1.13 Describe important events and movements that changed life in Indiana from the mid-1900s to now.

4.1.18 Research and describe the contributions of important Indiana artists and writers to Indiana's culture.

4.3.10 Identify immigration patterns and describe the impact of diverse groups on Indiana.

Many Hoosiers recognized that it was wrong to treat African Americans differently because of their race. By the 1960s, Indiana became a leading state in passing civil rights laws. In 1961, the state legislature passed a law banning discrimination in hiring. Other new laws banned segregation in parks and other public places.

Starting in the 1960s, African Americans also became more active in politics and government in Indiana. In 1965, Daisy Lloyd became the first African American woman in the Indiana General Assembly. In 1967, the people of Gary elected Richard G. Hatcher as their mayor. He became one of the first African Americans elected to run a major city in the United States. Hatcher won the support of voters of all races. Then he faced challenges in running a city struggling with poverty and unemployment. He worked hard to meet the challenges and was reelected four times. Mayor Hatcher served for 20 years.

In 1982, Katie Hall from Gary became the first African American woman to represent Indiana in the U.S. House of Representatives. Julia May Porter Carson was the second African American woman elected to Congress in Indiana. She served in the Indiana General Assembly for many years before she was elected six times to the U.S. House of Representatives.

Richard Hatcher, mayor of Gary

This Korean War memorial stands in Sunset Park in Evansville to honor Hoosiers who fought in the war.

The Cold War

During the Civil Rights Movement, the United States faced new conflicts overseas. Following World War II, the United States had become the most powerful nation in the world. The Soviet Union was its main rival. In the decades that followed the war, both nations tried to win allies. They often did this by providing aid to countries in need. The period from about 1947 until 1991 is known as the Cold War. It was a tense time, but no direct fighting occurred between the two nations.

The United States and the Soviet Union had very different political and economic beliefs. The Soviet Union had a communist government with a powerful leader who was not elected by the people. Communists believed that the state, not individuals, should control the economy. The United States has a democratic government in which the people elect leaders. It follows a capitalist economic system. Under capitalism, individuals own and run companies.

Indiana and the Korean War

During the Cold War, allies of the two rivals often had conflicts. One conflict began in 1950. Troops from North Korea, a small communist country supported by the Soviet Union, invaded its neighbor South Korea. The United States quickly agreed to send in troops to defend South Korea.

Many people saw the Korean War as a battle between communism and democracy. The fighting continued for three years with neither side defeating the other. About 1.3 million armed service members died in the war, including nearly 37,000 Americans.

In all, about 62,000 men and women from Indiana served in the Korean War. More than 900 died in the fighting. There are several memorials in Indiana that honor those who died. One impressive memorial is located in the Indiana War Memorial Museum in downtown Indianapolis. Others are in Evansville, Fort Wayne, and Marion.

2. Explain why many people in the United States felt the Korean War was worth fighting.

....

....

....

....

Vietnam War Divides Hoosiers

Soon after the Korean War ended, another war began in Southeast Asia. Like Korea, Vietnam was divided into two parts. North Vietnam had a communist government. South Vietnam did not. Starting in the late 1950s, North Vietnam began sending troops across the border into South Vietnam, hoping to take over the country.

The United States had agreed to support South Vietnam if it needed help. At first, the United States sent in advisors to help train South Vietnam's troops. Then, in 1965, U.S. Marines entered the fighting. By 1969, more than 500,000 American troops were serving in Vietnam. The war lasted until 1975. During those years, nearly 170,000 Hoosiers served in the American armed forces.

Some Americans supported the war. Others thought the United States should not be fighting in Vietnam. Some people in Indiana and other states marched in protest against the war. They carried signs and chanted anti-war slogans. At first, most of the protests involved college students. Then the protests spread. Many Americans wrote letters to their representatives in Congress, demanding that the United States bring its troops home. Many members of Congress opposed the war. Indiana senator Birch Bayh was one outspoken opponent. In 1973, the United States decided to stop fighting in Southeast Asia.

The protests for peace in Vietnam and for civil rights affected life in Indiana and the rest of the country. They showed the power of the American democratic system. In the United States, people have the power to bring about important changes.

3. **Summarize** how the Vietnam War affected life in Indiana.

Vietnam War protesters march outside the auditorium at Indiana University in Bloomington.

Indiana's New Citizens

The Top Ten Countries of Birth

1. Mexico
2. India
3. Philippines
4. China
5. Burma (Myanmar)
6. Bosnia and Herzegovina
7. Nigeria
8. Canada
9. Vietnam
10. United Kingdom

Source: U.S. Department of Homeland Security, 2012

Immigration From Asia and Latin America

During the 1970s and 1980s, Indiana continued to change. Back in the 1940s and 1950s, many immigrants had come to Indiana from China and Japan. In addition, some Japanese Americans moved to Indiana from other parts of the country. Then, following the Korean and Vietnam wars, people from other parts of Asia began arriving. They immigrated from Korea, Vietnam, Laos, Burma, and Cambodia to escape wars. Other people came from India and the Philippines. Students came to attend Indiana colleges, and then many of them stayed in the state to work and raise families.

Many people who come to Indiana today are from Latin America. Most emigrate from Mexico. They come in search of a better life for themselves and their families. Immigrants contribute to Indiana's culture with their arts and native foods. Many immigrants start new businesses and work in highly-skilled jobs. They help make Indiana's economy stronger, and through taxes, they provide money for the state. In 2010 alone, new immigrant businesses earned more than $725 million.

4. **Look** at the map below. **Circle** the top three countries from which Indiana's new citizens come, based on the chart above.

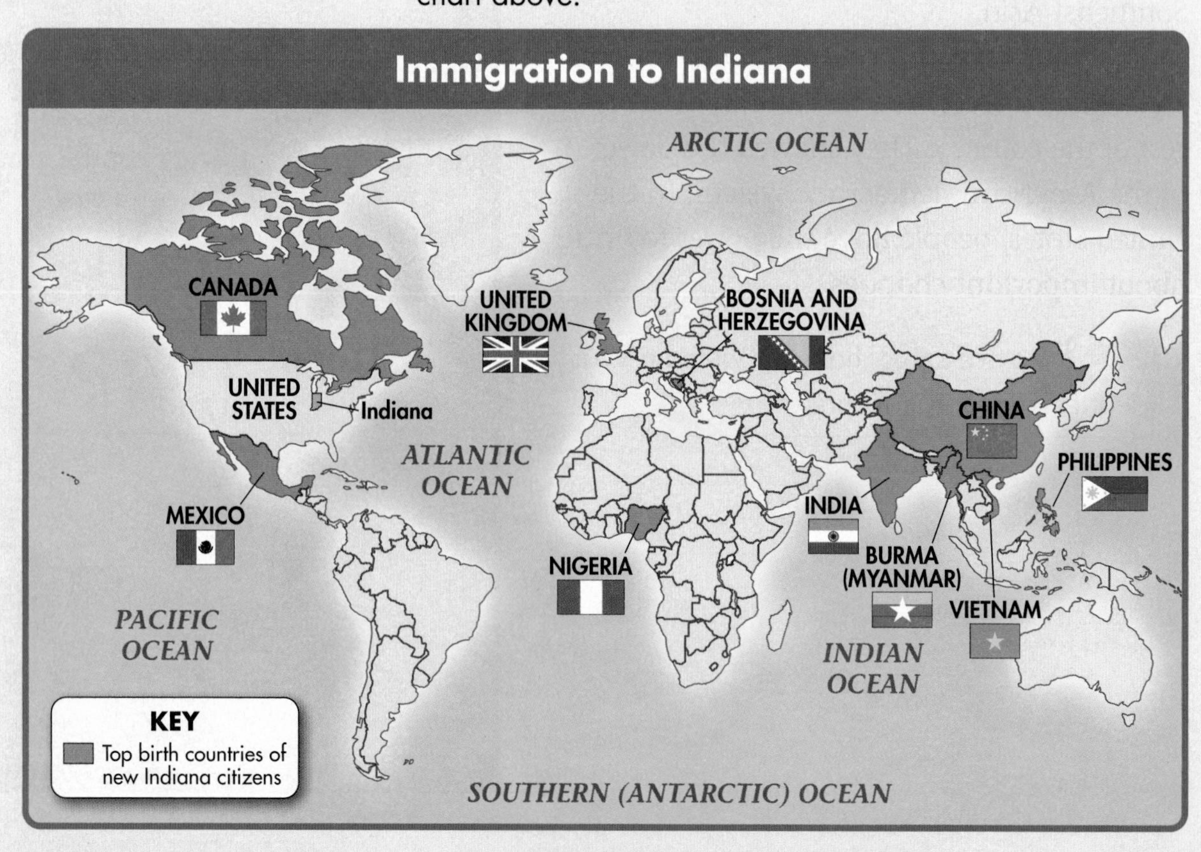

Indiana Writers, Artists, and Entertainers

Throughout decades of change, Indiana's artists, writers, and entertainers have been eyewitnesses. The beautiful landscape and people of Indiana inspire them. Poet James Whitcomb Riley from Greenfield often wrote about nature in Indiana. In his verses, he tried to copy the way people in Indiana spoke.

The artist Robert Indiana was born Robert Clark in 1928 in New Castle. He changed his name to honor his home state. In his work, Indiana tried to convey feelings. He designed the LOVE sculpture, shown on this page, that stands at the entrance to the Indianapolis Museum of Art.

Comedian Richard Bernard "Red" Skelton of Vincennes was a star in radio and television programs. Skelton, a former circus clown, often performed pantomime during his weekly television show, "The Red Skelton Show," from 1951 to 1971.

Robert Indiana expressed his love for Indiana in sculpture.

Got it?

5. **Cause and Effect** **Explain** why many immigrants from Asian countries came to Indiana.

....

....

....

6. **Write** why school desegregation was important in Indiana in the 1950s.

my Story Ideas

....

....

....

Stop! I need help with ....

Wait! I have a question about ....

Go! Now I know ....

Primary and Secondary Sources

To learn about events or people in history, we refer to two kinds of sources: primary sources and secondary sources.

A **primary source** is a firsthand account. This means that it comes from a person who was present at an event and experienced it directly. Primary sources can be eyewitness accounts, letters, speeches, e-mails, autobiographies, diaries, letters, or government documents.

A **secondary source** is a secondhand account of history. It comes from someone who has read about or studied events but did not experience them directly. Secondary sources can include articles, biographies, Internet resources, nonfiction books, and some films. Both primary and secondary sources teach people about history from different perspectives.

The following primary and secondary sources are about the tornadoes that struck northern Indiana on Palm Sunday, April 11, 1965. This was a tragic event in Indiana history.

"I was only seven years old and living east of South Bend . . . . I can still recall the neighborhood out playing in the warm weather but all the parents looking at the sky. . . . I am not sure how many times we hid in the basement but it was more than once. . . ."

—Robert Rohloff, April 12, 2009

"On Palm Sunday, April 11, 1965, Indiana was one of six Midwest states to be raked [swept] by deadly tornadoes. . . . In Indiana, 137 people were killed and over 1,200 injured by ten tornadoes during the late afternoon and evening hours that day.

[One] tornado formed just south of South Bend and tracked to just south of Elkhart. This tornado killed 45 in the town of Dunlap. . . ."

—National Weather Service

Learning Objective

I will know how to identify and use primary and secondary sources.

IN **4.1.17** Construct a narrative about an Indiana history event using primary and secondary sources.

To identify whether a text is a primary or secondary source, ask yourself questions such as:

- Is this a document, photograph, or other item from the event itself? Was the writer or photographer at the event? Does the writer use words such as *we* or *I*? If so, then the material is probably a primary source.
- Does the writer use words such as *he, she,* or *it* to talk about events? Does the writer provide general facts about the event and draw conclusions? If so, then the material is probably a secondary source.

Try it!

1. How is the account about the tornadoes in the first box different from the account in the second box?

....

....

....

....

2. Which source would be best to use to report facts about the tornadoes? .... Which source would be best to use to report how the tornadoes affected people? ....

3. On the previous page, **identify and label** each source as a primary source or a secondary source on the lines provided.

4. **Apply Write** a short story, or narrative, about the Palm Sunday tornadoes on a separate sheet of paper. Use information from the primary and secondary sources on the previous page in your narrative.

myworldsocialstudies.com ▶ Experience ▶ Skills

Chapter 5
Study Guide

Lesson 1

World War I and the 1920s

- After the United States joined the fighting in World War I, soldiers from Indiana fought in Europe. Indiana industries produced needed goods for the war.
- Life at home was difficult during the war. Many people worked new jobs to take the place of soldiers fighting overseas.
- After many years of struggle, women finally gained the right to vote in Indiana and the rest of the country.
- During the 1920s, people enjoyed a time of prosperity during the Roaring Twenties.

Lesson 2

The Great Depression and World War II

- During the Great Depression in the 1930s, many Hoosiers lost their jobs and went through hard times.
- Hoosier men and women served in World War II, and Indiana industries produced steel, fuel, and vehicles for the war.
- On the home front, people bought war bonds, collected metal and rubber for recycling, and planted Victory Gardens to help with food shortages.
- After the war, Indiana industries boomed. Many people moved from cities to the suburbs.

Lesson 3

A Changing State

- The Civil Rights Movement resulted in changes to laws in Indiana and other states. African Americans won rights that had been denied to them.
- Indiana men and women served during the Korean and Vietnam wars. Some Hoosiers protested the Vietnam conflict.
- Many immigrants from southern Europe, Asia, and Latin America began arriving in Indiana in the late 1900s.
- Indiana writers, artists, and entertainers gained national attention in the late 1900s.

Chapter 5
Review and Assessment

Lesson 1

World War I and the 1920s

1. Write examples of Indiana industries that geared up to help the American war effort in World War I. What did they produce?

....

....

....

....

....

....

2. Write the name of the movement that led to the passage of the Nineteenth Amendment to the Constitution.

....

3. Which of the following best describes life in Indiana in the 1920s? **Circle** the correct answer.

A. People worked hard but had time for leisure activities.

B. Industries were busy gearing up for war.

C. More people lived on farms than in cities.

D. People worried about losing their jobs and their savings.

Lesson 2

The Great Depression and World War II

4. **Cause and Effect** **Identify** two causes of the stock market crash in 1929.

....

....

....

....

....

5. Fill in the blanks.

During World War II, people on the

....

planted ....

to feed their ....

and save food for the ....

6. Describe two important developments that changed the population of Indiana after World War II.

....

....

....

....

....

....

Review and Assessment

Lesson 3

A Changing State

7. **Match** each Indiana person with his or her occupation.

.... Richard Hatcher	a. painter and sculptor
.... Robert Indiana	b. African American mayor
.... Red Skelton	c. African American Congresswoman
.... Julia Porter Carson	d. comedian and pantomimist

8. **Use** the numbers 1, 2, 3, and 4, to put the following events in the order that they happened.

.... Many immigrants arrive from Southeast Asia.

.... The Korean War begins.

.... Richard Hatcher wins first election.

.... The Vietnam War ends.

9. **Describe** two characteristics of the poetry of James Whitcomb Riley.

....

....

....

....

....

10. **What causes are worth fighting for?**

This photograph shows people protesting against the Vietnam War in Indiana. Use the photograph and question below to think about the chapter's Big Question.

Why might people protest to support a cause or oppose a cause?

....

....

....

....

....

....

....

....

Go online to write and illustrate your own **myStory Book** using the **myStory Ideas** from this chapter.

What causes are worth fighting for?

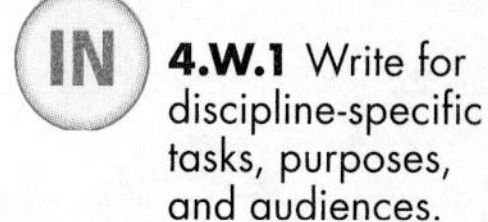

Throughout their history, Hoosiers have fought for causes they believed in. Many people from Indiana were active in the Civil Rights Movement. They believed it was wrong that African Americans were not treated fairly in Indiana and in other states. Their efforts in the Civil Rights Movement helped African Americans win equal rights.

Think about the causes people have fought for in Indiana in the past. **Write** about a cause that you would like to fight for to make Indiana a better place today.

Draw a picture that shows one way you can support your cause.

While you're online, check out the **myStory Current Events** area where you can create your own book on a topic that's in the news.

Chapter 6

Indiana Today

my Story Spark

What goals should states set?

Describe a goal you set for yourself and what you did to achieve your goal.

The Indianapolis skyline

Lesson 1 Indiana's Government
Lesson 2 Citizens of Indiana
Lesson 3 Indiana's Economy
Lesson 4 Entrepreneurs and Artists

Myra Selby

Lawyer and State Supreme Court Justice (1955–Present)

Myra Selby once said, "Your dreams can change. Your dreams can grow. When you have those dreams, you'll have something that you will [work] hard for that you'll set goals to achieve." Selby had her own dreams and set goals when she moved to Indiana in 1983 to practice law. Twelve years later, in 1995, she made history when she was appointed to serve on the Indiana Supreme Court. She was the first woman and the first African American in Indiana to gain this position. Others have since followed in her path.

Myra Selby was the first woman to serve on the Indiana Supreme Court.

Selby served on the court for four years. During that time, she wrote more than 100 decisions about issues important to Indiana citizens. These were issues in areas such as tax, insurance, and property. She also took a special interest in helping make sure Indiana courts treated women and minority members fairly.

Selby stepped down from the court in 1999 to return to private law practice. However, she has continued to push the courts in Indiana and other states to treat everyone fairly and equally. In 2000, an Indiana women's organization named Selby one of Indiana's "Trailblazing Women." This meant that they recognized that she had opened opportunities for others and helped them succeed.

Think About It What did Myra Selby see as a goal for Indiana's judicial branch? As you read this chapter, think about the goals that Indiana's leaders and citizens should set to help the state grow and improve.

Lesson 1

Indiana's Government

Envision It!

Indiana's state legislators, or lawmakers, meet to set goals for the state. They also make decisions about issues important to the citizens of Indiana.

Indiana's government serves and protects the people of the state. Some government leaders are elected. Others are appointed. They all have important duties to perform. The people of the state have responsibilities too.

What Is Government?

Our government is the system that makes the rules and laws that guide our country, state, or city. Government includes the people who make the laws and those who make sure the people obey the laws.

Indiana and the United States have a type of government that is called a republic. In a **republic**, citizens have the power to elect the leaders who represent them. A **citizen** is an official member of a state or country.

Our republic is a democracy. A **democracy** is a government in which citizens have the power to make political decisions. Elected leaders represent the people. If people become unhappy with the government, they can choose new leaders at the next election. Voting is one of the most important responsibilities that citizens of a democracy have.

Stained-glass rotunda in the Indiana Statehouse

Write one reason why it might be important for governments to set goals.

UNLOCK THE BIG ? I will understand the purposes and responsibilities of Indiana's government.

Vocabulary

republic	legislative branch
citizen	executive branch
democracy	judicial branch
preamble	veto

Indiana's Constitution

As you have learned, a constitution provides a plan for a government to follow. Indiana's early leaders wrote the state's first constitution in 1816 when Indiana became a state. Leaders rewrote it in 1851. The Constitution of 1851 remains the basis for the state's law and government today. It is one of the oldest state constitutions still in effect. However, it has been changed over the years by passing amendments, or changes to a constitution. For example, as you learned, one amendment in 1921 allowed women to vote in elections in the state. It was added a year after the 19th Amendment to the U.S. Constitution was approved.

The Indiana Constitution includes a preamble. A **preamble** is an introductory statement. The preamble explains the purposes of the constitution: to establish justice, maintain public order and preserve liberty. It also makes clear that the people of Indiana have the power to choose their form of government.

PREAMBLE to the INDIANA CONSTITUTION

TO THE END, that justice be established, public order maintained, and liberty perpetuated [preserved]; WE, the People of the State of Indiana, grateful to ALMIGHTY GOD for the free exercise of the right to choose our own form of government, do ordain this Constitution.

IN Indiana Academic Standards

4.2.1 Explain the purposes of Indiana's Constitution as stated in the Preamble.

4.2.3 Explain the responsibilities of the branches of state government as written in the Indiana Constitution.

4.2.4 Identify major state offices, their duties and powers, and how they are chosen.

4.4.9 Identify goods and services provided by state and local governments by identifying how tax revenues are used.

1. **Main Idea and Details List** the three purposes of the Indiana Constitution as set forth in the preamble.

2. The Indiana Statehouse in Indianapolis is the center of Indiana's state government. All three branches of Indiana's government conduct business inside this building. **Circle** on the picture the branch that carries out the laws.

The Three Branches and Their Responsibilities

Like the federal government, Indiana's government has three different branches. Each branch has responsibilities. The three branches work in different parts of the Indiana Statehouse in Indianapolis, as shown in the picture above.

The **legislative branch** makes the laws, or rules, that everyone in Indiana must obey. The General Assembly is Indiana's legislative branch. It is made up of two groups, or houses—the Senate and the House of Representatives. The Senate has 50 members elected to four-year terms. The House of Representatives has 100 members elected to two-year terms. The two houses have equal powers, except that all bills about taxes must start in the House of Representatives.

Voters elect their senators and representatives within districts. Each district has about the same number of people. Every 10 years, these districts are adjusted to allow for population changes.

Indiana's **executive branch** is the branch that carries out the laws. The governor is the leader of the executive branch. The governor is elected to a four-year term and can serve no more than eight years out of a twelve-year period. Other elected officials of the executive branch include the lieutenant governor, the secretary of state, the attorney general, the treasurer, the auditor, and the superintendent of public instruction. The governor must decide who will head most of the state's commissions and agencies. These state leaders are appointed, and not elected.

The **judicial branch** decides what laws mean and makes sure that laws are applied fairly. The Indiana Supreme Court, the Court of Appeals, and many lower courts make up the state's judicial branch. The governor appoints 5 justices to sit on the Supreme Court and 15 judges to sit on the Court of Appeals. Each new judge first serves a two-year term. After two years, voters decide whether the judge should serve a 10-year term or be replaced.

The branches of government work together to help run the state through a system of checks and balances. This means that each branch can check, or limit, the actions of the other two. These checks keep any one branch of government from gaining too much control. The checks and balances work for each branch of government. The General Assembly has to pass all laws. This keeps the power of the governor in check. In a similar way, if the governor objects strongly to a law that has been passed, the governor can **veto**, or reject, the law. In addition, laws passed by the General Assembly cannot go against the state constitution. If they do, the judicial branch can declare the laws unconstitutional. The judicial branch can also review rules made by state agencies to make sure they are fair.

3. In what branch of Indiana's government are people first appointed and then elected?

....

Indiana Government

Executive Branch	Legislative Branch	Judicial Branch
• Governor • Lieutenant Governor • Attorney General • Secretary of State • Treasurer of State • Auditor of State • Superintendent of Public Instruction • Clerk of Indiana Supreme Court, Court of Appeals, and Tax Courts	**General Assembly** • Senate: 50 members • House of Representatives: 100 members	• Indiana Supreme Court: 5 justices • Court of Appeals: 15 judges • Indiana Tax Court • Trial Courts • Small Claims Courts • Town Courts • City Courts

Responsibilities to Citizens

Indiana's state government has many responsibilities to its citizens. The people who work for the state carry out these responsibilities through different departments. The departments include public education, health, state police, agriculture, transportation, and homeland security (public safety and disaster relief). Public education is one of the state's biggest responsibilities—and one of its biggest expenses. The state provides money for public schools and state colleges. The next highest expense involves healthcare programs.

The money to pay for education, healthcare, and other programs comes mostly from taxes paid by the people who live and/or work in Indiana. People pay property tax on property they own, such as a home or land. People pay a sales tax on goods and services they buy in stores, restaurants, and other businesses. People and businesses also pay an income tax, which is a tax on the money they earn.

The state provides many different goods and services for state residents and state employees. For example, Indiana uses state funds to build and maintain state highways. Indiana maintains state museums and historic sites, too. Through the homeland security department, the state provides training for firefighters, emergency medical technicians (EMTs), and search and rescue squads. The state provides healthcare benefits for current state workers. It also provides retirement benefits for retired workers.

4. Look at the graph. On what does Indiana's government plan to spend the most in 2015? How does Indiana's government pay for most of these services?

....

....

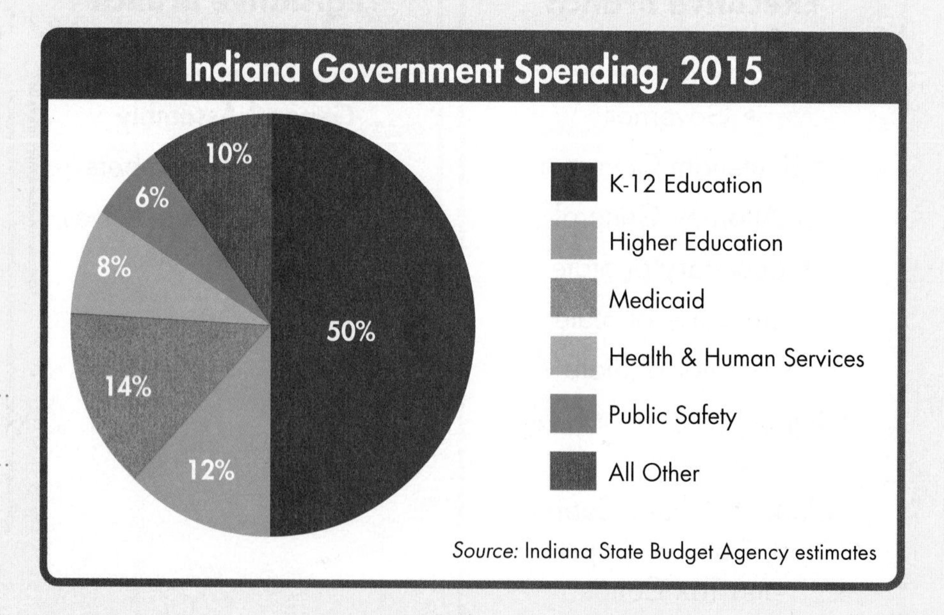

Indiana's Local Government

Indiana is made up of local governments, too. A three-member board of commissioners governs most of the state's 92 counties. Voters elect the commissioners to four-year terms. Residents pay taxes to the county. In return, county governments provide services to their residents. They maintain and repair roads and run hospitals and libraries. They also keep records of births, marriages, and deaths.

Within counties, there are cities, towns, and townships. A mayor and city council govern cities. A town council governs most towns. Trustees usually manage townships.

Residents of cities, towns, and townships also pay local taxes. These funds are used to help pay for services such as police and fire departments, water, and public transportation.

The city of Indianapolis has a special government structure known as Unigov. Its government is combined with that of Marion County. A mayor and a 29-member council run the city and county.

Local taxes pay for services such as police departments. Here, a police officer in Elwood, Indiana, helps assure the safety of his city's residents.

5. **Underline** the services provided by county governments in Indiana.

Got it?

6. **Draw Conclusions** Indiana has 92 counties, each with its own government. What is one advantage of organizing the state into counties?

....

7. One goal of local government is to provide services to the people. **Describe** one way your local government could meet that goal.

....

....

Stop! I need help with ....

Wait! I have a question about ....

Go! Now I know ....

Lesson 2

Envision It!

Citizens of Indiana

Voting is one of many important ways that citizens take part in government.

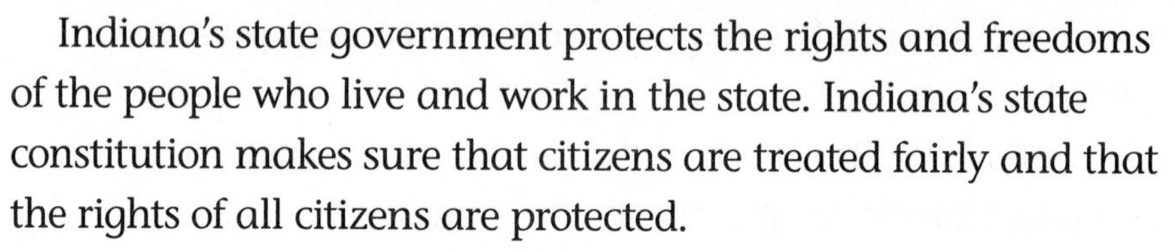

Indiana's state government protects the rights and freedoms of the people who live and work in the state. Indiana's state constitution makes sure that citizens are treated fairly and that the rights of all citizens are protected.

Indiana citizens take advantage of their freedom of speech to rally at the Indiana Statehouse.

Rights of Indiana's Citizens

In the United States, each state has its own constitution. State constitutions are often modeled after the federal Constitution, but they also include issues specific to their state. The Indiana Constitution, which was written and approved in 1851, makes sure that all Indiana citizens are treated fairly and that their rights are protected.

The first article of Indiana's constitution is called the **Bill of Rights.** The Indiana Bill of Rights lists 37 different rights that Indiana citizens are guaranteed by law. For example, Indiana citizens, like all United States citizens, have freedom of speech. People in Indiana are free to speak, think, and write as they wish. As with the federal Bill of Rights, however, there are limits. People cannot make threats or encourage actions that would harm others.

I will know the rights and responsibilities of Indiana's citizens.

Vocabulary

Bill of Rights	candidate
jury	naturalization
civic virtue	diverse

Write some of the things that you might vote on with your friends. Why does it matter that you vote?

IN Indiana Academic Standards

4.2.2 Describe individual rights included in Article I of the Indiana Constitution.

4.2.5 Give examples of how citizens participate in state government and explain the right and responsibility of voting.

4.2.6 Define and provide examples of civic virtues in a democracy.

4.3.10 Identify immigration patterns and describe the impact of diverse groups on Indiana.

Indiana citizens also have the right of assembly and petition under Article I. This means they are free to meet together in a peaceful manner to talk about issues of importance to them. They may also send petitions, or written requests, to elected leaders about laws they would like to be changed. Indiana citizens also have freedom of religion. All citizens are free to worship however they wish. No law can be passed that forces people to choose one religion over another.

Another important section in Article I protects any citizen accused of a crime. Any citizen accused of a crime has the right to a speedy trial before a jury. A **jury** is a group of citizens who are called on to make a decision in a court of law. A jury listens to facts that are presented by lawyers. A jury's decision is based on these facts and the law.

Article 8 in the Indiana Constitution describes the right to a free public education. Early leaders of Indiana believed that a free government could not exist without free public education for all.

1. **Complete** the sentence by filling in the blank. Citizens have the right to send letters and petitions to elected leaders. This right is called the

   ....

The Indiana Constitution includes the right to public education.

Citizens and Their Responsibilities

In a democracy, citizens have responsibilities as well as rights. To work well, schools, communities, and government need everyone's participation. Citizens' responsibilities include showing civic virtues. A **civic virtue** is a personal quality of a citizen that helps a democracy work. Some examples of civic virtues include individual responsibility, courage, patriotism, honesty, respect for the law, and respect for the rights and dignity of other people. Civic virtues contribute to the common good and help make a community successful.

2. **Explain** how voting is a right and a responsibility.

....

....

....

....

....

....

....

....

The most important right and responsibility for citizens involves voting. When citizens turn 18, they have the right to vote in a public election. Before a voter casts a vote, however, he or she has a responsibility to learn about the issues and candidates. **Candidates** are the people who run for a position in government. Voters can learn about the issues by reading newspapers, researching candidates online, watching television, or talking with community members. Voters can then vote for a candidate they agree with on the issues.

Citizens also have a responsibility to obey laws. When people do not obey laws, communities can become more dangerous and disorderly. Adult citizens meet another responsibility when they serve on a jury. The right to a jury trial in America means that most adults must serve on a jury at some point.

Paying taxes is another civic responsibility. As you learned, a tax is money that the government collects to pay for services such as roads, parks, schools, police, and the courts. Like adults, young people have responsibilities, too. They are required to obey the law. Some laws are made specifically to take care of children. For example, the law requires children to go to school or be educated at home.

All people, whatever their age, have a responsibility to treat others with respect. This includes people who are different from you. In a strong, healthy democracy, all people benefit from a society that they themselves work to create and improve.

Citizens in Action

Students have a civic responsibility to take part in their communities. Here, children help paint a park bench.

Indiana's state government needs all citizens to play an active role. Citizens have a civic responsibility to take part in their communities by solving problems and making decisions. They can volunteer to work on committees or projects. For example, they might work to raise money for the school library or volunteer at an animal shelter. By being active in their communities, citizens make sure their homes, towns, and cities are good places to live.

How can you and other students take action and participate in your schools and communities? In school, you might join the student council and help make the rules for your school. You can also work together with other students to start healthy lunch programs. In your community, you might help organize a recycling program.

3. Fill in the citizenship to-do list with how you can help improve both your school and community.

My Citizenship To-Do List

To help improve my school, I can:	To help improve my community, I can:
1. join the student council.	1. help organize a recycling program.
2.	2.

4. **Draw Conclusions** The people in the picture are taking an oath to become citizens of the United States. Why do you think people who become naturalized citizens are required to take a test and an oath?

The Path to Citizenship

Both the U.S. and Indiana constitutions make sure that all citizens are treated fairly and that their rights are protected. In return, citizens agree to follow the laws of the country and state. People who are born and live in the United States are considered American citizens. Some people who were born in other countries and immigrated to Indiana can become American citizens, too. To do so, they must follow a citizenship process called **naturalization.** As part of this process, they must pass a test by answering questions about American history and government.

Indiana is a good example of the American motto, *E Pluribus Unum,* which means "out of many, one." This is because Indiana's citizens come from many different backgrounds. Many citizens have ancestors who came to Indiana as immigrants. Recall that immigrants came from northern and western Europe in the mid-1800s and from eastern and southern Europe in the late 1800s. Some Chinese immigrants also came to help build railroads. In the twentieth century, immigrants came from Mexico, Puerto Rico, and also from Southeast Asia.

These immigrants, many of whom became citizens, brought their customs, languages, and foods to their new homes. This blending of traditions means that Indiana is becoming more **diverse,** or varied. People with different backgrounds are working and living together as neighbors.

Every year, thousands of immigrants decide to become naturalized citizens. Becoming a citizen has advantages. Citizens have the right to vote. Citizens can also travel freely in and out of the country.

To become a naturalized American citizen, immigrants must live in the U.S. for at least five years. If they are married to a U.S. citizen, they can become a citizen after three years as a resident. Most new citizens must be able to read, write, and speak basic English. They also must know some important facts about American history.

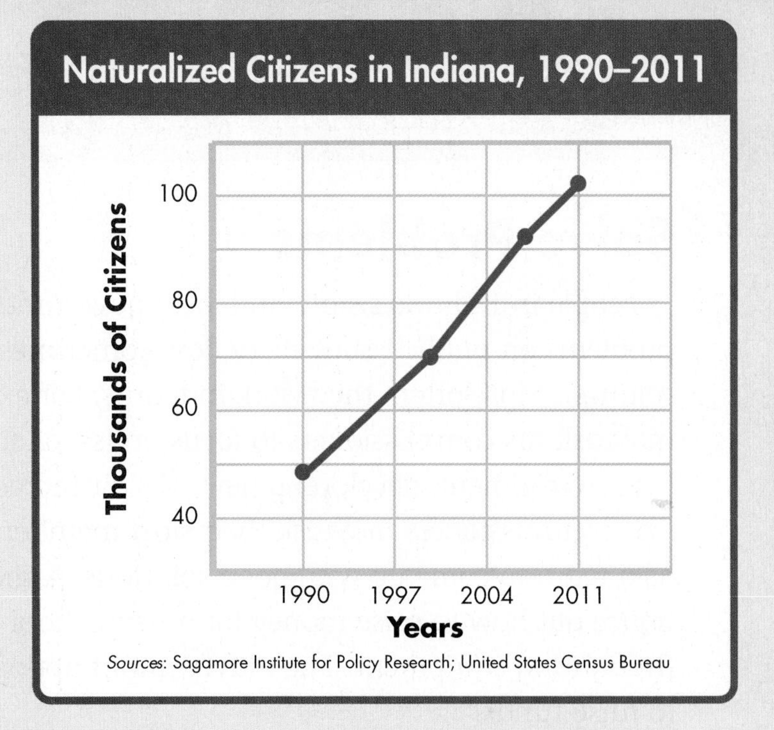

5. Look at the graph. What citizenship trend does it show?

....

....

Got it?

6. Draw Conclusions **Write** an example of a civic virtue and **explain** why civic virtues are needed to make a democracy work.

....

....

7. **Explain** how immigrants in Indiana have made the state more diverse. **Write** a goal for how to bring diverse ethnic and cultural groups together in your community.

....

....

....

Stop! I need help with ....

Wait! I have a question about ....

Go! Now I know ....

Collaboration and Creativity Skills

Solve Problems

People in Indiana's state and local governments work to solve problems on public issues every day. Sometimes they work alone on a solution. More often, they work in teams. For example, the governor may ask his commissioners to focus on issues such as improving the environment, developing new jobs, or increasing school success. The commissioners may ask their staff members to work together as a team to come up with good solutions. A mayor might need to figure out how to raise money for a new school or to pay for new firefighting equipment. The mayor might appoint a team to find ways to raise funds.

By following a series of steps, you can make informed decisions when working to solve a problem.

1. Identify the problem. Ask *who, what, when, where, why,* and *how* questions. You might want to work with others as a team to brainstorm questions.
2. Research to gather information about possible solutions. Discuss which resources may be best for your research, such as newspapers, magazines, books, videos, or Internet sites. Then assign team members to different sources to read them and take notes.
3. Discuss the pros and cons of possible solutions. Why might one solution be better than another?
4. Take a stand. Recommend a course of action.

Students often work as a team to solve problems together.

Learning Objective

I will know how to solve a problem and take a position.

IN **4.2.7** Use resources to take a position on or recommend a course of action on a public issue relating to Indiana's past or present.

Read the issue. Then **answer** the questions.

A study has shown that Indiana factories pour chemicals into the state's waterways each year. As a result, the state's rivers are polluted, even though we have laws against pollution, including the national Clean Water Act. What should the state do to reduce the amount of pollution in its rivers without closing the factories?

1. What is the problem or issue?

2. **Write** two sources where you could research the issue.

3. **List** two possible solutions based on your research.

4. **Circle** the solution above that you think is the best one. **Explain** why you support that solution.

5. On a separate sheet of paper, **write** an editorial for the school or local newspaper discussing the problem and explaining why your group's course of action can help solve the problem.

Lesson 3

Indiana's Economy

Envision It!

Workers at the Chrysler factory in Tipton, Indiana, assemble car parts.

When you buy or sell something, you are taking part in our economy. The economy is the way a place uses its resources to produce goods and services. Every town, region, and state has an economy. How does Indiana's economy affect you?

Understanding the Economy

Economies are set up to satisfy people's needs and wants. Needs are the things you must have to survive, such as food, clothing, and shelter. Wants are things you would like to have but can do without, such as a skateboard or a ticket to a movie.

There are two types of needs and wants that are called goods and services. Recall that goods are actual products that you buy, such as a car, shoes, or apples. Services are things that other people do for you, such as giving you music lessons or cutting your hair.

All economies produce, or make, goods. They offer services for people to buy and use. A person or a company that makes a good or service to sell to others is known as a **producer.** A person or a company that buys a good or service is known as a **consumer.**

Needs
• drinking water
•
•
•

Wants
• lemonade
•
•
•

1. **Classify** the following items as either needs or wants by adding them to the correct place on the chart: backpack, home, shoes, vacation, food, dance class.

Write three adjectives that describe the workplace shown in the photograph.

I will know how Indiana's economy is changing and growing in the twenty-first century.

Vocabulary

producer
consumer
currency
supply
demand
productive resources
interdependent

The Role of Money

Money is a key part of any economy. Producers use money to pay for machinery, raw materials, and workers. Consumers use money to purchase goods and services. The type of money used in a particular place is called its **currency**. The first currencies were not coins or paper bills. As you read, Native Americans once used clamshells as currency. Other groups used beans, stones, or seeds.

Some currencies did not work well. Shells broke into pieces. Seeds blew away or spoiled. People selling and buying goods needed a type of currency that was easy to carry and long-lasting. Eventually, people began using rare metals such as gold or silver to make coins. Then they agreed on the value that each coin would have.

Today, people can use different types of currency. These include coins and paper bills. Countries use coins and bills that are unique and have different values. In all cases, the currencies are usable because buyers and sellers agree on their value.

IN Indiana Academic Standards

4.1.13 Describe important events and movements that changed life in Indiana from the mid-1900s to now.

4.1.14 Research Indiana's modern growth.

4.3.11 Examine Indiana's international relationships.

4.4.1 Give examples of goods and services produced in Indiana in different historical periods.

4.4.2 Define productivity and provide examples of how it has changed in Indiana during the past century.

4.4.4 Explain that prices change as a result of changes in supply and demand.

4.4.5 Describe Indiana's emerging global connections.

4.4.6 List the functions of money and compare and contrast what was used as money in the past.

4.4.8 Define profit and describe how profit is an incentive for entrepreneurs.

2. Compare and Contrast **Fill in** the chart with what has been used as money in the past and what is used today.

Money: Then and Now

Past	Present

Supply and Demand

A free enterprise system like the economy in the United States is based on supply and demand. **Supply** is the amount of a product that businesses have available to sell. **Demand** is the amount of a product that consumers are willing to buy.

Successful businesses create products or services that have high demand. If products are in great demand, people are more likely to pay a high price for them. Businesses that provide this product or service have little risk. Businesses can also charge a price well above what it costs to produce the item. This will result in larger profits.

Think about a very popular toy or brand of sneakers that everyone in your school wants. Store owners often charge more for these items because demand is high. If the toy or sneakers are hard to find—if supply is low—stores may also increase their prices.

If there is low demand for a product or service, the situation is reversed. People will not be willing to pay a high price for the item. Businesses will be taking a larger risk. The business owner might look to investors to provide money to help pay to make the product or service. This will help the owner reduce some of the risk. The business might also be forced to lower prices to attract customers. The business's profits might be small.

Supply usually responds to demand in a pattern. If the number supplied is low and the number demanded is high, the price of an item will rise. For example, the price of snow shovels might increase during the winter months when there is more demand. What can a store do if it has a large supply of goods on hand? A sale can increase the demand for those goods.

A store displays a supply of snow shovels and sleds to meet the demands of its customers.

3. **Explain** why a store might have a sale.

....

....

....

Measuring Productivity

In every economy, producers use resources to create goods and services. These resources can be natural resources, human resources, or capital resources. Recall that a natural resource is something in the environment that people use. The people who do the work are human resources. The things they need to get the job done, such as money or an oven in a bakery, are capital resources. When natural, human, and capital resources are used to make products, they are known as **productive resources.**

A baker uses resources to create her products.

One way to measure the strength of an economy is to measure its productivity. As you learned, productivity is the amount of goods and services that companies can make or provide in a period of time. Economies that produce more products while using fewer resources have higher productivity.

4. **Circle** productive resources shown in the picture above. **Write N** above natural resources, **C** above capital resources, and **H** above human resources.

Indiana's Changing Economy

Indiana's productivity has changed over time. As you learned, in the 1800s, improvements to farm equipment made farming more productive. Farms produced more food. There was so much food available that farmers had to reduce their prices in order to sell their products. This reduced profits.

In the twentieth century, technology helped Indiana industries, such as the automobile industry, become more productive. In the twenty-first century, Indiana businesses have been increasing productivity by using their resources to produce new products in high demand. Examples are high-tech medical equipment and biofuels. Biofuels are fuels made from living products such as corn.

5. Indiana has three ports such as the one shown below in Portage. Most cargo from Indiana's ports is shipped to and from countries outside of North America. Go online to **research** Indiana's ports. **Write** one fact about the ports, and share it with the class.

A Global Economy

Some of the goods that your family uses probably come from your community. Your milk might come from a local dairy or your bread from the neighborhood bakery. Most goods, however, come from other places. Today, most countries in the world are part of a global economy. That means that countries around the world are connected to each other economically. In today's global economy, the world has become one giant market. Nations are **interdependent,** which means they rely on each other for goods, services, or resources.

A global economy is built on imports and exports. As you learned previously, imports are goods that are brought in from another country to be sold here. Exports are goods that are shipped to another country to be sold there. For example, bananas and figs might be imported into the United States. At the same time, corn and apples may be exported to other countries. Similarly, electronic equipment might be imported into Indiana and other states, while medical machinery is exported.

Sometimes companies in different countries work together to produce products sold in other parts of the globe. For example, a company in Indiana, such as Cummins Engine in Columbus, might import engines built by one of its plants in China. Cummins then exports the engines to Germany. The engines might then be used in automobiles exported from Germany to Canada.

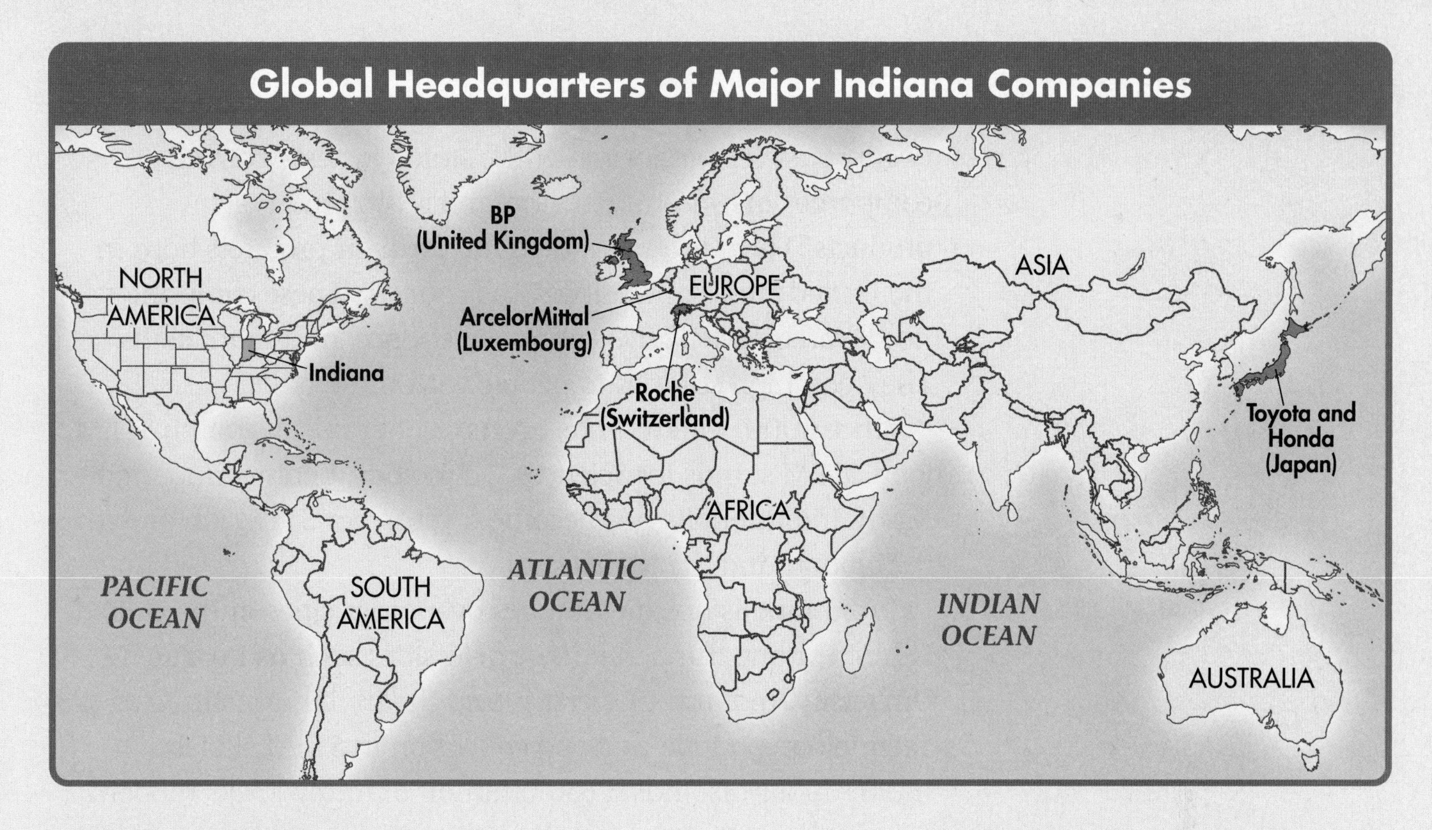

Indiana and the World

Global connections between Indiana and the rest of the world are important for Hoosier workers. One out of every four workers in manufacturing companies in Indiana work on products for export. Their companies do business around the world. Two well-known global companies are Eli Lilly and Company in Indianapolis and Biomet in Warsaw. The major exports from Indiana are vehicles and parts, pharmaceuticals (medicines), factory machinery, and medical instruments.

Indiana's farmers are also part of the global economy. Indiana farmers export soybeans, corn, animal feed, and other farm products to different countries around the world.

Many foreign companies have also built factories in Indiana. They employ Indiana workers to produce their products for sale in the United States or for export to other countries. Five large companies with factories in Indiana are Toyota and Honda from Japan, Roche from Switzerland, BP from the United Kingdom, and ArcelorMittal from Luxembourg. The location of these companies' headquarters are shown on the map above. Companies want to build plants in Indiana because of its skilled workers and its history of manufacturing products.

6. What does the map tell you about Indiana's global connections?

....

....

....

....

....

....

New Jobs for a New Century

Indiana is making important economic changes in the twenty-first century. Some of the state's fastest-growing companies are manufacturing and selling high-tech products. There is a great demand for their products both in the United States and outside the country. These companies need workers who have computer, science, and math skills. They pay high salaries to people with these skills.

Since 2000, Indiana has been a leader in developing STEM jobs. STEM stands for Science, Technology, Engineering, and Math. Indianapolis has become a center for STEM job growth in Indiana and the Midwest.

Indianapolis has advantages over other cities in the United States. For one thing, nearby universities such as Purdue University, Indiana University, and the Indiana Institute of Technology provide a strong education in STEM subjects. Indianapolis also has a combination of many large, modern companies and a strong cultural life. This combination has attracted many of the best engineers and scientists to the city.

Students attend the University of Notre Dame and Purdue University to earn degrees in aerospace engineering. These engineers explore ways to improve aircraft and spacecraft. In the 2000s, Indiana has also become a leader in developing products used for transportation and medical treatment around the world.

More Hoosiers today work in manufacturing jobs than any other profession. Smaller numbers work in fields such as construction and finance.

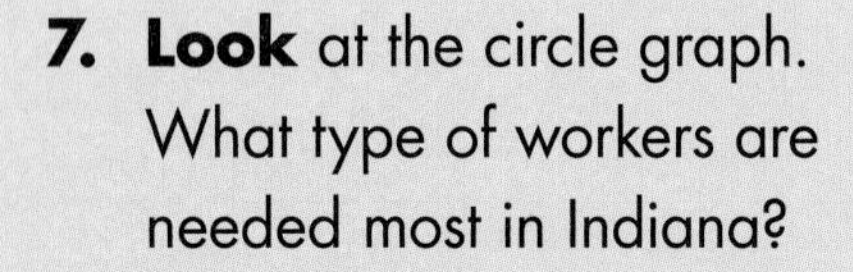

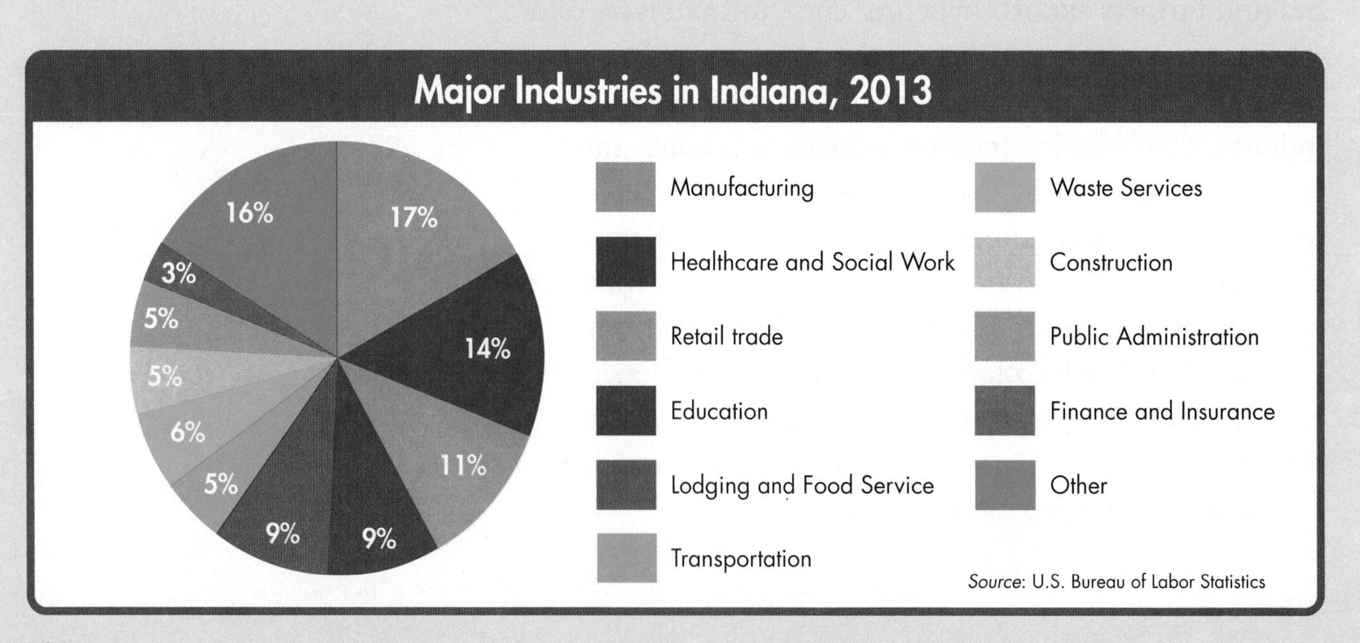

Life Sciences Industry Develops

One of the fastest-growing business areas in Indiana in the 2000s has been the life sciences industry. More than 50,000 Hoosiers currently work in the life sciences industry, and the number keeps rising. People who work in the life sciences help create medicines and medical tools. These products are designed to improve people's health. Doctors, dentists, and researchers around the world use products made in Indiana.

Many life science professionals in Indiana work in plants that manufacture medicines or equipment. Others help sell the products made in the plants. Others do research in laboratories located in companies or universities. Still others teach students courses related to life sciences.

Life sciences researchers work in a lab at the University of Notre Dame.

Got it?

8. **Draw Conclusions** How has the development of the life sciences industry improved life for producers in Indiana and for consumers around the world?

....

....

....

9. **Write** one way Indiana's economy has changed from the 1800s to today.

my Story Ideas

....

....

....

Stop! I need help with ....

Wait! I have a question about ....

Go! Now I know ....

myworldsocialstudies.com

Lesson 4

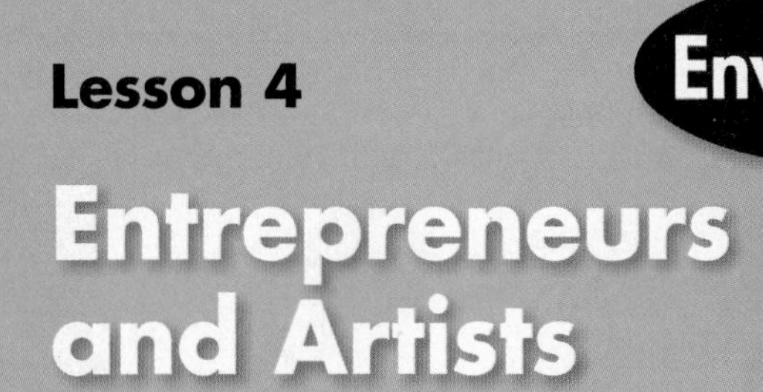

Entrepreneurs and Artists

Mark Cuban, a graduate of Indiana University, is a successful entrepreneur. He mentors, or helps, young entrepreneurs start companies.

In 2014, Indiana governor Mike Pence declared that Indiana would now have a special focus on building new businesses. "Indiana is on the move," Pence said. "The season of the entrepreneur has begun in the Hoosier State."

The Importance of Entrepreneurs

Entrepreneurs are people who risk money to start new businesses. All through Indiana's history, entrepreneurs shaped the state's economy in many ways. They built hotels and railroads. They brought jobs to the state. They also started new companies. These entrepreneurs all have something in common: they influenced Indiana and its economy.

Because entrepreneurs are so important, Indiana established a Young Entrepreneur Program in 2011. College-age students can apply for this program. In their applications, they describe their ideas for new businesses. Students whose business plans are accepted receive free rent, advice, and even money to help begin their new businesses. In exchange, the students locate their new companies in Indiana. This program benefits both the state and young entrepreneurs. The state keeps exciting, new businesses in local areas, and the students get help launching their companies.

Indiana's National Association of Women Business Owners (NAWBO) hopes to get younger students excited about starting their own businesses. NAWBO's Young Entrepreneurs Academy is for middle- and high-school students. Participants learn how to transform their ideas into successful new businesses.

Write the name of a company you would like to start. Explain why you think your company will be a success.

I will know that entrepreneurs improve Indiana's economy and that artists contribute to Indiana's culture.

Vocabulary

budget
incentive
modified
environment
contemporary

Traits of Entrepreneurs

Entrepreneurs need certain traits, or qualities, in order to succeed. They are hard-working and have unique ideas. They are willing to take risks and are flexible, or open to changing their plans.

Entrepreneurs are more likely to be successful if they have solid financial skills. These skills are important for anyone to have. One skill involves developing a plan to save money. A savings plan helps to make sure there is money available to use when needed. The key to a savings plan is to establish financial goals. The goals include knowing how much money is needed to start a business, deciding what part of one's earnings to put aside as savings, and determining if there are ways to spend less and save more.

Another important skill involves creating and balancing a budget. A **budget** is a plan for managing money. A budget includes income, expenses, and savings. Income is money earned. Expenses are moneys spent. When a budget is balanced, it means that the money you are earning is equal to the money you are spending. By creating a budget, people can figure out the best way to use their money in order to meet their needs and wants.

1. **Draw Conclusions** Why do you think it is important for an entrepreneur to have good financial skills?

....

....

IN Indiana Academic Standards

4.1.9 Give examples of Indiana's increasing agricultural, industrial, political and business development in the nineteenth century.

4.1.18 Research and describe the contributions of important Indiana artists and writers to Indiana's culture.

4.3.8 Identify the challenges in the physical landscape of Indiana to early settlers and economic development today.

4.3.12 Create maps of Indiana showing regions and features; give examples of how people have modified their environment over time.

4.3.13 Read and interpret texts to answer geographic questions about Indiana in the past and present.

4.4.7 Identify entrepreneurs who have influenced Indiana and the local community.

4.4.8 Define profit and describe how profit is an incentive for entrepreneurs.

4.4.10 Explain how to save, develop a savings plan, and create a budget.

My Budget

Week	Income	Expenses	Savings
1	$18	$6	$12
2	$18	$2	$16
3	$18	$10	$8

A simple budget helps people plan how to spend and save.

Indiana Entrepreneurs

Entrepreneurs with good ideas and courage have been building businesses in Indiana since the 1800s. You read earlier about the Studebaker brothers and Elwood Haynes who were pioneers in building automobiles. They built businesses in the late 1800s and early 1900s.

Two women who made important business contributions in the early 1900s were Madam C.J. Walker and Marie Webster. You read about Walker earlier. Recall that she developed a line of hair care products especially for African American women. She became one of the first female millionaires in the United States.

Marie Webster was an expert on designing and making quilts. Her patterns were printed in a leading magazine, *Ladies' Home Journal*. She also published the first book of quilt history in 1915. Webster inspired thousands of American women to begin sewing quilts. Her successful mail-order business sold patterns, kits, and finished quilts.

You also read about several Indiana entrepreneurs whose businesses are an important part of Indiana's economy today. For example, after the Civil War, entrepreneur Eli Lilly founded a company in Indianapolis to make and sell medicines. Eli Lilly and Company has grown and expanded. Today, it is one of the biggest pharmaceutical manufacturers in the world. The company earns more than $23 billion each year. It is especially well known for the medicines it has created to help treat diabetes, a medical condition that causes high blood sugar levels.

This Marie Webster quilt pattern, "Grapes and Vines," was included in her book *Quilts: Their Story and How to Make Them*, published in 1915.

2. Name one Indiana entrepreneur and his or her contribution.

....

....

....

....

Santiago Jaramillo is an entrepreneur who created a successful company in Indiana. He started his first business at age 7.

An important Indiana entrepreneur today is Santiago Jaramillo. He is an immigrant from Colombia, a country located in South America. He came to Indiana to study at Indiana Wesleyan University in Marion. Jaramillo's company creates high-tech computer applications (apps). Many of these apps are used by nonprofit organizations. In 2013, a business publication named Jaramillo one of the top businesspeople under age 30 in the United States.

Entrepreneurs like Jaramillo, Lilly, Webster, and Walker took risks to open new businesses. Their **incentive**, or what encourages one to take an action to do something, was to make a profit. The biggest risk of entrepreneurs is that they spend their own money. They use the money to rent or buy a workspace, pay for machinery and materials, and hire employees. If the business fails, the entrepreneur's money will be lost.

3. Write one risk of entrepreneurs.

The Impact of Entrepreneurs

4. Limestone mining is an important industry that has changed the environment of the state. **List** two ways Indiana's entrepreneurs have impacted the state.

All of the entrepreneurs that you have read about have had an impact on Indiana. Their companies created jobs to be filled by Indiana workers. Their products have been sold all over the United States and have also been exported to other countries. Their companies play an important role in Indiana's economy.

Entrepreneurs have also had an impact on the land in Indiana. Some have built factories, plants, and office buildings around the state. They first needed to clear the land in order to put up buildings. Lumber companies in the southern part of the state have cleared forests. Mining companies in the south and west have dug into the land to find coal. Others have mined limestone. Oil and natural gas companies have drilled into the land, causing changes above and below ground. These businesses have **modified**, or changed, Indiana's environment. The **environment** is the natural world in which humans and animals live. The business executives believe that the changes to the environment have been necessary to build Indiana's economy.

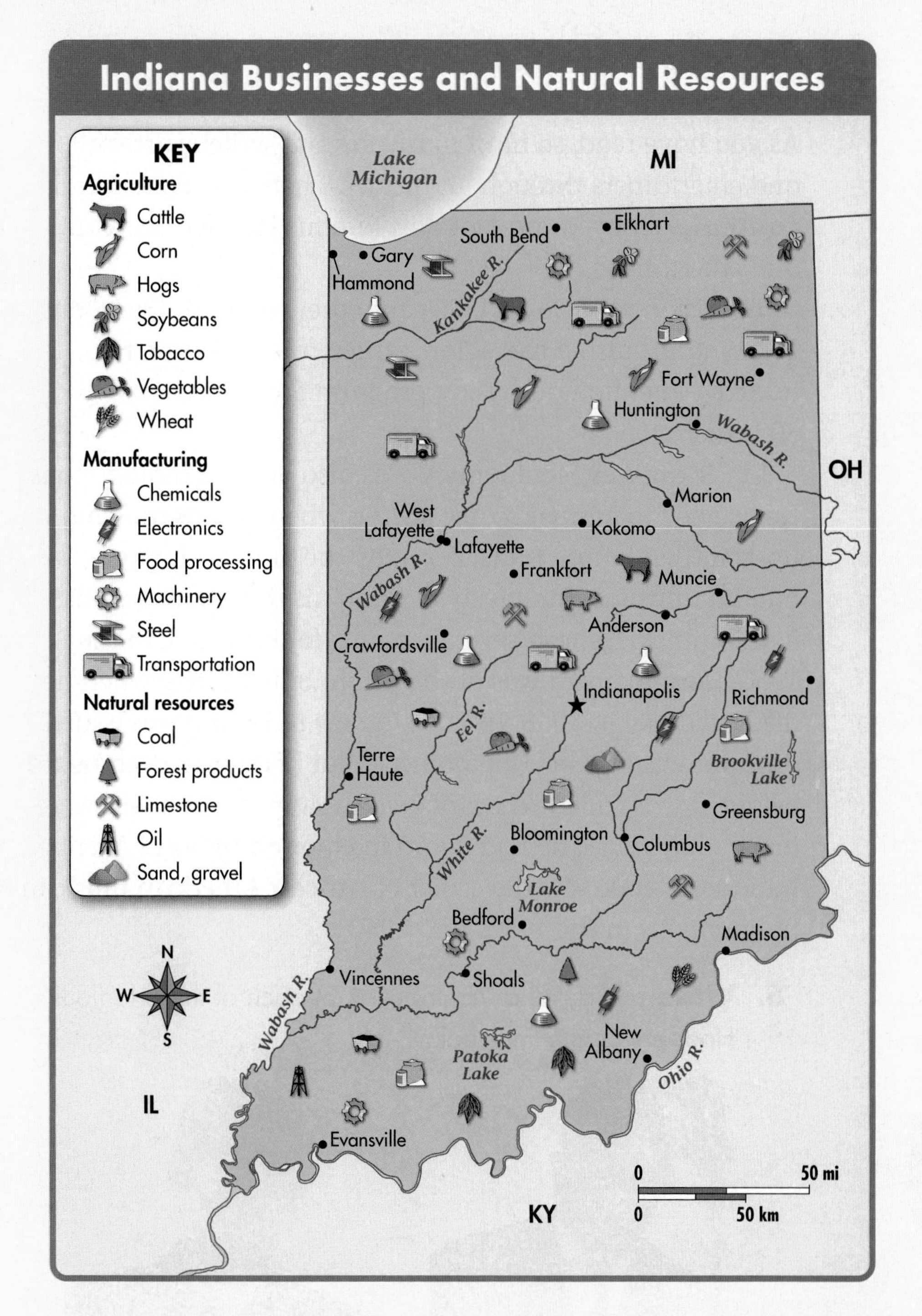

5. **Study** the map of Indiana. On a separate sheet of paper, **trace** a map of Indiana. Based on the key, **write** on your map the letter **M** where businesses have modified the environment through mining, the letter **D** where they have drilled for oil, the letter **F** where they have built factories, and the letter **C** where they have cut down forests.

Famous Hoosiers

Many important entrepreneurs have come from Indiana. As you have read, so have many famous writers, artists, and entertainers throughout history. There are also several **contemporary,** or present-day, famous Hoosier musicians and entertainers.

Television host David Letterman grew up in Indianapolis. Letterman is also a comedian, writer, and producer. He hosted a late-night television program for more than 30 years.

Musician Wes Montgomery was also born in Indianapolis. He listened to many jazz recordings when he was growing up and then taught himself to play the guitar. Montgomery had an unusual playing style, using his thumb instead of a guitar pick. He won several awards for his music in the 1960s. Montgomery was at the height of his career when he died suddenly in 1968. In 2012, a new recording was issued containing songs by Montgomery that had never been heard before. It was called *Echoes of Indiana Avenue*. The songs were inspired by music he had heard in clubs on Indiana Avenue. Indiana Avenue was the center of African American music in Indianapolis in the 1950s and 1960s.

6. **Write** one detail or contribution of each of these famous Hoosiers on the lines below.

David Letterman

....

....

....

Wes Montgomery

....

....

....

Joshua Bell

....

....

....

Musician John Mellencamp from Seymour has been entertaining people around the world since the 1980s. Words from his song "Small Town" capture feelings about living in rural Indiana: "No I cannot forget where it is that I come from . . . . I can be myself here in this small town. And people let me be just what I want to be."

Born in Bloomington, Joshua Bell is another well-known musician from Indiana. Bell is one of the most famous classical violin players in the world today. When Bell was four years old, he would stretch rubber bands around the handles of his dresser drawers. Then he would pluck the strings to make sounds. His parents were impressed and decided to buy him his first violin. By the time he was 14, Bell was playing violin in concerts with several different large city orchestras. At 19, he made his first recording. Today, Bell plays a rare, special violin made in Italy in 1713 when he performs. Bell and the other famous Hoosiers you have learned about have contributed greatly to the cultural landscape in Indiana today.

Violinist Joshua Bell plays his rare violin during a concert.

Got it?

7. **Draw Conclusions** What made entrepreneur Marie Webster a successful businesswoman?

....

....

....

8. You want to start a successful business in Indiana. Where should you start in order to meet this goal?

my Story Ideas

....

....

Stop! I need help with ....

Wait! I have a question about ....

Go! Now I know ....

Chapter 6

Study Guide

Lesson 1

Indiana's Government

- The Preamble establishes the purposes of the Indiana Constitution: justice, public order, and liberty.
- Indiana's government has three branches: legislative, executive, and judicial. Each branch has different responsibilities.
- There are many government leaders in Indiana's government. Some leaders are elected, while others are appointed.
- Both state and local governments use tax revenues to provide services, such as education and law enforcement, to their citizens.

Lesson 2

Citizens of Indiana

- Article I of Indiana's constitution includes 37 rights of Indiana citizens.
- Good citizens in Indiana demonstrate civic virtues, such as honesty, respect for the law, and respect for others.
- Citizens can participate in state government by volunteering, voting, staying informed, and writing letters or petitions.
- Immigrants can become citizens of the United States by a process called naturalization. Immigrants contribute to Indiana's diversity.

Lesson 3

Indiana's Economy

- Economies are set up to satisfy people's needs and wants. The cost of products is impacted by supply and demand.
- Indiana's economy and productivity have changed over time. Productivity is determined by how an economy uses resources.
- Indiana businesses are part of a global economy. Many new jobs require STEM skills (science, technology, engineering, and math).

Lesson 4

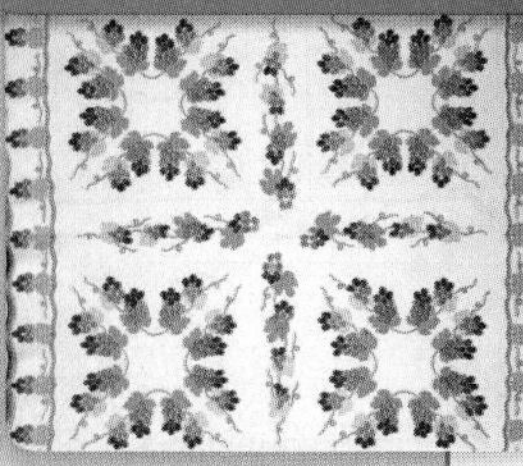

Entrepreneurs and Artists

- Entrepreneurs risk their own money and time to establish new businesses. They know how to save money and create budgets.
- Entrepreneurs such as Eli Lilly, Madam C.J. Walker, Marie Webster, and Santiago Jaramillo have built successful businesses in Indiana.

Chapter 6

Review and Assessment

Lesson 1

Indiana's Government

1. Which branch of Indiana's state government decides what laws mean and makes sure that laws are applied fairly?

....

2. What is the beginning of Indiana's constitution called? Why is it included?

....

....

....

3. Which of the following best describes the role of the General Assembly in Indiana?

A. It carries out the laws.

B. It determines whether the laws are constitutional.

C. It decides if people have been treated fairly.

D. It makes the laws.

4. **Fill in** the blanks of the following sentence.

Indiana's county governments use money from .... to pave and repair .... and run hospitals and public ....

Lesson 2

Citizens of Indiana

5. **Draw Conclusions** What might result if only a small number of people vote in a state election?

....

....

....

....

6. **Write** three of the rights included in Article I of Indiana's constitution.

....

....

....

....

....

7. **Circle** which of the following is an example of a civic virtue.

A. Becoming a naturalized citizen

B. Respecting the rights and dignity of others

C. Buying products from a local store

D. Watching local news shows on television

8. From which parts of the world did many immigrants to Indiana come in the late 1900s?

....

Review and Assessment

Lesson 3

Indiana's Economy

9. Contrast goods produced in Indiana in the mid-1800s with those produced today.

....

....

....

....

....

10. Match each economics term with its definition or purpose.

.... supply and demand	a.	when countries are connected in global economy
.... productivity	b.	used to determine price of goods
.... interdependent	c.	can show an economy's strength

Lesson 4

Entrepreneurs and Artists

11. Fill in the blanks.

Entrepreneurs risk their own .... in hopes of making ....
To help manage their money, they create .... Marie Webster was an Indiana entrepreneur who created a successful business designing ....

12. Name an industry that has modified the environment in Indiana, and **describe** the changes made.

....

....

....

....

13. Which modern jazz musician from Indianapolis helped capture the spirit of the city's African American community?

....

14. What goals should states set?

Why should it be a goal of states such as Indiana to support programs that recognize young entrepreneurs?

....

....

....

....

....

Go online to write and illustrate your own **myStory Book** using the **myStory Ideas** from this chapter.

my Story Book

What goals should states set?

Good citizens are important in a state such as Indiana and in a school such as yours. Think about how a state or a school is stronger when all of its citizens work together and help each other.

IN **4.W.1** Write for discipline-specific tasks, purposes, and audiences.

Think of a time you acted as a good citizen in your community or in your school. How did you work with others to accomplish a goal? **Write** about your actions and the benefits of those actions.

....

....

....

....

Now **draw** a picture to illustrate your writing.

While you're online, check out the **myStory Current Events** area where you can create your own book on a topic that's in the news.

Atlas

The United States of America, Political

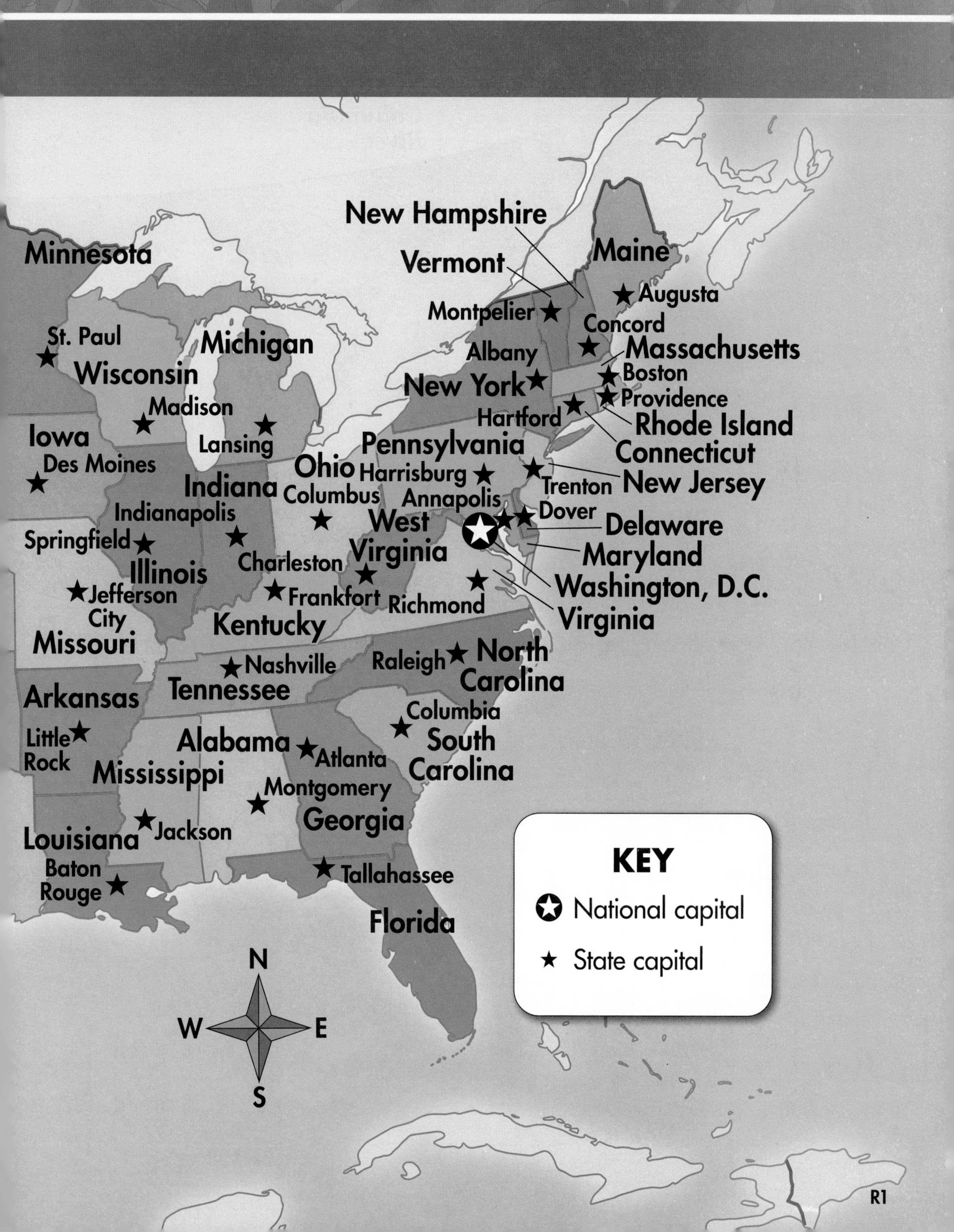
New Hampshire
Minnesota
Vermont
Maine
Augusta
Montpelier
Concord
St. Paul
Michigan
Massachusetts
Albany
Wisconsin
Boston
New York
Providence
Madison
Hartford
Rhode Island
Iowa
Lansing
Pennsylvania
Connecticut
Des Moines
Ohio
Harrisburg
Indiana
Trenton
New Jersey
Columbus
Annapolis
Indianapolis
West
Dover
Delaware
Springfield
Virginia
Maryland
Charleston
Illinois
Washington, D.C.
Jefferson City
Frankfort
Richmond
Virginia
Kentucky
Missouri
Raleigh
North Carolina
Nashville
Tennessee
Arkansas
Columbia
Little Rock
Alabama
South Carolina
Atlanta
Mississippi
Montgomery
Georgia
Jackson
Louisiana
Baton Rouge
Tallahassee
Florida
KEY
National capital
State capital
N
W
E
S

The United States of America, Physical

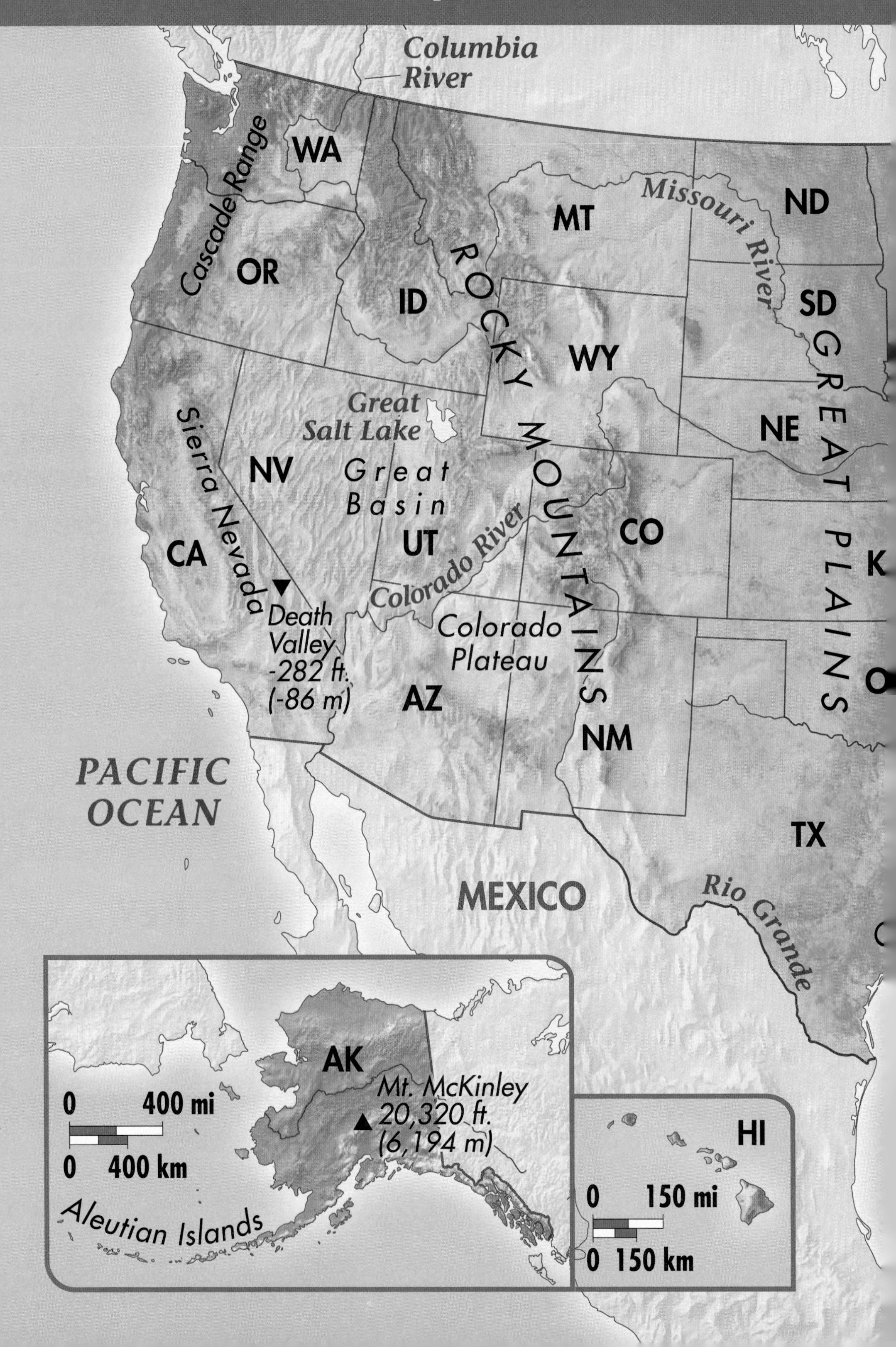

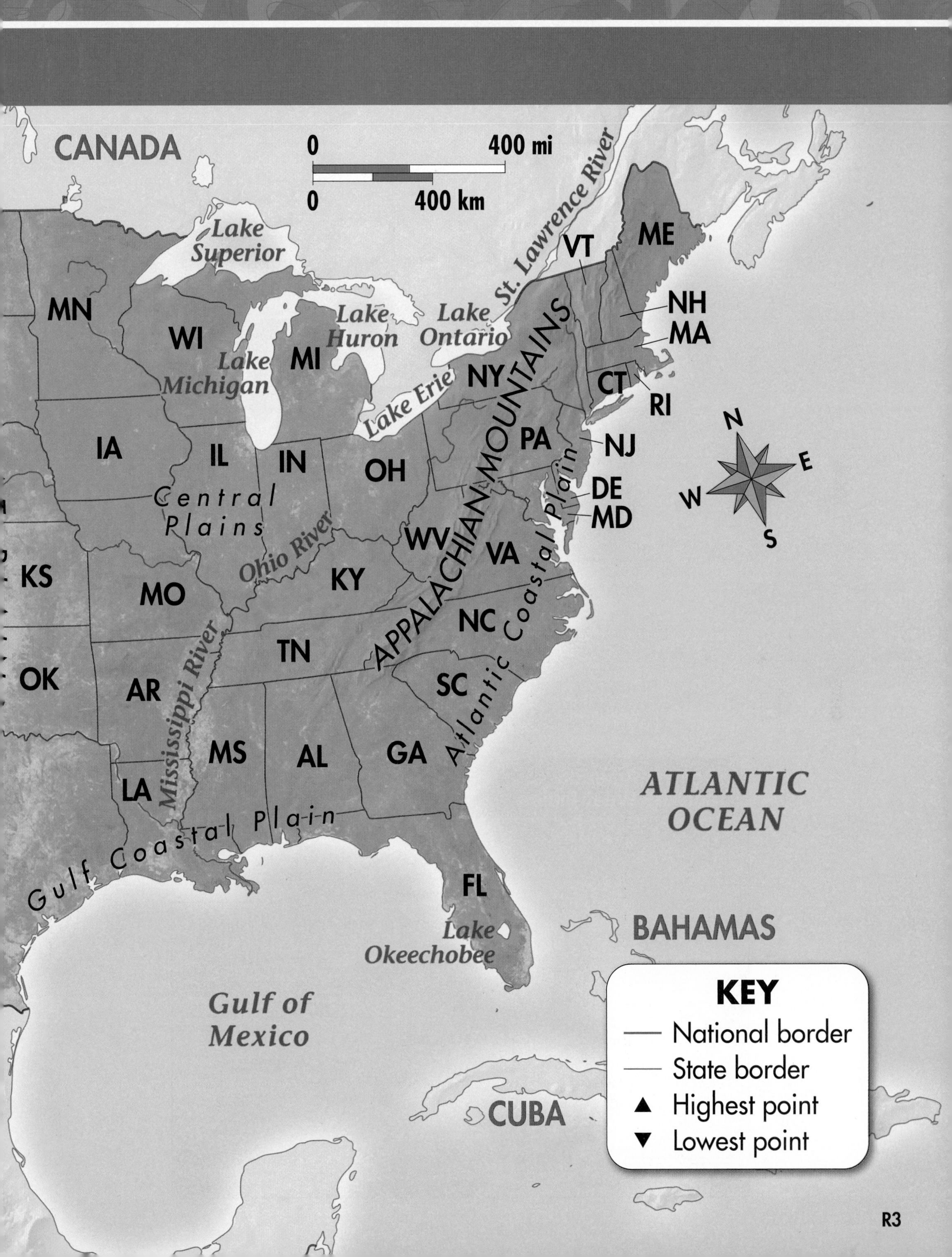
CANADA
0
400 mi
0
400 km
Lake Superior
Lake Michigan
Lake Huron
Lake Ontario
Lake Erie
St. Lawrence River
MN
WI
MI
IA
IL
IN
OH
NY
PA
VT
ME
NH
MA
CT
RI
NJ
DE
MD
WV
VA
KY
KS
MO
OK
AR
TN
NC
SC
MS
AL
GA
LA
FL
Central Plains
Ohio River
Mississippi River
APPALACHIAN MOUNTAINS
Atlantic Coastal Plain
Gulf Coastal Plain
N
E
W
S
ATLANTIC OCEAN
BAHAMAS
Lake Okeechobee
Gulf of Mexico
CUBA
KEY
National border
State border
Highest point
Lowest point

The World

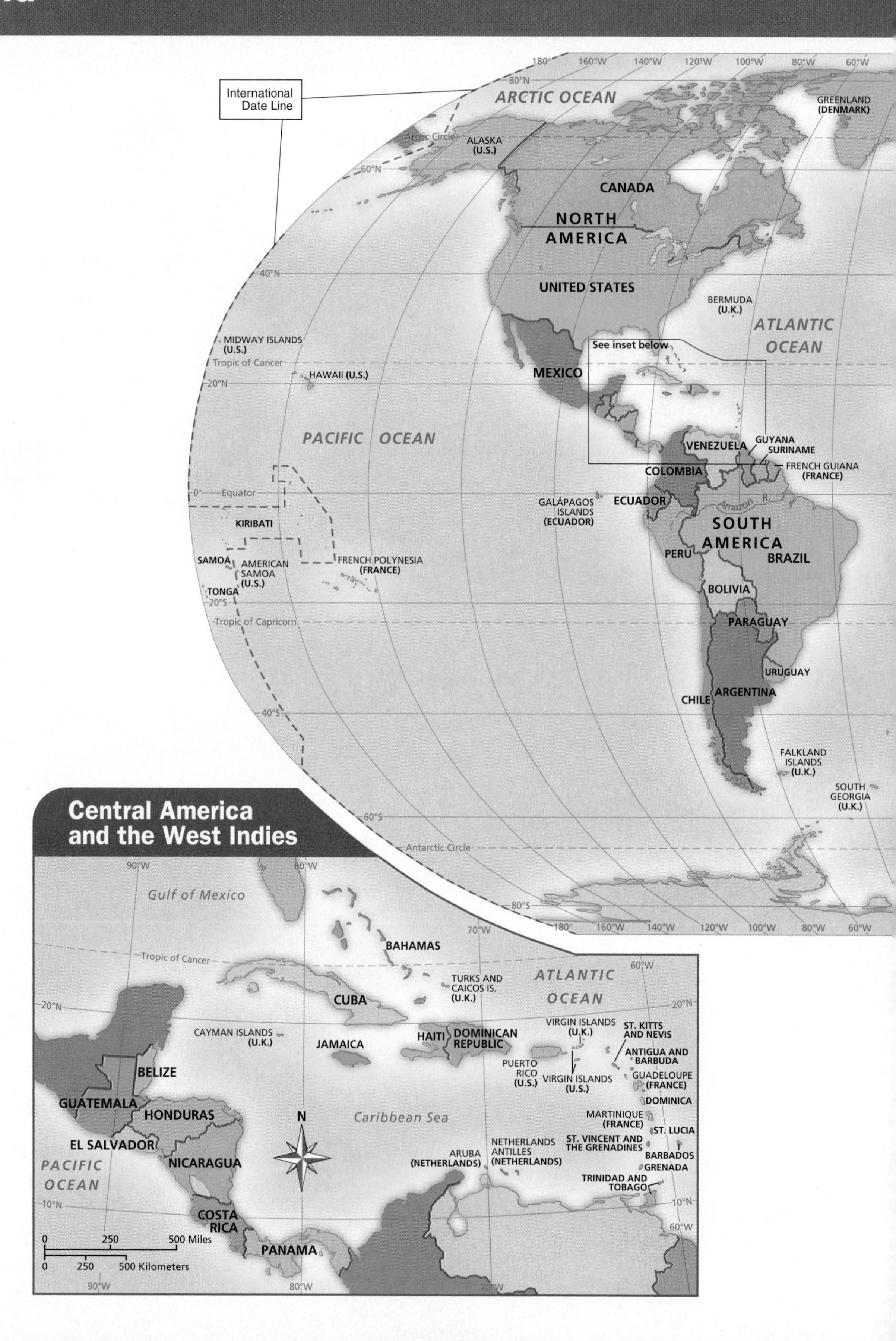
International Date Line
ARCTIC OCEAN
GREENLAND (DENMARK)
Arctic Circle
ALASKA (U.S.)
CANADA
NORTH AMERICA
UNITED STATES
BERMUDA (U.K.)
ATLANTIC OCEAN
MIDWAY ISLANDS (U.S.)
Tropic of Cancer
HAWAII (U.S.)
MEXICO
See inset below
PACIFIC OCEAN
VENEZUELA
GUYANA
SURINAME
FRENCH GUIANA (FRANCE)
COLOMBIA
Equator
GALÁPAGOS ISLANDS (ECUADOR)
ECUADOR
Amazon R.
KIRIBATI
SOUTH AMERICA
SAMOA
AMERICAN SAMOA (U.S.)
FRENCH POLYNESIA (FRANCE)
PERU
BRAZIL
TONGA
BOLIVIA
Tropic of Capricorn
PARAGUAY
URUGUAY
CHILE
ARGENTINA
FALKLAND ISLANDS (U.K.)
SOUTH GEORGIA (U.K.)
Antarctic Circle
Central America and the West Indies
Gulf of Mexico
BAHAMAS
Tropic of Cancer
TURKS AND CAICOS IS. (U.K.)
ATLANTIC OCEAN
CUBA
CAYMAN ISLANDS (U.K.)
JAMAICA
HAITI
DOMINICAN REPUBLIC
VIRGIN ISLANDS (U.K.)
ST. KITTS AND NEVIS
ANTIGUA AND BARBUDA
PUERTO RICO (U.S.)
VIRGIN ISLANDS (U.S.)
GUADELOUPE (FRANCE)
DOMINICA
BELIZE
GUATEMALA
HONDURAS
EL SALVADOR
NICARAGUA
Caribbean Sea
MARTINIQUE (FRANCE)
ST. LUCIA
ST. VINCENT AND THE GRENADINES
BARBADOS
GRENADA
ARUBA (NETHERLANDS)
NETHERLANDS ANTILLES (NETHERLANDS)
TRINIDAD AND TOBAGO
PACIFIC OCEAN
COSTA RICA
PANAMA
0 250 500 Miles
0 250 500 Kilometers

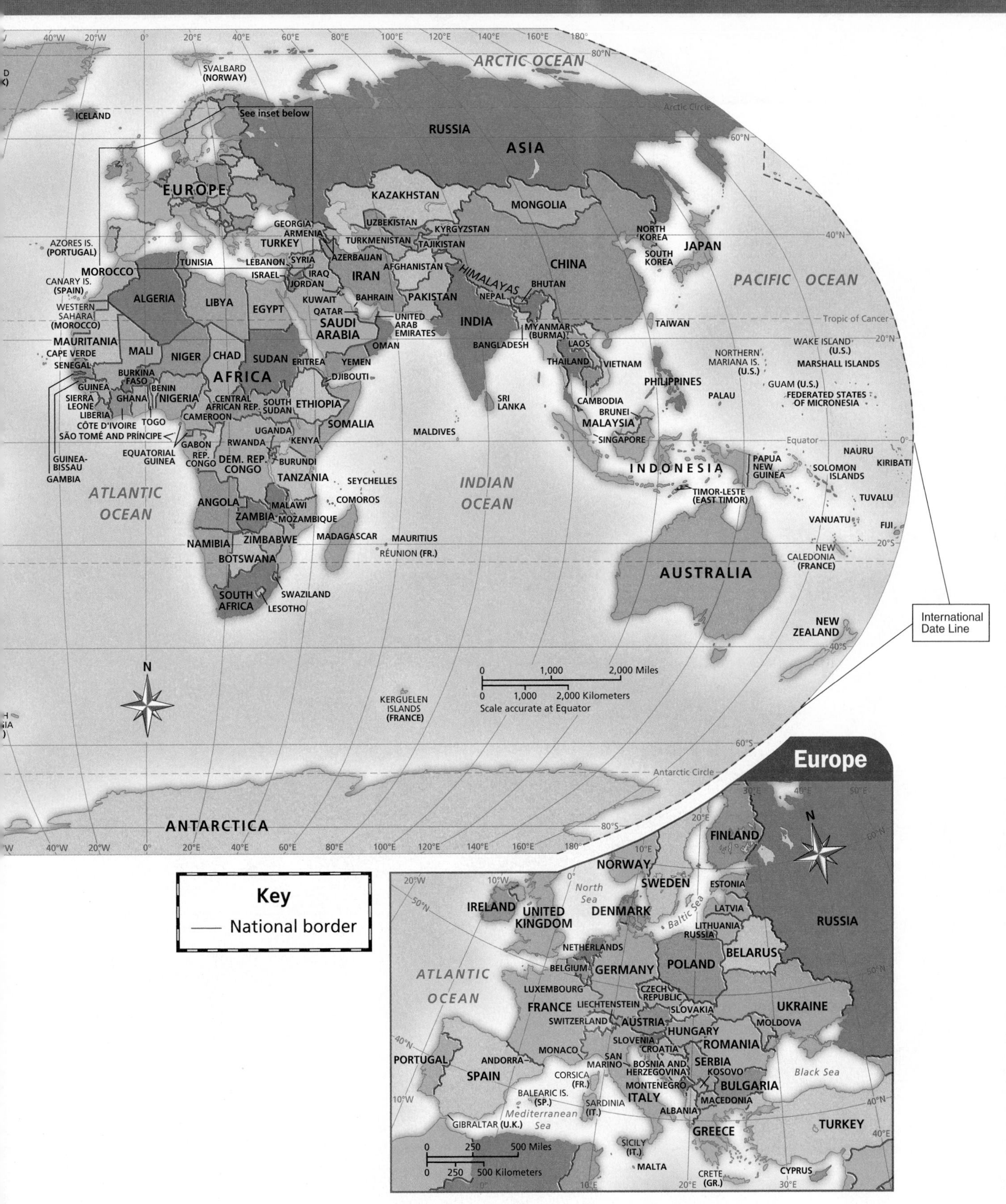
ARCTIC OCEAN
SVALBARD (NORWAY)
ICELAND
See inset below
RUSSIA
ASIA
EUROPE
KAZAKHSTAN
MONGOLIA
GEORGIA
ARMENIA
UZBEKISTAN
KYRGYZSTAN
TURKMENISTAN
TAJIKISTAN
NORTH KOREA
SOUTH KOREA
JAPAN
AZORES IS. (PORTUGAL)
TURKEY
AZERBAIJAN
AFGHANISTAN
CHINA
MOROCCO
TUNISIA
LEBANON
SYRIA
IRAQ
ISRAEL
JORDAN
IRAN
HIMALAYAS
BHUTAN
NEPAL
CANARY IS. (SPAIN)
ALGERIA
LIBYA
EGYPT
KUWAIT
BAHRAIN
QATAR
PAKISTAN
INDIA
PACIFIC OCEAN
WESTERN SAHARA (MOROCCO)
SAUDI ARABIA
UNITED ARAB EMIRATES
OMAN
MYANMAR (BURMA)
BANGLADESH
TAIWAN
Tropic of Cancer
MAURITANIA
CAPE VERDE
SENEGAL
MALI
NIGER
CHAD
SUDAN
ERITREA
YEMEN
LAOS
THAILAND
VIETNAM
NORTHERN MARIANA IS. (U.S.)
WAKE ISLAND (U.S.)
MARSHALL ISLANDS
AFRICA
BURKINA FASO
GUINEA
BENIN
DJIBOUTI
PHILIPPINES
GUAM (U.S.)
SIERRA LEONE
GHANA
NIGERIA
CENTRAL AFRICAN REP.
SOUTH SUDAN
ETHIOPIA
SRI LANKA
CAMBODIA
PALAU
FEDERATED STATES OF MICRONESIA
LIBERIA
CÔTE D'IVOIRE
TOGO
CAMEROON
SOMALIA
BRUNEI
MALAYSIA
SÃO TOMÉ AND PRÍNCIPE
GABON
UGANDA
KENYA
MALDIVES
SINGAPORE
Equator
NAURU
KIRIBATI
GUINEA-BISSAU
EQUATORIAL GUINEA
REP. CONGO
RWANDA
DEM. REP. CONGO
BURUNDI
INDONESIA
PAPUA NEW GUINEA
SOLOMON ISLANDS
GAMBIA
TANZANIA
SEYCHELLES
INDIAN OCEAN
ATLANTIC OCEAN
ANGOLA
MALAWI
COMOROS
TIMOR-LESTE (EAST TIMOR)
TUVALU
ZAMBIA
MOZAMBIQUE
VANUATU
FIJI
NAMIBIA
ZIMBABWE
MADAGASCAR
MAURITIUS
RÉUNION (FR.)
NEW CALEDONIA (FRANCE)
BOTSWANA
AUSTRALIA
SOUTH AFRICA
SWAZILAND
LESOTHO
International Date Line
NEW ZEALAND
N
0 1,000 2,000 Miles
0 1,000 2,000 Kilometers
Scale accurate at Equator
KERGUELEN ISLANDS (FRANCE)
Arctic Circle
Antarctic Circle
ANTARCTICA
40°W 20°W 0° 20°E 40°E 60°E 80°E 100°E 120°E 140°E 160°E 180°
80°N 60°N 40°N 20°N 0° 20°S 40°S 60°S 80°S
Key
National border
Europe
FINLAND
NORWAY
SWEDEN
ESTONIA
North Sea
IRELAND
UNITED KINGDOM
DENMARK
Baltic Sea
LATVIA
LITHUANIA
RUSSIA
NETHERLANDS
BELARUS
BELGIUM
GERMANY
POLAND
ATLANTIC OCEAN
LUXEMBOURG
CZECH REPUBLIC
SLOVAKIA
UKRAINE
FRANCE
LIECHTENSTEIN
SWITZERLAND
AUSTRIA
MOLDOVA
HUNGARY
SLOVENIA
CROATIA
ROMANIA
MONACO
SAN MARINO
BOSNIA AND HERZEGOVINA
SERBIA
KOSOVO
PORTUGAL
ANDORRA
SPAIN
CORSICA (FR.)
MONTENEGRO
BULGARIA
Black Sea
BALEARIC IS. (SP.)
SARDINIA (IT.)
ITALY
MACEDONIA
ALBANIA
Mediterranean Sea
GIBRALTAR (U.K.)
GREECE
TURKEY
0 250 500 Miles
0 250 500 Kilometers
SICILY (IT.)
MALTA
CRETE (GR.)
CYPRUS

Canada, Political

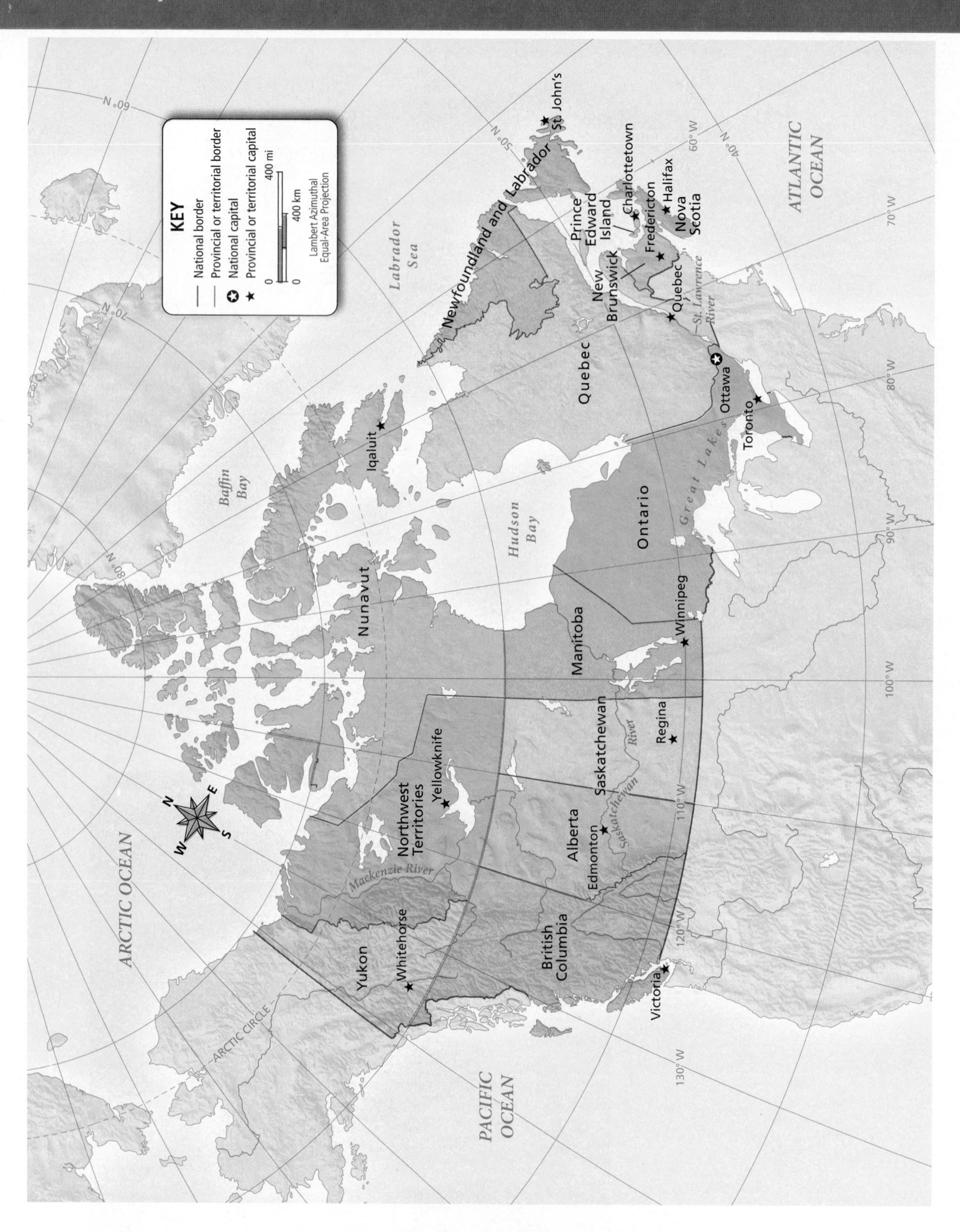

Canada, Physical

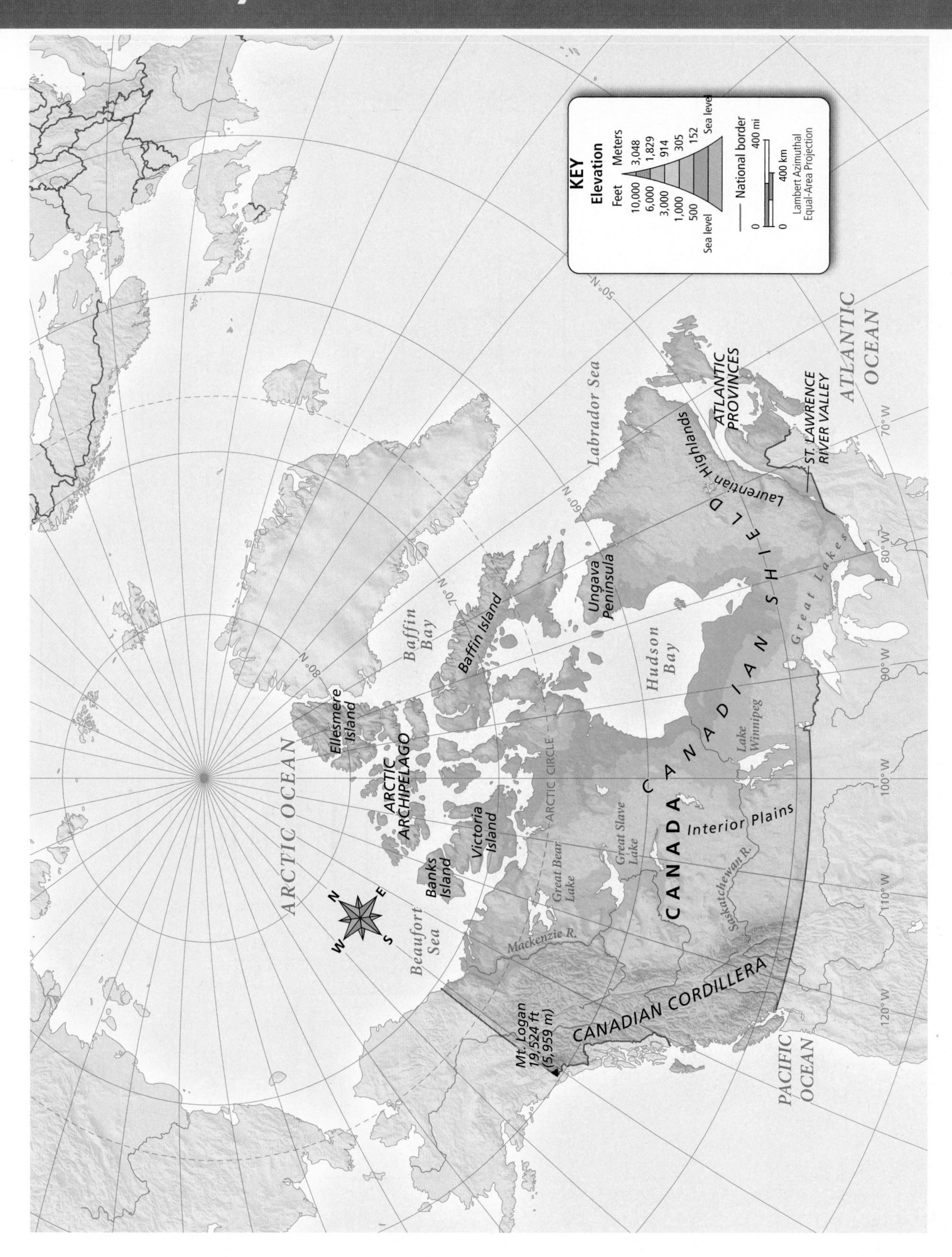

Mexico, Political

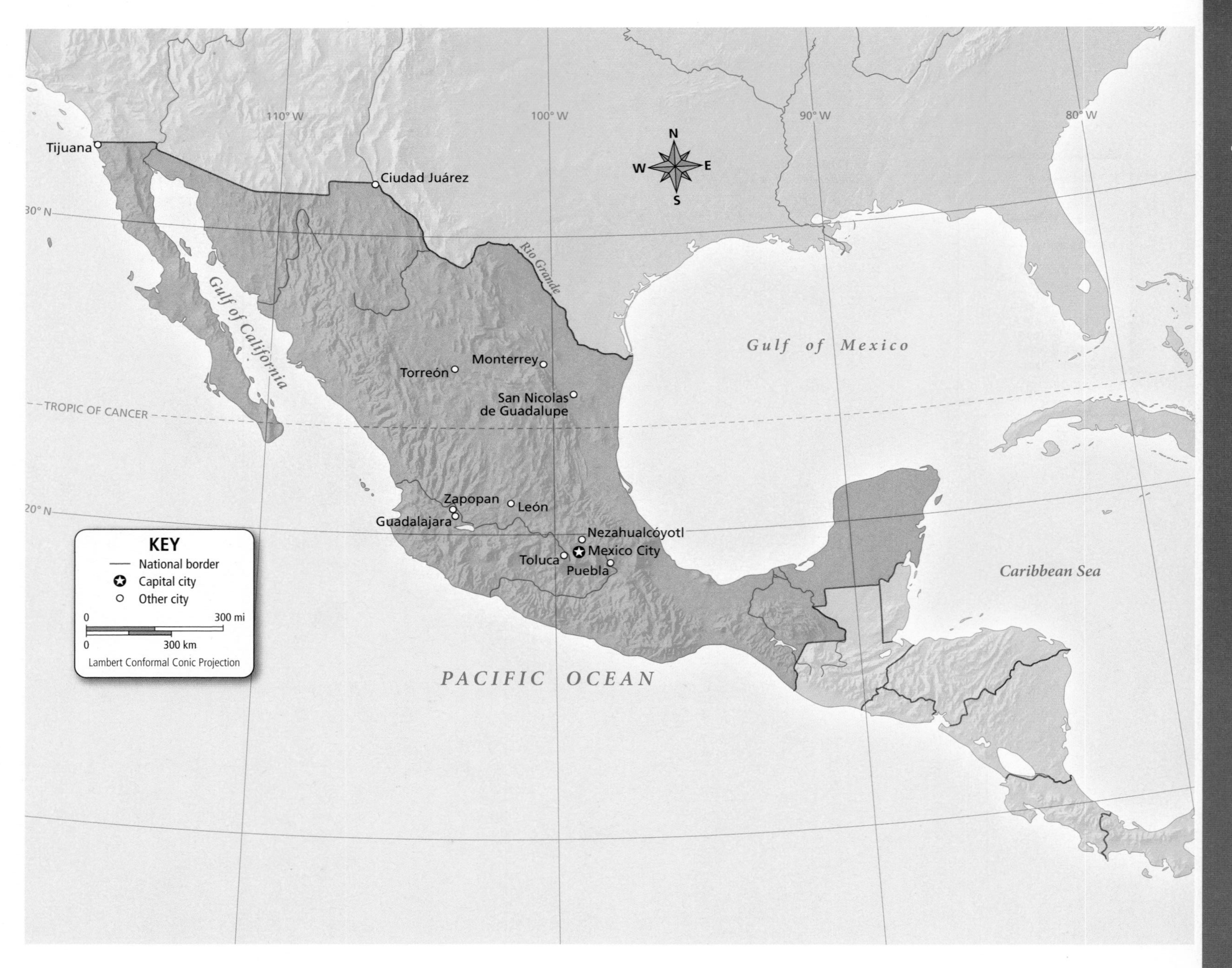

Mexico, Physical

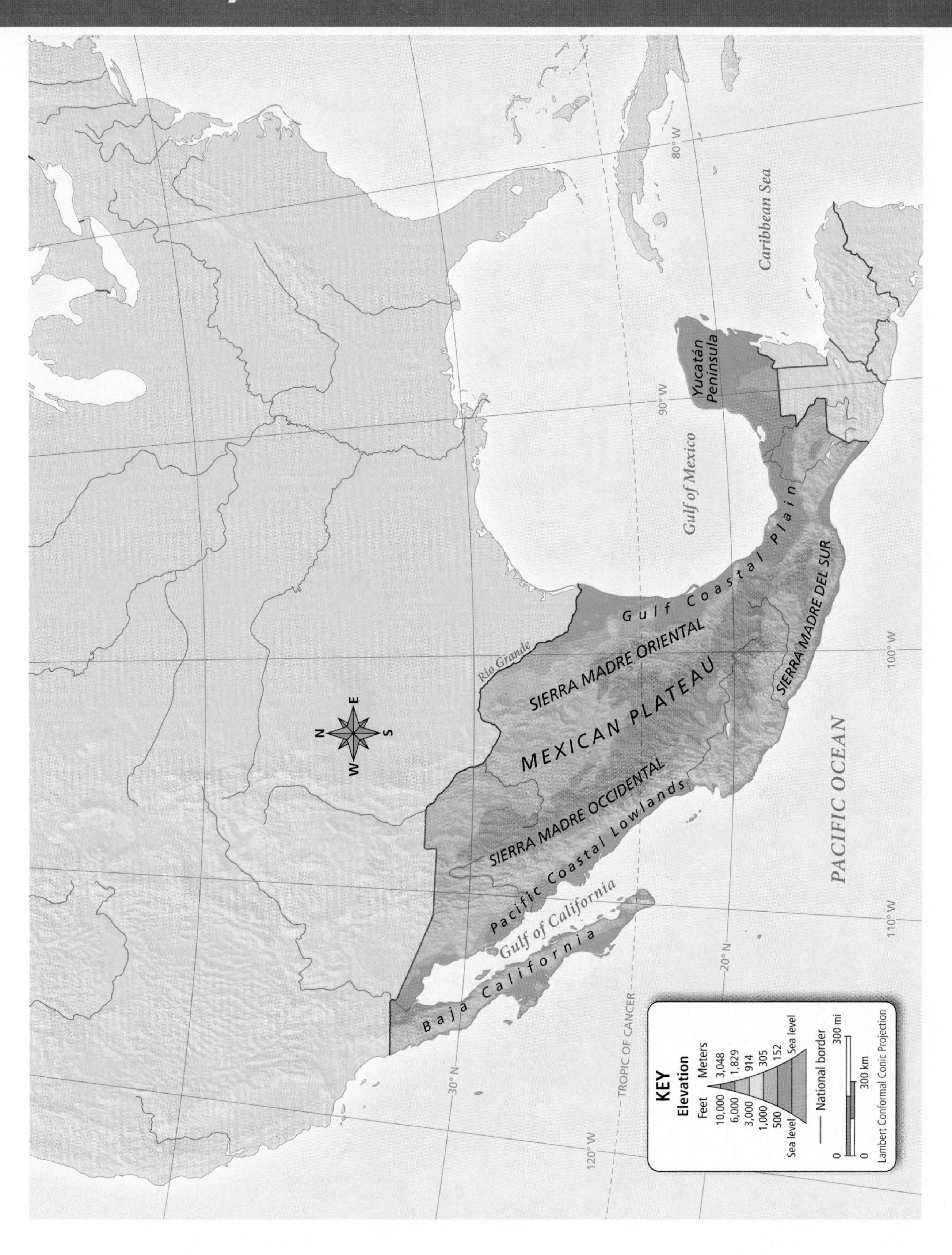

Caribbean, Political

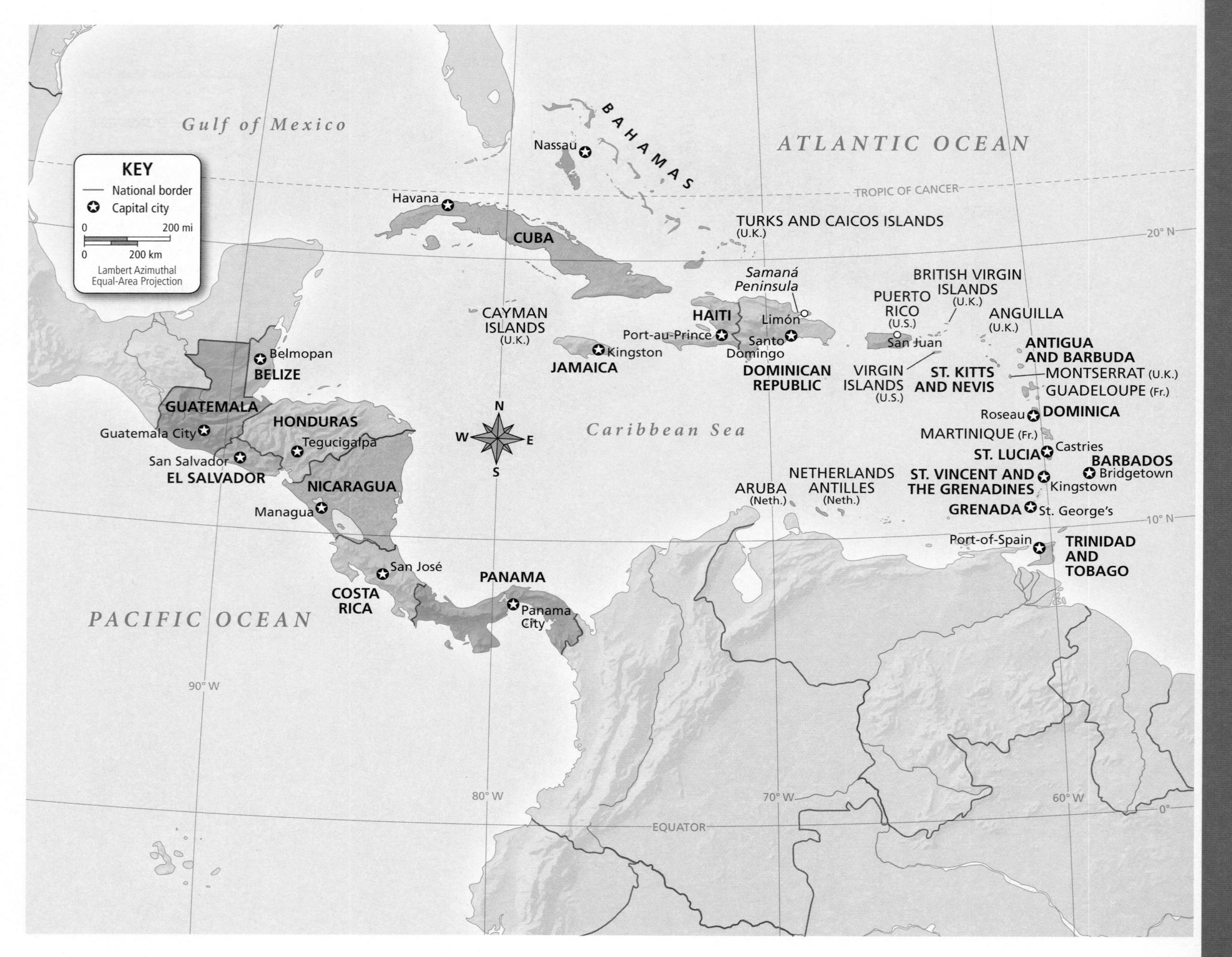

Glossary

A

abolition (ab′ə lish′ən) The act of ending or abolishing something, such as slavery.

adapt (ə dapt′) To change to fit new situations.

agriculture (ag′ri kul′chər) Farming.

ally (al′ī) A partner or supporter who pledges friendship or help.

amendment (ə mend′mənt) A change or improvement.

archaeologist (är′kē äl′ə jist) A person who studies artifacts and sites to learn about ancient people.

artifact (ärt′ə fakt) An object made by humans.

atlas (at′ləs) A collection or book of maps.

B

Bill of Rights (bil uv rīts) Amendments to the U.S. and Indiana Constitutions that protect citizens' basic rights.

biosphere (bī′ō sfir′) All of the plants and animals living on Earth's surface.

budget (buj′it) A plan for managing money.

C

canal (kə nal′) A human-made waterway dug across land.

candidate (kan′də dāt) A person who runs for a position in government.

cardinal direction (kärd′'n əl də rek′shən) One of the four main compass points north, south, east, and west.

citizen (sit′ə zən) An official member of a state or country.

civil rights (siv′əl rīts) Rights guaranteed to citizens of the United States.

civil war (siv′əl wôr) A war between different groups of people in the same country.

civic virtue (siv′ik vʉr′cho͞o) A personal quality of a citizen that helps a democracy work, such as courage, patriotism, honesty, respect for the law, and respect for the rights and dignity of other people.

clan (klan) A related group.

climate (klī′mət) The pattern of weather in a place over a long period of time.

colony (kä l′ə nē) A settlement in a new land where the people remain loyal to their home country.

compass rose (kum′pəs rōz) A symbol on a map that shows directions.

Pronunciation Key

a in hat	ō in open	'l in cattle
ā in age	ô in order	'n in sudden
ä in father	o͞o in tool	th in weather
e in let	u in cup	zh in measure
ē in equal	ʉ in reverse	
i in it	ə a in ago	
ī in ice	e in agent	
o in hot	o in collect	
	u in focus	

confederacy (kən fed′ ər ə sē) A group of people or several smaller groups joined together for a common purpose.

confederation (kən fed′ ər ā′shən) A union of states that agree to cooperate.

congress (kän′gres) A group of people responsible for making a country's laws.

constitution (kän′stə to͞o′shən) A plan of government.

consumer (kən so͞om′ər) A person or company that buys or uses goods and services.

contemporary (kən tem′pə rer′ē) Present day.

corporation (kôr′pə rā′shən) A company or organization designed for a specific purpose.

cultural exchange (kul′chər əl eks chānj′) An act of two different cultures sharing information with each other.

cultural group (kul′chər əl gro͞op) A group of people connected by a common language, religion, and culture.

culture (kul′chər) The way of life for a group of people.

currency (kur′ən sē) Money used in a particular place.

D

debt (det) Money that is owed.

degree (di grē′) A unit of measure. There are 360 degrees of latitude and longitude used to locate places on Earth.

delegate (del′ə git) Someone who represents a group of people.

demand (di mand′) The amount of a particular good or service that consumers want to buy.

democracy (di mäk′rə sē) A government in which citizens have the power to make political decisions.

depression (dē presh′ən) A time when business activity is slow and many people are out of work.

discrimination (di skrim′i nā′shən) Unfair treatment based on a person's gender, religious beliefs, or race.

diverse (də vurs′) Showing much variety.

draft (draft) A system in which men of certain ages are required to join the armed forces for a certain period of time.

E

economy (i kän′ə mē) The way a place uses its resources to produce goods and services.

elevation (el′ə vā′shən) The height above sea level.

entrepreneur (än′trə prə no͝or′) A person who risks money and time to start a new business.

environment (en vī′rən mənt) The natural world in which humans and animals live.

equator (ē kwāt′ər) A line drawn around Earth halfway between the North and South Poles. It divides Earth into Northern and Southern Hemispheres.

evaporation (ē vap′ə rā′shən) The process of water vapor rising into Earth's atmosphere and turning into clouds.

executive branch (eg zek′ yo͞o tiv branch) The branch of government that carries out the laws.

export (ek′spôrt) Goods that are shipped to another country to be sold there.

G

glacier (glā′shər) A huge mass of ice that moves slowly across the land.

globe (glōb) A round model of Earth.

grid (grid) A system of lines that cross each other to form a pattern of squares. On a map, grids are used to locate places.

H

hemisphere (hem′i sfir′) Half of a sphere. Earth's hemispheres are formed by the equator and the prime meridian.

hydrologic cycle (hī′drə läj′ik sī′kəl) The water cycle that describes the movement of water on, in, and above Earth.

hydrosphere (hī′drō sfir′) All the water on Earth's surface.

I

immigrant (im′ə grənt) A person who moves from one country to another.

import (im′port) Goods that are brought in from another country to be sold.

independence (in′dē pen′dəns) Freedom from being ruled by others.

integrate (in′tə grāt′) To bring together people of all races.

interdependent (in′tər dē pen′dənt) When nations rely on one another for goods, services, or resources.

intermediate direction (in′tər mē′dē it də rek′shən) A direction, such as northwest, that is between two cardinal directions.

J

judicial branch (jo͞o dish′əl branch) The part of government that decides what laws mean and makes sure that laws are applied fairly.

jury (joor′ē) A group of citizens who are called on to make a decision in a court of law.

L

labor union (lā′bər yo͞on′yən) A group of workers, usually in the same type of job, who have joined together to demand better wages and working conditions.

landform (land′fôrm) A natural feature of Earth's surface, such as a mountain, hill, valley, or even an island.

latitude (lat′ə to͞od) Lines that measure the distance north and south of the equator.

legislative branch (lej′is lā′tiv branch) The branch of government that makes the laws.

literacy (lit′ər ə sē) The ability to read and write.

lithosphere (lith′ə sfir′) The soil and rock that form Earth's surface.

loan (lōn) Money that is lent to someone, often from a bank.

longhouse (long′hous′) A large house built by Native Americans with trees and bark where many people lived.

longitude (län′jə to͞od) Lines that measure the distance east and west of the prime meridian.

M

manufacturing (man′yo͞o fak′chər ing) The making of goods by machines, usually in factories.

map key (map kē) A map legend; the boxed list showing what the symbols on a map represent.

map scale (map skāl) A line drawn on a map that shows the relationship between distance on the map and distance on Earth.

migrate (mī′grāt) To move from one place to another.

militia (mə lish′ə) A group of people who are not in the military but are still trained as soldiers.

modified (mäd′ə fīd) Changed.

moraine (mə rān′) A mass of dirt and rocks left behind by glaciers.

mound (mound) A pile of earth made by early cultures.

N

natural resource (nach′ər əl rē′sôrs) Something in the environment that people use.

naturalization (nach′ər əl i zā′shən) The process people follow to become citizens.

neutral (no͞o′trəl) Not choosing a side in a war.

New Deal (no͞o dēl) A federal program that created jobs and set up laws to make both the banking system and the stock market safer. It also created several relief programs to help those in need.

O

oil refinery (oil ri fīn′ər ē) A factory where oil is processed into gasoline and other products.

ordinance (ôrd′'n əns) A law.

P

physical map (fiz′i kəl map) A map that shows landforms and bodies of water.

political map (pə lit′i kəl map) A map that shows information such as borders, capitals, and important cities.

preamble (prē′am′bəl) An introductory statement.

precipitation (prē sip′ə tā′shən) The amount of moisture that falls as rain or snow.

prime meridian (prīm mə rid′ē ən) A line drawn from the North Pole to the South Pole through Europe and Africa. It divides Earth into Eastern and Western Hemispheres.

producer (prə do͞os′ər) A person or company that makes goods or services to sell.

productive resources (prə duk′tiv rē′sôrs) Resources that are used to make products.

productivity (prō′dək tiv′ə tē) The amount of goods or services workers can make or provide in a set amount of time.

profit (präf′it) The money a business earns after all its expenses are paid.

prosperity (präs per′ə tē) Success or good fortune.

public education (pub′lik ed yoo kā′shən) A system in which government provides free schooling for all children.

R

ratify (rat′ə fī′) To approve officially.

ration (rash′ən) To allow each person to have only a fixed amount of food or supplies.

regiment (rej′ə mənt) A military unit usually made of several groups of soldiers.

region (rē′jən) An area that has common features.

regulate (reg′yo͞o lāt) To control or maintain with rules and regulations.

republic (ri pub′lik) A form of government in which citizens have the power to elect the leaders who represent them.

reservation (rez′ər vā′shən) An area of land that the United States set aside for Native Americans.

rural (ro͞or′əl) Of or relating to the country.

secede (si sēd′) To separate from or leave a country.

segregation (seg′rə gā′shən) The enforced separation of different races.

slavery (slā′vər ē) The act of owning people and forcing them to work without pay.

states' rights (stāts rīts) The idea that the states had the power and the right to decide important matters for themselves.

steelworks (stēl′wʉrks) A factory where steel is made.

stock market (stäk mär′kit) A place where people buy and sell stocks.

stocks (stäks) Shares, or portions, of ownership in companies.

strategy (strat′ə jē) A careful plan.

strike (strīk) A protest in which workers refuse to work until their demands are met.

supply (sə plī′) The amount of goods or services available for a consumer to buy.

suffrage (suf′rij) The right to vote.

surrender (sə ren′dər) To give up and agree to stop fighting.

symbol (sim′bəl) A small drawing, line, or color that stands for something else.

tax (taks) Money that people pay to support the cost of government.

territory (ter′ə tôr′ē) An area of land that is controlled by an outside government.

till (til) The soil and rock that gets left behind after a glacier melts.

trade (trād) The buying and selling of goods and services.

U

unemployed (un em ploid′) Out of work.

urban (ûr′bən) Of or relating to cities.

utopia (yo͞o tō′pē ə) An imagined place in which everything is perfect.

V

veto (vē′tō) To reject.

W

weather (weth′ər) The condition of the air at a certain time and place.

wigwam (wig′wäm) A round house built by Native Americans from young, flexible trees and covered with bark and animal skins.

Index

In this index, the letter *c* indicates a chart or table, *d* indicates a diagram, *g* indicates a graph, *m* indicates a map, and *p* indicates a photograph or drawing. Bold page numbers indicate vocabulary definitions. The terms *See* and *See also* direct the reader to alternative entries.

A

Abolition, 74–75
Adams, John, 66
Adapting, 31
Adapting to the environment, 40, 53
Adena culture, 31, 32
Aerospace engineering, 166
African Americans.
- in American Revolution, 58
- Carson, Julia May Porter, 133
- Civil Rights Movement and, 132–133
- in Civil War, 78
- Hatcher, Richard, 133, 133*p*
- in Indiana Supreme Court, 145
- migration of/to urban areas, 96, 105, 130, 131
- Montgomery, Wes, 175, 175*p*
- musicians, 174
- Selby, Myra, 145, 145p
- Walker, Madam C. J. 94, 170
- in World War I, 120
- in World War II, 128

Agriculture
- after Civil War, 90, 93
- early cultures of Indiana and, **31**, 33, 34
- economy and, 165
- map of, 173*m*
- railroads and, 93
- state government and, 150
- trade and, 20

Agriculture belt, 12
Air raid drills, 129
Allied Powers, 118–119
Allies, 44
Amendments, 121
American Revolution, 58–61, 59*m*
Angel Mounds State Historic Site, 28*p*
Animals, 8–9, 45
Antietam, Battle of, 78, 78*p*
Appalachian Mountains, 56
Appomattox Court House, Virginia, 80, 80*p*
ArcelorMittal, 165
Archaeologists, 30
Arsenals, 80
Articles of Confederation, 62, 63
Artifacts, 30
Artists, 1, 89, 137. *See also specific artists.*
Asia, 136, 136*m*. *See also specific countries.*
Assembly and petition, right of, 152–153
Atlas, IN 33
Attorney general, 148, 149*c*
Auditor, 148, 149*c*
Austria-Hungary, 118
Automobile industry
- in Central Till Plain, 12
- entrepreneurs of, 170
- foreign companies in Indiana and, 165
- Great Depression and, 126
- in late 1800s in Indiana, 106
- technology and, 163
- trade and, 19*p*, 20, 21, 21*c*
- World War II and, 128

B

Ball brothers, 12
Ball Brothers Glass Manufacturing Company, 94, 101
Ball jars, 94*p*
Ballard, Greg, 151*p*
Baseball stadiums, 107
Bayh, Birch, 135
Bays, IN 33
Bell, Joshua, 174*p*, 175, 175*p*
Bill of Rights, 152
Bills, 161
Biofuels, 163
Biomet, 165
Biosphere, 8
Bloomington, 13
Bombing drills, 129
Bosse Field, 107
Boundaries, maps and, IN 32
BP, 165
Brazil, 22
Brickyard, 107
Buddhists, 19, 19*p*
Budgets, 169
Bull Run, First Battle of, 77
Burial mounds, 31, 32, 32*m*, 33*p*
Burma, 136

C

Calumet region, 11, 102*m*, 102–104
Calumet River, 102
Cambodia, 136
Canada, 20, 20*m*, 43
Canals, IN 27, 68*p*, 70*m*, **70**, 73, 97
Candidates, 155
Canoes, 44
Capes, IN 33
Capital of Indiana, 2, 2*m*, 12, 66–68
Cardinal directions, IN 33
Carmichael, Howard Hoagland (Hoagy), 123
Cars. *See* Automobile industry.
Carson, Julia May Porter, 133
Cartographers, 48
Cause and Effect, 73, 121, 123, 131, 137, 141
Caves, 3, 4, 4*p*, 10, 13
Central Till Plain region, 10, 12, 12*m*, 13*c*
Checks and balances, 149
Chiefs, 37, 37*p*, 38
Child labor, 108
China, 22–23, 136
Chrysler, 160*p*
Cities, 98*m*, 98–99, 131, 151
Citizens, 146, 150, 157*c*
Citizenship, 156–157
City councils, 151
Civic virtue, 154
Civil rights, 132
Civil Rights Movement, 132–133
Civil War
- beginning of, 76–77
- end of, 80–81
- important battles of, 77–78
- in Indiana, 79–80
- timeline of, 78

Civil wars, 75
Clans, 36, 38, 39
Clark, George Rogers, 59–61, 60*p*, 66
Clark, Robert, 137
Clark, William, 64
Clark County, 66
Clarksville, Indiana, 66
Clay, 32, 33, 41
Climate, 14–15, 40
Coal industry
- Central Till Plain region and, 13
- Great Depression and, 126
- immigrants and, 97
- map of, 173*m*
- railroads and, 94
- trade with China and, 23
- World War I and, 120

Coffin, Levi and Catharine, 75, 75*p*
Cold War, 134
Colfax, Schuyler, 109
Colombia, 136
Colonies, 43
Compare and Contrast, 8, 13, 39, 92, 95, 100, 101, 103, 109, 114, 161
Compare Viewpoints, 80–81
Compass rose, IN 30
Condensation, 7, 7*p*
Confederacies, 46

Confederate battle flag, *75p*
Confederate States of America, *76. See also* Civil War.
Confederations, 62
Congress, 62
Congressional Medals of Honor, 119, 129
Constitution, 62, 68, 73
Indiana, 68, 73, 100, 147–148, 152–153, 156
U.S., 62, 121, 132, 156
Constitutional Convention, 62
Consumers, 160
Contemporary, 174
Continental Army, 58
Copper, 33, 34
Corn, 12, 20
Corporations, 104
Corydon, Battle of, 79, *79p*
Corydon, Indiana, 67, 68
Council houses, 39
Council Oak, 29
Counties, 151
Court of Appeals, 149
Criminals, rights of, 153
Critical Thinking Skills, 80–81, 138
Crops, 11, 20, 71
Crossroads of America, 70
Cuba, 136
Cuban, Mark, *168p*
Cultural exchange, 22
Cultural groups, 31, *35c*
Culture, **22**
Adena, 31, 32
early in Indiana, 30–31
Hopewell, 31, 33
Mississippian, 31, 34
Cummins Engine, 164–165
Currency, 161

D

Dams, 6
Debts, 56
Declaration of Independence, *56–57, 57p*
Degrees, IN **36**
Delaware people, 38, 46
Delegates, 62
Demand, 71, 162
Democracy, 146, 154
Depression, 125
Descendants, 30
Detroit, Fort, 58
Direction on maps, IN 30
Discrimination, 132
Distance on maps, IN 31
Diversity, 156
Drafts, 119
Draw Conclusions, 156, 157, 167, 169, 175, 177
Duesenberg, 106

E

E Pluribus Unum, 156
Earth, hemispheres of, IN 29
"Echoes of Indiana Avenues" (Montgomery), 174
Economy, 90
entrepreneurs and, 172
global, 164–165
in Indiana over time, 163
productivity and, 163
role of money in, 161
supply and demand and, 162
understanding, 160
Education, 100–101, 132, 133. *See also* Public education.
84th Infantry Division, *118p*
El Salvador, 136
Elevation maps, IN 34
Eli Lilly and Company, 21, 165, 170
Ellis Island, 109
Emancipation Proclamation, *78*
Emergency medical technicians (EMTs), 150
England. See Great Britain.
Entertainers from Indiana, 174–175
Entrepreneurs
impacts of, 172
of Indiana, 170–171
in Indiana in late 1800s, **94,** 101
overview of, 168
traits of, 169
Environment, IN 27, **172**
Envision It!, 2, 10, 18, 30, 36, 42, 56, 62, 68, 74, 90, 96, 102, 118, 124, 132, 146, 152, 160, 168
Equator, IN 29, 16
Erie, Lake, IN 26, IN *26m*
Erie Canal, *68p*, 70
Europeans. *See also specific countries.*
arrival of in Indiana, 42–43
conflict and, 46–47
French, 44–45
Evansville, Indiana, 2, 13, 107, 130, 134
Evaporation, *7p*, **7**
Executive branch, 148, *149c*
Expenses, 169
Exports, *21g*, **21,** 164–165

F

Factories, 11, *11p*, 165
Facts, 80
Fairbanks, Charles W., 109
Fall of Vincennes, 59–60
Fallen Timbers, Battle of, 65
Farming
Adena culture and, 32
canals and, 70
Central Till Plain region and, 12
after Civil War, 90, 93
railroads and, 70, 93
trade and, 165
Farmland, 11
Fire engines, 99, *99p*
Firefighters, 150
Fires, cities and, 99
Fisher, Carl, 107
Flags, *75p*
Florida, 42
Forsyth, William, 13
Fort Wayne, Indiana, 66, 130, 134
France
French and Indian War and, 47, 56
settlers in Indiana, 44–45
World War I and, 118
World War II and, 127
Freedom of religion, 97, 153
Freedom of speech, 152
Freighters, 18
French and Indian War, 47, 56
Fur trade, 41, 45, 46

G

Gardens, *129p*
Gary, Elbert S., 104
Gary, Indiana
African Americans in, 131
Hatcher, Richard, and, 133, *133p*
location of, 2, *2m*
steel industry and, 104–105, *104p*, 108
strike in, 108
Wirt, William, and, 101
Gauchos, 22
General Assembly, 148, 149
General Electric, 130
Geography. *See also* Maps.
directions, maps and, IN 30
distance and, IN 31
elevation maps and, IN 34
events and, IN 37
five themes of, IN 26–IN 27
globes and, IN 28
grids on, IN 35
hemispheres and, IN 29
latitude and longitude and, IN 36
physical maps and, IN 33
political maps and, IN 32
Geography Skills, IN 28–IN 37

George III (King of England), 56, 58
German immigrants, 71
Germany, 118–119, 127
Gettysburg, Battle of, 78
GI Bill, 130
A Girl of the Limberlost **(Porter-Stratton),** 89
Glaciers, 3
Glass industry, 12, 94, 101, 108*p*
Global economy, 164–165
Globes, **IN 28**
Goods and services, 160
Gougar, Helen M., 121
Government, overview of, 146
Governor, role of, 148, 149*c*
Grange, 93*p*
Grant, Ulysses S., 80, 80*p*
Graph Skills, 110–111
Grasslands, 8, 9*p*
Great Britain
American independence from, 56–61
Native Americans and, 45, 46, 65
Virginia and, 43
World War I and, 118
World War II and, 127
Great Depression, 124–126
Great Lakes region, IN 26–IN 27, IN 26*m*
Great War Governor, 81
Greenville, Treaty of, 66, 66*p*
Grids on maps, **IN 35**
Guatemala, 136
Guthrie, Janet, 107

Hall, Katie, 133
Hamilton, Henry, 58, 59–61
Harmonists, 71
Harper, Ida Husted, 121, 121*p*
Harrison, Benjamin, *77*, 109, 109*p*
Harrison, William Henry, 55, 66–67
Harrison Land Act, 67
Hatcher, Richard, 133, 133*p*
Haynes, Elwood, 106, 170
Haynes-Apperson Automobile Company, 106
Health, state government and, 150
Healthcare industry, 166
Hemispheres, **IN 29**
Hendricks, Thomas, 109
High-tech industry, 166
Highways, 18, 70*m*, 130*m*, 150
Historic sites, 150
Hitler, Adolf, 127
Home front, 120, 129
Homeland security, 150
Honda, 165
Hoosier Group of painters, 1
Hoosier Hill, 4, 12, 12*m*
Hoosier National Forest, 8, 8*p*
Hopewell culture, 31, 33
Horses, 39
House of Representatives, 148, 149*c*
"The House of the Singing Winds," 1
Human interaction, geography and, IN 27
Hunter-gatherers, 30, 32
Hunting, 9, 30*p*, 33
Huron, Lake, IN 26, IN 26*m*
Hydrologic cycle, 7*c*, **7**
Hydrosphere, **7**

Ice Age, 3
Illinois Territory, 67
Immigrants
from Asia and Latin America, 136, 136*m*
citizenship and, 156–157
in early 1800s, **69**
steel industry and, 105
transportation and, 71
waves of to Indiana, 97
Immigration, to Indiana, 136, 136*m*
Imports, **21**, 164–165
Incentives, **171**
Income, 169
Income tax, 150
Independence, **56**
Index, maps and, IN 35
Indian Removal Act of 1830, 72
Indiana
American Revolution in, 58–61, 59*m*
artists from, 137. *See also specific artists.*
automobile industry and, 106
businesses and natural resources of, 173*m*
changes and challenges in cities of, 98–99
Civil Rights Movement and, 132–133
Civil War and, 79–80, 81
climate and precipitation in, 14–15
constitution of, 68, 73, 100, 147–148, 152–153
early cultures of, 30–31
economy of, 163–167, 166*c*
elevation map of, IN 34*m*
entertainers from, 137, 174, 174*p*. *See also specific entertainers.*
entrepreneurs from, **94**, 101, 168*p*, 170–172, 171*p*. *See also specific entrepreneurs.*
Europeans in, 42–47
farming and, 90, 93
government of, 148–150, 149*c*, 150*c*
government spending of, 150*g*
Great Depression and, 126
growth of, 69
immigrants in, **69**, 71, 97, 105
immigration to, 136, 136*m*
increasing population of, 96*c*, 98*m*
industry in, 166, 166*g*
Korean War and, 134
landforms of, 4–5
landscape of, 3
local governments of, 151
location of, 2
maps of, 2*m*, 12*m*, 14*m*, 16*m*, 32*m*, 36*m*, 98*m*, 102*m*, 130*m*, 173*m*
Miami people and, 72
motto of, 18
musicians from, 137. *See also specific musicians.*
Native Americans of, 36–41
naturalized citizens of, 157*g*
new industries and goods in, 94, 102–103
new machines and, 91
oil and, 95
physical map of, IN 33*m*
plants and animals in, 8–9
political leaders from, 109
political map of, IN 32*m*
population of, 96, 96*g*, 98*m*
ports of, 164*p*
Potawatomi people and, 72
railroad boom and, 92–93
regions of, 10–13, 12*m*, 13*c*, 102–103
relationship of with country and world, 18
Roaring Twenties and, 122–123
slavery and, 74–75
sporting events in, 107
statehood of, 68
as territory, 66–67
trade and, 19–22
transportation in, 70*m*, 70–71, 73
Vietnam War and, 135
water features and hydrologic cycle of, 6–7, 7*p*
women's suffrage movement and, 121
World War I and, 119, 120
World War II and, 128–129
World War II, after, 130
writers from, 137
Indiana, Robert, 137
Indiana Dunes National Lakeshore, 5*p*, 10
Indiana Dunes region, 8
Indiana Dunes State Park, 10
Indiana Institute of Technology, 166
Indiana Legion, 79
Indiana Territory, 66–67
Indiana Theater, 122*p*
Indiana University, 166
Indiana Wesleyan University, 171
Indianapolis, Indiana
as capital, 68
city map of, IN 35
government of, 151
industry and, 130
location of, 2, 2*m*, 12
sister cities of, 22

Indianapolis 500, 107
Indianapolis Motor Speedway, 107, 107*p*
Indianapolis Museum of Art, 137, 137*p*
Industry, in Indiana, 166*c*
Indy Sister Cities Fest, 22
Inland Steel, 102*p*, 103
Integration, 132
Interdependence, 164
Intermediate directions, IN 30
International Harvester, 130
International trade, 20, 20*m*
International War Memorial Museum, 134
Interpret Maps, 48–49
Interstate highways. *See* Highways.
Irish immigrants, 71
Iron industry, 103
Iroquois Confederacy, 46

J

Jackson, Andrew, 72
Jamestown, Virginia, 42*p*, 43
Japan, World War II and, 127
Jaramillo, Santiago, 171, 171*p*
Jefferson, Thomas, 57, 64
Jenckes, Virginia E., 121
Jennings, Jonathan, 68
Jewelry, 32
Judicial branch, 149*c*, **149**
Jury, 153, 155
Justices of the Supreme Court, 149

Kansas, 72
Katrina, Hurricane, IN 31, IN 31*m*
Kelley, Oliver Hudson, 93
Kennedy, John F., 22
Keys, on maps, IN 32
Kickapoo people, 39, 61
Knobs, 13
Kokomo, Indiana, 106
Korean War, 134
Korean War Memorial, 134*p*

La Salle, Robert de, 29, 29*p*, 43, 43*m*
Labor unions, 108
Lakes, 6–7
Land Ordinance of 1784, 63
Land Ordinance of 1785, 63, 63*p*, 67
Landforms, 4–5, IN 33
Laos, 136
Latin America, 22
Latitude, 16, **IN 36**
Laws, 149, 155
***A League of Their Own* (movie),** 107
Lee, Robert E., 78, 80, 80*p*
Legends on maps, IN 32
Legislative branch, 148, 149*c*
Lenape people, 38, 46
Letterman, David, 174, 174*p*
Lewis, Meriwether, 64
Liberia colonization movement, 75
Lieutenant governor, 148, 149*c*
Life sciences industry, 167
Lighting, cities and, 99
Lilly (Eli) and Company, 21, 165, 170
Lilly, Eli, 170, 170*p*, 171
Limestone belt, 13
Lincoln, Abraham, 69, 76, 78, 81
Lincoln, Tom, 69
Literacy, 100
Lithosphere, 4
Little Turtle (Chief), 65–66
Livestock, 90
Lloyd, Daisy, 131
Loans, 125
Local government, 150
Location, geography and, IN 26
Longitude, 16, **IN 36**
Louisiana, La Salle and, 29
Louisiana Purchase, 64, 65*m*, 74
Louisiana Territory, 64
LOVE sculpture, 137, 137*p*

Main Ideas and Details, 9, 15, 23, 26, 46, 129, 147
Main Street of America, 71
Mann Hopewell Site, 35*p*
Manufacturing, 20
Manufacturing sector, 166, 173*m*. *See also specific industries.*
Map keys, IN 32
Maps. *See also specific types.*
American Revolution in the West, 59*m*
The Calumet Region, 102*m*
direction on, IN 30
distance on, IN 31
elevation, IN 34
events on, IN 37
Explorers in the Americas, IN 37
French Trade Routes and Forts, 44*m*
Global Headquarters of Major Indiana Companies, 165*m*
globes, IN 28
of Great Lakes, IN26*m*
grids on, IN 35
hemispheres on, IN 29
Hurricane Katrina's Path, IN 31*m*
Immigration to Indiana, 136*m*
Indiana (location of), 2m
Indiana Businesses and Natural Resources, 173*m*
Indiana Elevation, IN 34*m*
Indiana Highways, 1960, 130*m*
Indiana: Physical and Human Features, 16*m*
Indianapolis, Indiana, IN 35*m*
Indiana's Plant Hardiness Zones, 14*m*
Indiana's Regions, 12*m*
Indiana's Top Trading Partners, 2013, 20*m*
interpreting, 48
La Salle's Explorations, 43*m*
latitude and longitude on, IN 36
The Midwest, Physical, IN 33*m*
The Midwest, Political, IN 32*m*
Mineral Resources in the Midwest, 94*m*
Mounds in Indiana, 32*m*
Native Americans Move to Indiana, 1600s–1800s, 48*m*
Native Americans of Indiana, 1600s–1700s, 36*m*
physical, IN 33
political, IN 32
Population of Indiana Cities, 1900, 98*m*
of United States, IN 30*m*
The United States, 1804, 65*m*
The United States, 1860, 74*m*
U.S. Roads, Canals, and Railroads, 1840, 70*m*
Map scale, IN 31
Map Skills, 16–17, 48–49
Marshall, Thomas R., 109
Marshes, 3
Massachusetts, 43
Maumee River, 39, 65–66
Mayors, 151
McNutt, Paul, 126
Meat-packing industry, 90
Medals of Honor, 119, 129
Medical industry, 163
Mellencamp, John, 175
Melons, 13
Metal, trade and, 41
Mexico, 20, 20*m*, 42, 136, 136*m*
Miami, Fort, 44*m*
Miami people
American Revolution and, 58, 61
Battle of Fallen Timbers and, 65–66
French and Indian War and, 46–47
New Purchase and, 69
overview of, 36–37
reservations and, 72
Michigan, Lake, 5, 6, IN 26, IN 26*m*, 11, 14–15

Michigan Central Depot, 92*p*
Migration to urban areas, 96, 105, 130, 131
Militias, 79
Millionaires, 94
Mills, 90
Mills, Caleb, 100, 100*p*
Mining industry, 172
Mint, 20
Mississippi River
American Revolution and, 59
geography of, 6
La Salle and, 29, 43
as link between Indiana and rest of world, 18
Mississippian culture, 31, 34
Missouri Compromise, 74, 74*m*
Modification, 172
Money, 40, 161, 171. *See also* Currency; Shells.
Monroe Lake, 6
Montgomery, Wes, 174, 174*p*
Monument Mountain, 4
Moraines, 10
Morgan, John Hunt, 79, 79*p*
Morgan's Raid, 79
Morton, Camp, 79
Morton, Oliver P., 77, 77*p*, 79, 80, 81
"Mother of Vice Presidents," 109
Mottos, 18
Mound Builders, 33
Mounds, 31, 32, 32*m*, 33*p*
Mount Baldy sand dune, 5, 5*p*
Mountains, IN 33
Movement, geography and, IN 27
Musicians from Indiana, 137, 174–175. *See also specific musicians.*

National Association of Women Business Owners (NAWBO), 168
National Road, 70, 71
Native Americans
adapting to land by, 40
American Revolution and, 58–59
Delaware people, 38, 46
French and British settlers and, 46
French settlers and, 44
Groups, 39*c*
Kickapoo people, 39, 61
La Salle and, 29
Lenape people, 38, 46
map of in 1600s–1700s, 36*m*
Miami people, 36–37, 46, 58, 61, 65–66, 69, 72
in Northwest Territory, 65–66
overview of, 36
Piankashaw people, 61
Potawatomi people, 38, 47, 58, 72*p*
Shawnee people, 39, 46, 55, 58–59
trade and, 40–41
Natural gas, 12, 94
Natural resources
of Central Till Plain region, 12
defined, **10**
map of, 91*m*, 173*m*
mineral, 91*m*, 94
of Northern Lakes and Moraines region, 10–11
productive, 163
of Southern Lowlands region, 13
trade and, 20
Naturalization, 156, 157*c*
NAWBO. *See* National Association of Women Business Owners.
Nazi Party, 127
Neutral, 118
New Deal, 126
New France, 43. *See also* Canada.
New Harmony, Indiana, 71, 71*p*
New Purchase, 69, 72
Newport, Indiana, 75
Nineteenth Amendment to the Constitution, 121
North Korea, 134
North Vietnam, 135
Northern Lakes and Moraines region, 10–11, 12*m*, 13*c*
Northwest Ordinance of 1787, 64
Northwest Territory, 63–64
Notre Dame, University of, 166

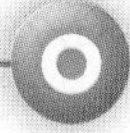

Ohio
location of, 2
Native Americans in, 39, 48*m*
statehood of, 67
Ohio River, 2, 2*m*, 6, 18, 79
Oil industry
Calumet region and, 11, 102*m*
environment and, 172
map of, 173*m*
Southern Lowlands region and, 13
Standard Oil and, 95, 103
Oil refineries, 95*p*, **95**
Oliver, James, 91
Ontario, Lake, IN 26, IN 26*m*
Opinions, 80
Ordinance, 63
Ornaments, 32
Ouiatenon, Fort, 44, 44*m*
Owen, Robert, 71

P

Painters, 1, 1*p*, 13
Palm Sunday tornadoes, 138
Partners of the Americas, 22
Patrick, Danica, 107, 107*p*
Pearl Harbor, attack on, 127
Pence, Mike, 168
Pershing, John, 118, 119
Petitions, 152–153
Petroleum. *See* Oil industry.
Pharmaceutical industry, 21, 21*c*. *See also* Eli Lilly and Company.
Philadelphia, Pennsylvania, 56, 57, 62
Photography, 89
Physical maps, IN 33, 48
Piankashaw people, 61
Pilgrims, 43
Place, geography and, IN 26
Plants
USDA hardiness zones of, 14*m*
in Indiana, 8–9
Native Americans and, 31, 32
Plastics Valley, 13
Plows, 91
Plymouth Colony, 43
Poland, 127
Police, 150
Political leaders from Indiana, 109
Political maps, IN 32, 48
Population growth, 96, 96*c*, 98*m*
Portage, 18
Porter, Charles, 89
Porter, Cole, 123
Ports, 18, 164*p*
Potawatomi people, 38, 47, 58, 72*p*
Pottery, 31, 32
Preamble to the Indiana Constitution, 147*p*, **147**
Precipitation, 7*p*, **7**, 14–15
Primary sources, 138–139
Prime meridian, IN 29, 16, IN 36
Proclamation of 1763, 56
Producers, 160
Productive resources, 163
Productivity, 91, 163
Profit, 91
Prophet, The (Tenskwatawa), 55
Prophetstown, 55
Prosperity, 122
Protests, 132–133, 135, 135*p*
Public education, 100–101, 132, 150, 153
Public relief programs, 126
Puerto Rico, 136
Pulitzer Prizes, 117
Purdue University, 166
Pyle, Ernie, 117, 117*p*, 129

Q

Quayle, Dan, 109
Quilts, 170

R

Racetracks, 107
Railroads
- in 1800s, 70, 70*m*
- boom in Indiana, 92–93
- economy and, 90
- immigrants and, 97
- as link between Indiana and rest of world, 18, 90
- union strikes and, 108

Rainey, Elizabeth, 121
Ratification, 62, 121
Ration, 129
Reading Skills
- Cause and Effect, IN 22, 73, 121, 123, 131, 137, 141
- Compare and Contrast, IN 21, 8, 13, 39, 92, 95, 100, 101, 103, 109, 114, 161
- Draw Conclusions, IN 23, 156, 157, 167, 169, 175, 177
- Main Idea and Details, IN 18, 9, 15, 23, 26, 46, 129, 147
- Sequence, IN 20, 58, 61, 64, 67, 73, 81, 85
- Summarize, IN 19, 31, 35, 41, 47, 51, 135

Reeds, 38, 39
Refineries, 95
"Refrigerator capital of America," 130
Regiments, 76
Regions of Indiana, IN 27, **10**–13, 12*m*, 13*c*, 102–103
Regulation, 93
Religious freedom, 97, 153
Reporters, 117
Representatives, 148
Republican Party, 76
Republics, 146
Reservations, 72
Reservoirs, 6
Resources, 163. *See also* Natural resources.
Respect, responsibility to treat others with, 155
Retirement benefits, 150
Review and Assessment, 25–26, 51–52, 85–86, 113–114, 141–142, 177–178
Revolutionary War, 58–61, 59*m*
Riley, James Whitcomb, 137
Rio Grande do Sul, Brazil, 22
Rivers, 6–7. *See also specific rivers.*
Roads and highways. *See* Highways.
Roaring Twenties, 122–123, 124
Roche, 165
Roosevelt, Franklin D., 126
Roosevelt, Theodore, 109
Rothrock Cathedral, 4*p*
Rural, 96
Russia, World War I and, 118

S

Sachems, 38
Sackville, Fort, 59–60
Sand dunes, 5, 5*p*, 8
Sandhill cranes, 8, 9, 36
Saratoga, Battle of, 58
Savings plans, 169
Scale, maps and, IN 31
Schools. *See* Education.
Science, Technology, Engineering, and Math (STEM) jobs, 166
Search and rescue squads, 150
Secession, 75
Secondary sources, 138–139
Secretary of state, 148, 149*c*
Segregation, 132
Selby, Myra, 145, 145*p*
Senate, 148, 149*c*
Senators, 148
Sequence, 58, 61, 64, 67, 73, 81, 85
Services, 160
Sewall, May Wright, 121
Shamans, 37
Sharpsburg, Maryland, 78
Shawnee people, 39, 46, 55, 58–59
Shells, 32–34, 34*p*, 40, 161
Shipping industry, 18
Sister cities and states, 22, 22*m*
Skelton, Richard (Red), 137
Slavery, 64, 74*m*, 74–75, 78
Snow, 15
Solve Problems, 158–159
Sources, primary and secondary, 138–139
South Bend, Indiana, 29, 106, 120, 128, 131
South Korea, 134
South Vietnam, 135
Southern Lowlands region, 10, 12*m*, 13, 13*c*
Southwind Maritime Center, 18
Soviet Union, 127, 134
Soybeans, 20
Spanish explorers, 42
Spears, 30*p*
Speech, freedom of, 152
Sports and recreation, 107
St. Lawrence Seaway, 18
Stamp Act, 56
Stamps, 129
Standard Oil Refinery, 95, 95*p*
State government, 148–150, 149*c*
Statehood, 67, 68
Statehouse, 54*p*, 146*p*
States' rights, 75
Steel industry
- Calumet region and, 11, 102*m*
- Great Depression and, 126
- trade and, 20, 23
- U.S. Steel Corporation and, 103–105
- World War I and, 120
- World War II and, 128

Steel plow, 91
Steele, T. C., 1, 1*p*, 13
Steelworks, 104, 105*p*
STEM jobs, 166
Stock market, 124
Stock market crash, 124–125
Stockades, 44
Stocks, 124
Stone points, 30*p*
Strategies, 60
Stratton-Porter, Gene, 89, 89*p*
Streetcars, 98, 98*p*
Strikes, 108
Studebaker Corporation, 106, 128, 170
Study Guide, 24, 50, 84, 112, 140, 176
Subaru, 19*p*
Suffrage, 121
Summarize, 31, 35, 41, 47, 51, 135
Sumter, Fort, 76, 77
Superintendent of Public Instruction, 148, 149*c*
Superior, Lake, IN 26, IN 26*m*
Supply, 71, 162
Supreme Court, Indiana, 145, 149
Surrendering, 61
Surveyors, 63
Swamps, 3, 89
Symbols, IN 32

T

Taxes
- as civic responsibility, 155
- defined, **56**
- education and, 100
- income, 150
- local, 151

Technology, changing economy and, 163, 166–167
Tecumseh, 55, 55*p*, 58–59, 66
Tenskwatawa (the Prophet), 55
Territories, 44

Thematic maps, 48
Till, 12
Timelines
of Civil War battles, 78
interpreting, 110–111, **110**
of statehood, 68
War for Independence, 58*p*
Tippecanoe, Battle of, 55
Tombs, 30
Tompkins, Alan, 126
Tools, 33
Tornadoes on Palm Sunday, 138
Town councils, 151
Towns, 151
Townships, 63, 151
Toyota, 165
Trade
Adena culture and, 32
benefits of, 19
culture and, 22–23
defined, **19**
French and, 44*m*
French explorers and, 44, 44*m*, 45
Hopewell culture and, 33
International, 20, 20*m*
Mississippian culture and, 34
Native Americans and, 40–41
top imports and exports and, 21, 21*c*
Trail of Death, 72
"Trailblazing Women," 145
Transportation. *See also* Canals; Highways; Railroads; Rivers.
improvements in during 1800s, 70*m*, 70–71
as link between Indiana and rest of world, 18
planning for, 73
state government and, 150
Trappers, 44, 45
Treasurer, 148, 149*c*
Treaty of Greenville, 66, 66*p*
Trench warfare, 119
Trenton, Battle of, 58
Trustees, 151
28th Regiment of the U.S. Colored Troop, 74*p*, 78
21st Century Skills
Compare Viewpoints, 80–81
Interpret Maps, 48–49
Interpret Timelines, 110–111
Primary and Secondary Sources, 138–139
Solve Problems, 158–159
Use Latitude and Longitude, 16–17
Twightwee, 36

Underground Railroad, 75
Unemployment, 125*g*, **125**
Union flag, 75*p*
Unions, 108
United States Colored Troops, 78
Urban, 96
USDA Hardiness Zones, 14, 14*m*
U.S. Steel Corporation, 104–105
Utopia, 71*p*, **71**

Valley Forge, Pennsylvania, 58
Vehicle manufacturing industry. *See* Automobile industry.
Veto, 149
Vice Presidents, 109
Vicksburg, Siege of, 78
Victory Gardens, 129*p*
Vietnam War, 135, 135*p*
Vincennes, Fort, 44*m*, 59–60, 59–60*p*
Vincennes, Indiana, 66
Volunteer soldiers, 77
Voting, as responsibility, 146, 155
Voting rights, 121, 147. *See also* Suffrage.
Voyageurs, 44

Wabash Canal, 68*p*, 70
Wabash River, 2, 2*m*, 6, 6p, 59
Walker, Madam C.J., 94, 101, 101*p*, 170
Wallace, Lew, 77
War bonds, 129
Washington, George, 58, 58*p*
***Washington Daily* News,** 117
Washington Street, Indianapolis, 88*p*, 90*p*
Water, cities and, 99
Waterways, 18
Wawasee, Lake, 6
Wayne, Anthony, 65–66
Wayne, Fort, 66
Weapons, 34
Weather, 14, 40
Webster, Marie, 170
Wellington Mills, 90*p*
Wigwams, 37, 38*p*, 39
Wildflowers, 8
Wilson, Woodrow, 109, 118
Wirt, William, 101
Women
auto racing and, 107
Civil War and, 80
entrepreneurs, 170
in government, 133, 145, 145*p*
labor unions and, 108
in life sciences industry, 167*p*
steel industry and, 105
voting rights and, 121, 147
World War I and, 119, 120
World War II and, 128
writers, 89, 89*p*
Women's suffrage, 121
Woodfill, Samuel, 119, 119*p*
Wool, 41
Works Progress Administration (WPA), 126
World War I, 117, 118–120
home front and, 120
World War II, 105, 127–129
home front and, 129
WPA. *See* Works Progress Administration.
Writers from Indiana, 137. *See also specific writers.*
Wyandotte Cave, 4, 4*p*, 13

Y

Yorktown, Virginia, 58
Young Entrepreneur Program, 168
Young Entrepreneurs Academy, 168

Z

Zhejiang Province, China, 22–23

Credits

Every effort has been made to locate the copyright owners of the material produced in this component. Omissions brought to our attention will be corrected in subsequent editions.

Maps

XNR Productions, Inc.

Photographs

Every effort has been made to secure permission and provide appropriate credit for photographic material. The publisher deeply regrets any omission and pledges to correct errors called to its attention in subsequent editions. Unless otherwise acknowledged, all photographs are the property of Pearson Education, Inc.

Photo locators denoted as follows: Top (T), Center (C), Bottom (B), Left (L), Right (R), Background (Bkgd)

Cover

Front Cover (TR) American Spirit/Shutterstock; (TL) Todd Taulman/Shutterstock; (CR) Michael Ochs Archives/Getty Images; (B) Rudy Balasko/Shutterstock; **Back Cover** (TC) Paul John Fearn/Alamy; (TR) Walter Bibikow/Corbis; (CL) Bettmann/Corbis; (B) Robin Jerstad/Reuters/Corbis

Front Matter

IN5 Alexey Stiop/123RF; **IN6** Robert Harding Picture Library Ltd/Alamy; **IN7** World History Archive/Alamy; **IN8** Lake County Museum/Fine Art Museums/Corbis; **IN9** George Marks/Retrofile RF/Getty Images; **IN10** HenrykSadura/Shutterstock; **IN26** Jim West/Alamy; **IN27** (BR) HenrykSadura/Shutterstock, (TL) RWP/Alamy Images, (CL) Walter Bibikow/mauritius images GmbH/Alamy Images; **IN28** (B) Morgan Lane Photograph/Shutterstock, (T) Stockbyte/Thinkstock

Text

ii Old Studio (oil on canvas), Steele, Theodore Clement (1847–1926)/Huntington Library and Art Gallery, San Marino, CA, USA/The Huntington Library, Art Collections & Botanical Gardens/Bridgeman Images; **1** T.C. Steele/Mary Lakin/Indiana Historical Society **2–3** Don Smetzer/Alamy; **3** Brad Whitsitt/Shutterstock; **4** Richard Wong/Alamy; **5** Russell Kord/Alamy; **6** Kate Rose/Alamy; **8** Cathy Melloan Resources/PhotoEdit, Inc.; **9** NatPar Collection/Alamy; **10** (TR) Cathy Melloan Resources/PhotoEdit, Inc., (BL) Kenneth Keifer/Shutterstock, (BL)Trout55/iStock/Getty Images Plus/Getty Images; **11** (TL) Alexey Stiop/123RF, (TC) Charles Fenno Jacobs/The LIFE Images Collection/Getty Images, (BR) Liane Harrold/123RF; **12–13** Alexey Stiop/Shutterstock; **15** Bob Wellinski/The News Dispatch/AP Images; **18** Daniel Dempster Photography/Alamy; **18–19** Blickwinkel/Alamy; **19** Ty Wright/Bloomberg/Getty Images; **23** David Snodgress/Bloomington Herald Times/AP Images; **24** (TL) Russell Kord/Alamy, (BL) Blickwinkel/Alamy, (CL) Cathy Melloan Resources/PhotoEdit; **28** Steve Wiltsie/Angel Mounds State Historic Site; **29** Pictorial Press Ltd/Alamy; **30** (CL) OleksiyMaksymenko/Alamy, (TR) Tom Uhlman/Alamy; **31** North Wind Picture Archives/Alamy; **33** (B) Matt Meadows/Getty Images, (TR) Robert Harding Picture Library Ltd/Alamy; **34** Werner Forman/Getty Images; **36** SuperStock; **37** Digital image © 2003 Indiana Historical Society. All Rights Reserved; **38** MyLoupe/UIG Via Getty Images; **40** North Wind Picture Archives/Alamy; **41** North Wind Picture Archives/Alamy; **42** (TR) North Wind Picture Archives, (B) SuperStock/Getty Images; **44** Stephen Goodwin/Alamy; **45** Berlin Bpk/Art Resource, NY; **46** North Wind Picture Archives; **50** (TL) Matt Meadows/Getty Images, (BL) North Wind Picture Archives, (CL) MyLoupe/UIG Via Getty Images; **52** MyLoupe/UIG/Getty Images; **47** HIP/Art Resource, NY; **54** Rudy Balasko/Shutterstock; **55** North Wind Picture Archives/Alamy; **56** (TR) Encyclopedia Britannica/UIG/Getty Images, (BL) Everett Collection Historical/Alamy; **57** GL Archive/Alamy; **58** World History Archive/Alamy; **60** North Wind Picture Archives/Alamy; **63** Steve Geer/iStock/360/Getty Images; **64** North Wind Picture Archives/Alamy; **66** The Treaty of Greenville on August 3, 1795 (oil on canvas), 1805, American School, (19th century)/© Chicago History Museum, USA/Bridgeman Images; **68** Indiana Register of Historic Sites/USA.gov; **69** Paul John Fearn/Alamy; **71** Chronicle/Alamy; **72** Universal Images Group/Art Resource, NY; **74** PF/Alamy; **75** The Underground Railroad, 1893 (oil on canvas), Webber, Charles T. (1825–1911)/Cincinnati Art Museum, Ohio, USA/Subscription Fund Purchase/Bridgeman Images; **76** (TL) Pictorial Press Ltd/Alamy, (BL)Universal History Archive/UIG/Getty images, (BR) YAY Media AS/Alamy; **77** Indiana Historical Society; **78** Archive Images/Alamy; **79** John Hunt Morgan's (1825–64) Raiders (litho), American School, (19th century)/Private Collection/Peter Newark Military Pictures/Bridgeman Images; **79** (TR) North Wind Picture Archives/Alamy; **80** Everett Collection Historical/Alamy; **84:** World History Archive/Alamy, (TC) North Wind Picture Archives/Alamy, (BC) Indiana Register of Historic Sites, (B) Archive Images/Alamy; **86:** John Hunt Morgan's (1825–64) Raiders (litho), American School, (19th century) / Private Collection / Peter Newark Military Pictures / Bridgeman Images; **88** Washington Street, Indianapolis at Dusk (oil on canvas), Groll, Theodor (1857–1913)/Indianapolis Museum of Art, USA/Bridgeman Images; **89** Chronicle/Alamy; **90** (BL) Historic Map Works/Getty Images, (TR) North Wind Picture Archives/Alamy; **91** (BR) Ralph Henry Gabriel, 1926 (engraving), American School, (19th century) (after)/Private Collection/Bridgeman Images, (TL) Everett Collection Historical/Alamy; **92** Lake County Museum/Fine Art Museums/Corbis; **93** Niday Picture Library/Alamy; **94** Jason Lindsey/Alamy; **95** Library of Congress Prints and Photographs Division Washington, D.C. 20540 USA;

96 The New York Public Library/Art Resource, NY; **97** Lewis Wickes Hine/Bettmann/Corbis; **98** PrismaArchivo/Alamy; **99** (TR) Bettmann/Corbis, (BR) Everett Collection Historical/Alamy; **100** (TL) courtesy of Wabash College/USA.gov, (B) PhotoQuest/Contributor/Getty Images; **101** Michael Ochs Archives/Getty Images; **102** Schenectady Museum/Hall of Electrical History Foundation/Corbis; **103** Library of Congress Prints and Photographs Division Washington, D.C. 20540 USA; **104** Library of Congress Prints and Photographs Division Washington, D.C. 20540 USA; **105** Margaret Bourke White/The LIFE Picture Collection/Getty Images; **106** Library of Congress Prints and Photographs Division Washington, D.C. 20540 USA; **107** (TR) Patrick Smith/NASCAR/Getty Images, (B) Tom Uhlman/Alamy; **108** Bettmann/Corbis; **109** North Wind Picture Archives/Alamy; **110** Peter Stackpole/Contributor/Getty Images; **112** (T) Ralph Henry Gabriel, 1926 (engraving), American School, (19th century) (after) / Private Collection / Bridgeman Images, (C) Everett Collection Historical/Alamy, (B) Schenectady Museum; Hall of Electrical History Foundation/CORBIS; **114** Bruce Leighty/Photolibrary/Getty Images; **116** National Archvies; **117** American Stock/ClassicStock/Alamy; **118** (TR) Chronicle/Robert Hunt Library/Alamy, (B) PF (bygone1)/Alamy; **119** (BR) Library of Congress Prints and Photographs Division Washington, D.C. 20540 USA, (TL) The LIFE Picture Collection/Getty Images; **120** Historical/Corbis; **121** Pictorial Press Ltd/Alamy; **122** Everett Collection Inc/Alamy; **123** Bettmann/Corbis; **124** (TR) Atomic/Alamy, (TC) H. Armstrong Roberts/ClassicStock/Alamy; **126** Smithsonian American Art Museum, Washington, DC/Art Resource, NY; **127** Glasshouse Images/Alamy; **128** Philip Gendreau/Bettmann/Corbis; **129** (BR) GalerieBilderwelt/War Gardens for Victory, 1942 (colourlitho), American School, (20th century)/Private Collection/Bridgeman Images, (BL) George Marks/Retrofile RF/Getty Images; **132** Bettmann/Corbis; **133** Bettmann/Corbis; **134** Andre Jenny/Alamy; **135** Richard J. Sroda/AP Images; **137** David R. Frazier Photolibrary, Inc./Alamy; **140** (T) Chronicle/Alamy, (C) War Gardens for Victory, 1942 (colour litho), American School, (20th century) / Private Collection / © Galerie Bilderwelt / Bridgeman Images, (B) ASSOCIATED PRESS; **142** Richard J. Sroda/AP Images; **144** RGB Ventures/SuperStock/Alamy; **145** Courtesy of Myra Selby; **146** (BL) HenrykSadura/Shutterstock, (TR) Michael Conroy/AP Images; **148** Rudy Balasko/Shutterstock; **151** John P. Cleary/The Herald Bulletin/AP Images; **152** (TR) Hill Street Studios/Blend Images/Corbis, (BL) The Star, Olivia Corya/AP Images; **153** Michael Conroy/AP Images; **154** Jeff Greenberg 2 of 6/Alamy; **155** Hill Street Studios/Blend Images/Corbis; **156** Michael Conroy/AP Images; **158** PhotoAlto/Alamy; **160** AJ Mast/AP Images; **161** Jeff March/Alamy; **162** Bob Caddick/Alamy; **163** Jim West/Alamy; **164** John Luke/The Times/AP Images; **167** Joe Raymond/AP Images; **168** Ronald Foster Sharif/Demotix/Corbis; **169** Roman Sotola/Shutterstock; **170** Grapes and Vines, 1914 (textile), Webster, Marie D. (1859–1956)/Indianapolis Museum of Art, USA / Gift of Mrs Gerrish Thurber/Bridgeman Images; **171** Jeff Morehead, Chronicle-Tribune/AP images; **172** The Herald-Times, David Snodgress; **174** (L) Ray Tamarra/Film Magic/Getty Images, (C) Everett Collection Historical/Alamy, (R) Everett Collection Inc/Alamy; **175** Chicago Tribune/Contributor/Getty Images; **176** (TL) Rudy Balasko/Shutterstock, (CT) The Star, Olivia Corya/AP Images, (CB) AJ Mast/AP Images, (BL) Grapes and Vines, 1914 (textile), Webster, Marie D. (1859–1956)/Indianapolis Museum of Art, USA/Gift of MrsGerrish Thurber/Bridgeman Images.